Only N

The Terry Oldfield Story

Only Now

The Terry Oldfield Story

Memoirs of a musician, fisherman and free-thinker

∞
Lemniscate

Only Now: The Terry Oldfield Story © Terry Oldfield and Joe McGowan, 2022.

All rights reserved. No part of this book may be reproduced or transmitted in any form or by any means, electronic or mechanical, including photocopying and recording, or held within any information storage and retrieval system, without permission in writing or granted licence from the authors.

© Terry Oldfield and Joe McGowan, 2022
Terry Oldfield and Joe McGowan assert their moral right to be identified as the authors of the work.

Terry Oldfield	Joe McGowan
32 Country Road	Rosebank
Palmwoods QLD 4555	Rutherglen
Australia	Glasgow

For information contact: www.terryoldfield.com
www.joemcgowan-jowrimu.com

Cover design by Joe McGowan. Cover photograph © Al Melville. All interior photographs © Terry Oldfield except page 358: top © Joe McGowan; middle and bottom © Michael McGrath. Reproduced with permission.

ISBN: 9798444267776

Praise for *Only Now: The Terry Oldfield Story*

'Your Book is amazing and I am so enjoying it and having to force myself to put it aside now and then so as to continue with the days... Such a great experience for me to review your remarkable life in this manner.'

— Kevin McGrath, Poet in residence, Harvard University

'Just finished your book, all of it – which is rare for me! It's so beautifully crafted just like your moving music. You've led an extraordinary life all the better for the struggles you went through to get there. I think I will take up fishing!'

— Sir Richard Branson, British entrepreneur and business magnate

'...an amazing journey to reach the current times with such peace and spiritual coherence. It provides me with hope and a path to follow; a way to make sense of the wrinkles and so-called imperfections of life. There is a destination, and it is a good one.'

— Jon Valdivia, Creative freelancer

'What a testimonial to the journey of a lifetime lived in consciousness... You take the reader on a physical and simultaneously spiritual path, the journey of the personality into the realm of the soul. And all the while the music is playing, rising and falling in the background.'

— Colette Green, MA Integrative Psychotherapist

'...absolutely amazing. Clear and exciting to read. It is an extraordinary piece of writing, Terry, and I honour you.'

— Graeme Whiting, Headmaster, Acorn School. Gloucestershire

Contents

Foreword by Sally Oldfield xiii

Introduction. The Four Stages of My Life 1

1: Awakening in The Dream 3
    12th August 1949 9
    Baby Michael 13
    Angling DNA 15
    Moving Times 17

2: Lost in The Dream 21
    Holy Hell 23
    Requiem for Joy 24
    The Hidden Side 37
    1969. One Small Step... 40
    A New Platform 42
    Take up Thy Bed and Walk 45

3: Awakening to The Dream 47
    Hydra 49
    India 55
    War 56
    The Promise of the East 60
    A Land Down Under 62
    Farewell Tennant Creek 70
    Rome 71
    Return to Hydra 72
    For Whom the Bell Tolls 76

A New Motivation 78
Baptism of Fire 83
Family Ties 86
Rachel Oldfield, Welcome to the World 91
Different Outlooks 94
Terry Oldfield, Shop Assistant 99
Changes 103
Sacred Geometry 107
Moving On 116
Spiral 117
A Beginning 120
Travels with my Brother 125
Exegesis 128
Paddling to Success 136
A Hard Realisation 139
A New Start in an Old Place 140
Survival of the Fittest 143
Island of the Soul 146
A Trip Back in Time 149
Message in a Bottle, by Telegram 151
The Journey Begins 154
And Baby Makes Four 157
An Experience Out Of Body 160
All is Not Lost 166
My Turn in the Recording Studio 168
1984 170
Bears, Tigers, Rabbits, a Bit of Silence & Some Climbing 172

High as a Kite and Still Rising 175
The Wicked Stepmother 176
Pirating 178
An Unexpected Call 179
A New Age 185
A Fresh Mission 196
Rekindling an Old Passion 199
Autumn Salmon 201
Lost Worlds and New Horizons 208
Writing Film Music to a Brief 210
Into the '90s 212
Time for a Little Enlightenment 217
Trout and Salmon Magazine and 'Wet Cel Tel' 219
The Wildman Alters My Attitude 224
My Darling Clementine 227
School's Out 231
Music for the Time Machine 238
The Relentless March of Progress 241
The Wall 243
Man and Soul Reunited 246
Underneath the Arches with Bernard Cribbins 248
The Bells are Ringing… Again 255
1999 256
A Dawning 260
Goodbye 266
Exodus 271
Turning Point 274
Ebb and Flow 277

Meeting with a Soulmate 279
Precognition 281

4: Awakening from The Dream 287
Sad Endings, Joyous Beginnings 293
The Celtic Curse 296
A New Dawn and a Tin Shed 298
A Different Life Begins 302
The Ultimate Tragedy 305
Mangalam 306
He Ain't Heavy 308
Inspirations and Challenges 310
Another Farewell 314
A Hole in the Sky 315
Return to Celtic Roots 329
A Long-Awaited Confrontation 335
2020. Challenges and Opportunities 345
Isolation and the 'Doing' Energy 348

Reflections 359
Glimpses of Truth 361
Awakening, Life, Death and Meditation 363
Addictions 370
Creating Music 373
Why the Flute? 377
My Way of Composing Music 380
My Peaceful Passion 384
Family 397
Now 403

Time and continuity are the great mesmerisation

That keep the dream alive.

— Terry Oldfield

Foreword

It was getting late on a bright winter's afternoon when I was about nine years old. Suddenly I heard my father's voice calling out anxiously, 'Where's Terry?'

My younger brother was only seven, but his lifelong love affair with fishing had recently begun in earnest. On this particular day he had gone off alone on his bike to his favourite haunt near a tributary of the River Kennet called *The Holy Brook*.

We were all worried now, as dusk was falling fast. My father set off in a panic to search for him and luckily, after an anxious wait, they both returned safe and sound. Dad had found Terry standing stock-still in a trance on the frozen water, lost to everything but the pure magic he had discovered in the beauty of rivers and in the world of nature.

Over the course of his life this passion would gradually become mystical in intensity and inspire much of his music. His beautiful album, *All the Rivers Gold*, is a blossoming of his first childhood encounter with the divine stillness he would often experience on the banks of the wonderful rivers of the world.

Terry and I had been close companions and soulmates in our early childhood before our younger brother Michael (Mike) was born, a child destined to become one of the most successful and original musician/composers of the 20th century. His debut album, *Tubular Bells*, sky-rocketed him to fame and fortune at the age of just twenty, and it was this meteoric trajectory of our younger brother's life and music that sometimes wove a challenging thread through Terry's own story.

However, it was only when he sent me the manuscript of his memoir that I began to fully understand the depth of his struggle and the great inner strength and courage he found within himself to rise to that challenge and forge his own successful life and career in music.

Following Mike's dizzying rise to fame at such a young age, Terry recalls his determined attempts to bridge the huge gap between the two brothers' fortunes, and how he helped Mike with emotional support when the pressures of his sudden celebrity became overwhelming, sharing with us the long therapeutic road trips they took together around Ireland and Greece. Terry, who played flute on some of Mike's early albums as well as at the world premiere of *Tubular Bells*, also recants a number of hilarious anecdotes about his involvement with the legendary tycoon/prankster, Richard Branson, as *Tubular Bells* began to pave the way for the Virgin Empire.

As Terry starts to find his feet in the world, he takes the reader on a breathtaking journey, both inner and outer, travelling alone across continents to India, Greece and through his growing, inner spiritual landscape. We travel with him all the way from the searing heat of an Australian mining camp where, by a stroke of fate, he is rescued from destitution, to the eventual joy of a shopping spree for a dinner jacket to attend his first nomination for an Emmy award for his film music.

He takes us to the beautiful Greek island of Hydra where so many of the great artists of the seventies found solace and inspiration. Here he meets Leonard Cohen and other luminaries of that fecund time of music and the arts and where, most significantly, he discovers the instrument that finally gives voice to his soul – a beautiful silver flute! He then shares with us how this flute becomes his saving grace, his best friend when disaster strikes, and finally his way out of the financial stress that periodically threatens to derail his life. Within a few years he has created his own successful career and settled down to marriage and raising a family.

However, the demons of our traumatic childhood, our mother's prescription drug addiction and his banishment to the horrors of an abusive Catholic boarding school continue to haunt him over the ensuing years. This generates a mental and emotional crucible that gradually percolates into a rich brew of spiritual optimism and sardonic humour that has inspired others and often lightened my own life.

As he increasingly follows his own inner guidance, destiny finally takes him to Queensland, Australia where he meets his soulmate, life companion and wife, Soraya Saraswati. Together they have formed an inspiring partnership and musical collaboration in which mutual support and sharing with many other people have become their guiding light.

Terry's book, the writing of which was ably assisted by his close friend Joe McGowan, is an enthralling read that engages us with a cornucopia of life experience, taking us to the operating theatre in 2016 when my brother lost his right eye to a melanoma and faced the long-haul, dark journey of healing the grief of losing half his eyesight. We also learn about the fascinating background to many of his albums and how each one is a special landmark on his personal journey, giving meaning to the challenges and troubles he faced.

Yet with every bright summit and every dark chasm that weaves its way through his often turbulent life there shines an abiding commitment to always find the diamond at the heart of human consciousness that is untouched by it all – the pure, unsullied moment of Now. It is this quest that lies at the heart of Terry's moving memoir and is the silver thread that can be heard loud and clear in his spiritually inspired albums that shimmer with the joy he has always found in music and in playing his beloved flute.

Reading *Only Now* has been an eye-opener for me. Even though Terry is my brother and I have known him since birth, there are many aspects to his nature, his life and music that were hitherto unknown to me. I feel sure his memoir will be a source of discovery for many of his friends and fans, as well as all those who have followed the lives of The Oldfield Family since the birth of *Tubular Bells* in 1973.

Now is the time to open this book and delve into the secret life of an original and courageous soul who I am blessed to be able to call my brother.

— Sally Oldfield, March 2022

Introduction

— The Four Stages of My Life —

It seems to me now that there have been some distinct periods or eras in my life. And that life itself is the Great Dream.

Awakening in The Dream is the time of the innocent baby who has no sense of identity or separation, and who essentially has no idea of what is going on.

Getting *Lost in The Dream* is that period of accumulation of knowledge about the Self in relation to the dream that we call childhood or growing up.

Awakening to The Dream is basically the spiritual path that began for me in my late teens. This period takes us into the labyrinth of life with only Ariadne's thread of consciousness to guide us into the Minotaur's lair to face our fears and see the beast for what it really is; our resistance to life itself. This is the tricky one because until we face our fears – the Minotaur – there is no way back out of the labyrinth since the thread of Ariadne, consciousness itself, is the only thing that can guide us towards the final step.

Awakening from The Dream is where consciousness itself is now living through the body-mind with no resistance to the still mysterious flow of creation in the present moment.

— *Terry Oldfield*

1. Awakening in The Dream

1: Awakening in The Dream

A big white face glared in our direction as we hid beneath a single frosty bush in the vast forest, trying to stay out of sight of the danger we ourselves had invoked. Afraid. But that was okay. I was with Sally; best friend, companion, sister and fellow adventurer.

The dog inched forward, pushing his muzzle through the wooden posts in the meagre garden fence that separated us, eagerly sniffing the air to pick up the scent of his prey. That was okay, too, for we knew that, just like our other stalker, Jack Frost – whom we had conjured from spider webs woven onto twigs in the early morning dew – next door's dog was only another player in the game. Part of the magic we loved to create...

∞

A trip to the local department store to visit Father Christmas... His long white beard and bright red clothing... Very scary to this little boy who cried when he was lifted up onto his knee... Mum and Dad smiling... All so harmless and amusing to those around me...

∞

Like fragments in a dream the memories of childhood melt away the more I try to grasp hold of them. These magic pebbles, dropped as random markers of my apparent history, remind me of the child within who remains innocent at the heart of it all.

∞

The thing about childhood is that it is lived mainly in the present moment, meaning that strong memory lines aren't always firmly laid down since most things are experienced fully as a child and therefore complete. I'm sure there is a reason why memory chooses to retain access to some moments more than others on our journey through life. I feel that lingering childhood memories often seem to concern experiences that have been stored for possible future reference in terms of survival, or, in the case of an unhappy or insecure childhood, where more memories were established as a consequence of uncomfortable or threatening situations.

Until about the age of eleven my childhood was pretty much a happy experience in which I had very little resistance to life as it presented and flowed through me. That's why, I suppose, only certain fragments were laid down indelibly from time to time; perhaps for future reference, just in case they might come in handy. It's the same with dreams; they often seem to be the mind's way of completing an event that was not fully experienced at the moment it was current, or 'live'.

Looking back on my childhood now I feel that I am mostly only picking up those fragments in time, those archetypes of my early life that were somehow deemed useful. There are happenings that I have been told about my youth that are not really true memories for me, although I suppose they, too, are stored somewhere, locked away in the vaults for some unconscious purpose. Then there are the other snippets here and there; quite a few based around frequent visits to Margate, the seaside town in Kent where my paternal grandparents had retired to live. These were happy, endless days spent on the beach collecting shells and building sand castles. I particularly remember the awesome expanse of black seaweed amongst which my sister Sally and I would wander in search of crabs and other jewels. This was a world that I lost at some forgotten point in time, or rather it was swept away in the rising tide of complexity that we call 'growing up'.

I was so happy and immersed in life. But horrendous changes lay in store.

1: Awakening in The Dream

— 12th August 1949 —

I awoke to this particular dream in a nursing home in Alderman's Hill in Southgate, London, on 12th August 1949. In time Terence Raymond Oldfield would respond to just 'Terry', and understand that he was the second child of Maureen and Raymond Oldfield, that he had an elder sister, Sally, and that we all lived at 21 Monks Way in Reading. To adult eyes our three bedroom semi-detached house would have been considered rather small, but as I grew into a toddler I experienced it as a huge place with lots of stairs and an endless garden full of the promise of adventure.

I would learn that Daddy was a doctor and of course Mummy stayed at home to cook and clean and look after me and Sally, because that was what mummies did. Much later still I would come to know that my parents had met in the Royal Surrey County Hospital in Guildford where my dad was an intern and Mum a senior nurse. Dad came from Southgate and Mum from County Cork, right down on the southern coast of another country called Ireland. In later life I would also discover how difficult things had been for Mum and her family, and why she'd left the small town of Charleville as a young woman to make a new life for herself in England.

My earliest recollection of interacting with my mother, Maureen – 'Maisie' as she had been known to her family in Ireland – was on her birthday when I had toddled up to her, innocently proclaiming, 'Mummy I'm not going to tell you that your present is an umbrella..!' I have never forgotten the utter bemusement I felt when someone immediately told me off for saying that at the time.

Ashtrays full of lipstick-coated cigarette ends around the house are also a vivid memory as my mum always wore bright lipstick and seemed to smoke almost constantly; an activity that was both highly fashionable and benignly regarded in the 1950s.

Maisie was a very gregarious presence around the family home and she loved parties and general socialising. This was the era of the cocktail party to which, at Mum's instigation, our house was often host, and our dining room had a cabinet full of different coloured liqueurs and mixers and things, and of course the obligatory cocktail shaker. We children were allowed to use the soda fountain that formed part of the cocktail cabinet's armoury, a device that could make bubbly water because of the little gas canisters that were screwed into its base. For some obscure and forgotten reason I remember calling it 'fodanina'.

There were evenings when these cocktail parties were taking place that I can recall peeking out of my upstairs bedroom window at all the people arriving in their colourful dresses and smart suits. My sister and I sometimes sat on the stairs listening to the babble of voices while we played spontaneously invented games. Sally came up with the name *Syastairs* for me – derived from *Say a Stair* – which was part of a game where we had to give a particular name to each stair we elected to jump onto. We also had a game involving our garden hammock which resulted in my nickname for Sally becoming *Hamaka*. So *Syastairs* and *Hamaka* were our private names for each other in those early years.

Mum was also a keen cook, and I especially remember her rabbit stew and how every Christmas she'd make one of those huge, elaborate cakes full of glacé cherries, nuts and dried fruit that lasted nearly all year long. She once told me she could always tell when I was enjoying my food because I'd hum while I was eating. To entertain us all sometimes she would recite epic poems, of which *The Little Match Girl* was a party piece that I remember with great fondness.

Maisie's staunch Irish catholic upbringing meant that we all had to attend Mass every Sunday morning at the English Martyrs Church just up the road, next to Prospect Park. I always found this a rather confusing experience where I was made to remain quiet for about an hour while everyone kept standing up and sitting down, sometimes kneeling, for long periods. The Mass was in Latin, so of course I didn't understand anything the priest was saying either. I look back upon this as a valuable experience as it provoked the earliest beginnings of my questioning what on earth it was all about, which eventually became a trigger for looking beyond the pale. The first tiny glimpse of awakening to the dream.

Being the local GP, Dad was a very busy figurehead within our community at a time when the local doctor had a far more elevated status and greater responsibility than is typically the case nowadays. I was a little afraid of him as a young boy but not because he was a tyrant or anything; looking back I think perhaps it had more to do with our very different personalities. Dad was, largely through necessity, a pragmatic and orderly man, whereas I was more of a dreamer, a seeker of life's profound mysteries. He was a good parent in that he didn't want me to be held back in the same way he felt he had been by his own parents, Bertie and Mabel, known to us as Nana and Papa, both of whom were pleasant and amenable characters but very traditional and stuck in their ways.

Their outlook and, undoubtedly, support had helped my dad achieve his worldly ambition of becoming a doctor – a respected profession that most parents would be proud to see their child gravitating towards – but on the other hand, from them he also inherited the not uncommon handicap of bottling up his feelings and avoiding outward demonstrations of emotion. This somewhat characteristic English trait is often looked upon as a noble or courageous quality, yet it inevitably also spawns an inability to completely relax with people, especially strangers and, as in my dad's case, suppresses a great deal of emotion, anger and frustration that can be carried into later life.

Having experienced the damage all of that inflicted in himself, Dad obviously tried not to pass it on to his children, which is probably why I was destined to be sent to boarding school when I was twelve. This was most likely his attempt to give me the best education he could provide, a well-meaning act that would nevertheless have a negative effect on me from the very start. The fact that it was a Roman Catholic school, however, was undoubtedly the result of my mother's influence.

Dad's elder sister, my **Auntie** Audrey, was never a strong presence in my childhood as she spent a long period overseas in South Africa with her husband, Leslie. The couple eventually returned to England to run a post office in Norfolk, but I only recall ever meeting Audrey about two or three times when I was growing up. In later life I visited her in Cornwall when she was in her early eighties, living alone and painting water colours that she sold in local shops and galleries. This was a creative activity she shared with my dad as he would also take up painting after retiring.

Eventually dying at the ripe old age of ninety-five, longevity was, as it would turn out, something else Aunt Audrey had in common with Dad.

Although Mum was largely the source of entertainment in our household, on occasion Dad would take out his acoustic guitar and sing folk songs like *The Blue Tail Fly* and *Danny Boy*, and he once taught me a Scottish reel on the mouth organ which I can still play to this day. He also had an adventurous side which included skiing and a fascination for flying that led to him becoming a glider pilot. It was largely thanks to him that I too later learned to ski, but it was the fifth member of our family, yet to be born, who would inherit his flying bug.

— Baby Michael —

Three months before my fourth birthday, Mum brought someone back to Monks Way; a baby boy named Michael Gordon, my new little brother. Sally (now almost six) and I probably welcomed Michael in the way elder siblings – especially those who have become paired playmates – typically receive such disruptions to their status quo. I have very little memory of that particular time, but I suspect we remained rather aloof from baby Michael due to the age gap and the fact that he was now receiving the lion's share of our mother's attention. I do, however, remember him growing into a capricious toddler, a very happy-go-lucky child and a bit of a prankster. When he was two I convinced him one day that he could fly, upon which the intrepid Michael launched himself from the sofa, only to land badly on the coffee table. I got into serious trouble for that one.

However, considering that Michael – who later preferred to be called Mike – would one day have his own helicopter and private plane, not to mention help to launch Richard Branson's Virgin Empire, perhaps events of that day had a greater influence than any of us could have envisaged at the time!

At a stage in early childhood when two years of an age difference didn't seem to matter at all, Sally and I had been best friends and spent a great deal of our time together, but my sister, who had been going to ballet classes since the age of four, was now taking more of an interest in her dancing. We also attended different schools. Sally went to St. Joseph's Convent, then a girls' school, whereas I had been enrolled at St. Edward's Prep. The inevitable change in our childhood relationship took place all the more rapidly when my eight-year-old sister found a new best friend, Jane, and was immediately drawn away from our creative plains of fantasy into the real world, leaving me to remain a wanderer in the world of my own making.

Fortunately, though, the change didn't affect me too much as I was soon to discover a new interest which quickly grew into a passion that remains to this day... Fishing!

— Angling DNA —

Ours was a rather small family home, so when my paternal grandparents came up from Margate to visit us they stayed at a nearby guest house. I would often go out walking with Bertie and Mabel in the local parks and by the River Thames that ran through the town centre and away into the surrounding countryside of the Thames valley. One day as we were walking along the Thames promenade my grandfather, 'Papa' as I called him, noticed that I seemed to be fascinated by the activity of all the fishermen sitting on the river bank who were baiting up, casting and staring keenly at their floats bobbing away on the water. That very day I found myself the proud owner of a fishing rod, reel, line, floats, weights and hooks, all in one delightful, magical pack.

Papa showed me the basics of it all and I couldn't wait to set off on my bike and cycle down Cow Lane to the river about two miles away from our home. In those days even as a six-year-old boy I was free to wander the world at my pleasure, oblivious to all the dangers that seemed to materialise in later times. It was true bliss!

I was already aware from my mum that when she had been growing up her Dad, my other **grandfather** whom I would never meet, had been a fisherman and later a gamekeeper on the Blackwater in County Cork. As I raced down the lane towards the River Thames on that first ever fishing trip I recalled her telling us how some mornings when she'd come down to breakfast as a young girl in Ireland there would be a huge salmon lying on the table for that evening's family meal. So I pedalled faster.

I'll never forget catching my first ever fish that day, a species called a Pope. It was so small that I didn't realize I had caught anything until I reeled in the line. Not a specimen that any fisherman could ever find cause to boast about, but to me it was the jewel beyond all imagining. From then on I was literally hooked. My life had changed. I was now an angler. A true man of the river. A fisherman.

With Sally off exploring life with other girls now, and little Michael doing whatever his whimsical toddler mind dictated, I became something of a solitary, but very contented figure. I had friends, of course, but having now discovered fishing nearly all of my free time was spent exploring various parts of the River Thames close to home. I caught mostly small Perch, Roach and Rudd as I slowly acquired more skills with each unique and glorious little angling expedition.

It was whilst on one of these youthful fishing expeditions that I also had my first brush with death. (The second would occur thirty-seven years later – again, ironically, on a fishing trip.) I had just caught a magnificent Perch weighing about a pound down on the Thames promenade and was cycling back along Cow Lane with it, taking it home to triumphantly show my parents, when I came across some boys playing on a rope swing that was tied to a tree overhanging a small cliff. My friend James was among them and when he set eyes on me he immediately invited me to have a go. I can only remember snippets from the minutes and days that followed, but something caused me to slip off the rope swing and fall about thirty feet to the ground below. I remember one moment when I was cycling home and crying... then I was at home with my dad, vomiting into a bucket... one more moment I was in Battle hospital and a doctor was leaning over me looking rather concerned.

I had suffered a severe concussion and memory loss, and my jaw was broken (I still have a click in it to this day). Apparently I was lucky to have survived as the head injury was pretty bad and everyone said it was a miracle I had managed to cycle home. I remember everything before the fall and from about a week after, but nothing in between – apart from those sketchy scrapbook-like moments – and absolutely nothing of the fall itself. Maybe it will all come rushing back into my mind at some future date, triggered, perhaps, by a random event, and the mystery will be solved as to what actually happened on that day. If that does occur, hopefully I'll also remember what happened to the magnificent Perch I caught...

— Moving Times —

When I was about seven our family moved to a small detached house in Western Elms Avenue, which was only a short distance from Monks Way. At that age we don't pay much attention to these things, we just go where the adults take us, but I do remember that the new district had a more upmarket feel to it. I was far more preoccupied with my fishing at the time and had even managed to persuade my parents to have the *Angling Times* delivered to the house. Each week my newspaper would arrive through the letterbox alongside various popular glossy women's magazines, including *Health and Beauty* which catered for Mum's keen interest in this fashionable subject for which she now attended a local weekly class and bought lots of related material.

And so life continued happily, unremarkably, in the Oldfield family for several more years; Dad with his good job, Mum in her role as home maker and hostess, and Sally, Mike and I getting on with growing up in a stable and loving home environment.

Before I had reached my teenage years, however, all of that would change forever.

∞

In the spring of 1961 when I was eleven my parents gathered Sally, Mike and I together and announced that Mum was going to have another baby. I have no recollection of how we children felt about this, but with hindsight on that day we were receiving news of a pending event that would dramatically alter the course of all our lives.

As the weeks passed, baby clothes and other things were stored in our garage in preparation for the new arrival and life resumed pretty much as it had prior to the big announcement. This was a time when prenatal care was limited to periodic checks of the baby's heartbeat and position in the womb, as well as the mother's general health. There were no ultrasound scans that could provide more detailed information such as the sex of the developing fetus or detect underlying medical conditions or abnormalities. As a result, a greater element of mystery surrounded pregnancy, not to mention potential danger. For this reason we had no way of knowing that, hidden beneath the guise of the joyful prospect of Mum giving birth to her fourth child, there lurked a reality that would herald the irrevocable demise of our happy family.

And there was another horrendous experience in store. This one for me alone.

My first rod-caught eel! On a day outing in the 1950s with Sally

Best pals! Me and Sally on holiday

2. Lost in The Dream

— Holy Hell —

In September of that year, shortly after I had turned twelve, I found myself being sent away from my friends and family to a place that, even now, I can only best describe as an open prison. Run by Benedictine monks, Douai Abbey was a boarding school in Woolhampton, not far from where we lived, that was to be the bane of my life for the next couple of years. I hadn't done anything wrong and I wasn't being punished; my parents just believed that they were giving me the best education they could provide. Unable to comprehend this at the time, however, I wondered whether my being sent away had something to do with the approaching birth of the new baby.

From a place of happiness and contentment I had been delivered, bewildered and afraid, to this establishment run strictly, often cruelly, by the 'Brothers' of this Catholic order. I found it impossible to adapt to the regimented lifestyle here and the pressure of learning under the constant threat of corporal punishment. A lot of bullying existed, but the juniors were expected to accept and endure it almost as a ritualistic rite of passage, a means of becoming accepted into the regime. I would long for the end of each day and bed time when I could hide under the sheets and pray for morning never to come.

Sadistic is probably the most apt word to describe the monks who ran the place with their disturbingly assorted methods of punishment. My house master, Father Hilary, had various canes hanging on the wall of his study, each of which he had given a name that, in his mind, somehow represented their individual character. I remember the thickest and most menacing looking one was called *Benedict*, and even though I never became acquainted with this particular weapon, the first time I ever got caned Father Hilary told me that he was going to introduce me to *Lucy*, which turned out to be the thinnest, whippiest cane in his armoury.

There were of course some boys there who seemed fairly content to be controlled and herded about like sheep, but I could never understand them. I wondered if they were just conforming like zombies, making the best of a terrible situation, since no sane person, surely, could ever be happy in such a place. I was constantly miserable, my jotters full of handwritten days crossed off as a prisoner might carve them on a dungeon wall, each one laying open the way to a future date when I would be free. These dates would always be written bigger, always underlined, and always indicate a particular school holiday. That year, close to the anticipated arrival of my new brother or sister, my first holiday escape from Douai Abbey took place over Christmas.

— Requiem for Joy —

A baby boy.
David.
This news was not accompanied by joy because it came immediately after we children were told that our brother had not survived. He would never know me or Sally or Mike, the brothers

and sister who had been expecting him to arrive home any day as a tiny bundle in his mother's arms. Instead, my mum – or what appeared to be my mum, for she was never the same to us after that – came home alone from the hospital.

The once energetic socialite had been replaced by a sullen effigy of Maisie, the mother I had always known. We understood that this dramatic change in her demeanour was to be expected after what had just happened, and naturally assumed that she would slowly begin to heal and eventually return to her usual self. In the meantime she had been prescribed tranquilisers and had also **begun** to drink rather heavily. There were times when she became very emotional or just stared blankly into the near distance, experiencing something she alone could see. But a most puzzling thing to me was her inexplicable absences when she would go off somewhere, often in the car with Dad, for a few hours or even days at a time. We knew better than to ask too many questions, accepting that Mum was upset, and Dad always placated us with a fairly plausible reason for her absence.

Owing to the situation at Douai Abbey I had sufficient troubles of my own to contend with, added to which I had reached the age where childish innocence was giving way to adolescence and I was starting to take a mild interest in the opposite sex, so events at home did not fully impact upon me. At least not at this stage. Things at school of course didn't improve when I went back, and it now felt like all of the stability in my life had suddenly come adrift, making it a living nightmare. Before long I started running away from the hell hole and returning home, but each time I was taken back in disgrace as though I had made some dreadful error of judgment. I also developed a bit of an addiction to Mandrax pills, a tranquiliser my dad had innocently prescribed to help me sleep. Nobody knew the dangers of prescription drugs in those days, and my GP father would often hand out pills to us if he felt the situation required it. Rather like sending me off to boarding school this was just something else motivated by good intentions, and upon which hindsight really has no fair right to pass judgement. It was common in those days for local GPs to do such things, and even to perform minor surgery. I still have a small scar from the time when we were on a family picnic and I fell and split my chin on an old tree root while playing rounders; Dad had simply fetched his bag from the car and stitched my chin there and then without any hint of a trip to casualty. So no one would have given a second thought to the way he looked after us all at home. In that respect my mum was fortunate to have a doctor on hand who could offer medical support that didn't require countless visits to a surgery or hospital, but terribly unfortunate in that the standard treatment for her psychological condition back then was to prescribe barbiturates. Despite the associated high risk of dependency and overdose, these tranquilisers were the default drug given to patients suffering from anxiety, depression and insomnia, whose conditions were often perpetuated or aggravated by their use. Again only hindsight makes us wiser.

∞

2: Lost in The Dream

As time went on, it became obvious that Mum, rather than slowly improving, was in fact getting worse. She was suffering a serious emotional trauma. Oscillating between emotional outbursts, uncontrollable sobbing and long periods where she was uncommunicative, one evening things reached a peak and Dad had to call an ambulance. I have a vivid memory of standing at my parents' upstairs bedroom window with my dad that night, looking down on the scene below where, for the first of what would be several times, Mum was being guided into an ambulance. I remember saying, 'poor thing' out loud, at which point Dad broke down into uncontrollable sobbing. I did my best to comfort him as the true enormity of the situation first assaulted my own young understanding.

And so began a very long and cyclic period where Mum would come home after a spell in hospital, brighter and seemingly cured, only to slowly descend into a tranquiliser and alcohol fueled despair that inevitably resulted in her being carried off to hospital again. Many years later my siblings and I would discover the whole truth about this situation, and that our brother, David, was not stillborn but in fact had Downs Syndrome and, at the time when we were watching our poor mum disintegrate before our eyes, was alive and being taken care of in some medical facility. The child lived for about three years, during which time Mum kept her secret from us, all the while tormented and, perhaps because of her strict Catholic upbringing, feeling as though some kind of divine judgement was being meted out to her. This finally explained her periodic absences when Dad had spun various 'cover' stories for her; she was actually visiting her son in whatever institution he resided. A sad and painful comment about the times and, probably, the consequences of certain aspects of religious dogma. The official story told to us at the time was that our baby brother had a hole in his heart.

Another consequence of Mum's corrosive secret and her fragile condition was that we children now felt that any problems we had could no longer be openly voiced, so we just bottled up a lot of stuff that might otherwise have been vented. Our dad, too, was showing signs of the strain, but he always upheld a strong demeanour for our benefit. My situation at Douai Abbey was therefore rendered that bit more insurmountable, and all I could do was keep marking off the days to freedom in my school jotters and dream of future fishing trips.

Sally seemed to be using music as a means of escape from what was going on in the family home, and any time I was there now there always seemed to be something playing on the little record player in her room. *'And the Heaven's Cried,'* by Anthony Newley was a song that she had on repeat for ages!

Mike, on the other hand, was into making model planes at that stage and consequently gravitated more towards Dad who shared his passion.

∞

By the time I was fourteen I had reached a breaking point of my own. One day I ran away from Douai Abbey and rather than going home – only to be taken back to school – I hitched down to Bristol where Sally had just started University, turning up at her place at some ungodly hour. She was quite protective towards me in those days, so I knew I could rely on receiving an understanding ear.

I stayed with my sister for a day or so in her little flat, but of course my parents had alerted the police shortly after I'd been reported missing so it wasn't long before I was picked up and taken home. However, this desperate act on my part had the fortunate outcome of highlighting just how unhappy I was at Douai Abbey, and my parents, having finally got the message, gave me my freedom and enrolled me in the nearby Oratory School as a day pupil.

To this day I cannot understand how my frequent cries for help were not heeded sooner, or why my parents hadn't seemed to grasp that my miserable situation was going to remain as long as I attended Douai. Maybe they were hoping the situation would suddenly change the older I became, or that I would ultimately benefit from experiencing a bit of a tough regime. It could have been that they were so preoccupied trying to cope with their own degenerating domestic situation that they simply hadn't realised the extent of my suffering. As it happened, I was one of the lucky ones. Later on in life I would discover that certain others who had attended Douai Abbey had been repeatedly abused and that some of the monks were later prosecuted for their crimes.

The Oratory was an improvement on Douai, mainly because I could return home at the end of the day, but it still contained all the elements of bullying and harsh discipline I found disturbing. The school regime just wasn't for me. I didn't struggle academically or anything like that, I just seemed to be more acutely aware of, and therefore affected by, what I saw as inappropriate levels of exerted authority and punishment, religious hypocrisy and the mentality of teacher and student bullies.

I managed to stay at The Oratory until I reached the age of sixteen, though, after which my education became a bit fragmented. I went on to so-called higher education at Reading Technical College where I took some A-levels (it was either that or get a job which, for me, was a no-brainer) and spent most of my time in the common room playing cards and table tennis and chatting up girls. My dad also arranged for me to study A-level Spanish at St. Joseph's Convent, the girls' school Sally had attended. Being the only boy there for this one class I soon became the centre of attention, which was a delight for me, but not for my new girlfriend, Liz, who, as a student there, found it difficult to watch me receive so much attention from her schoolmates. I also got invited to a lot of parties and began smoking marijuana, albeit not too frequently just yet.

During the holidays Dad obtained permission for me to go shooting pigeons somewhere in Reading with a twelve bore shotgun he bought in a local second hand shop. Even at my age back then I didn't need any kind of firearms licence, and I also had an air rifle that I sometimes casually wandered around the streets with en route to some field or other. Very different days indeed. I can remember my friend James and I getting into trouble for shooting at cows in a distant field, and one night I shot a pellet at a lighted window across the railway track at the bottom of our garden, then watched in amusement as the owner came out with a torch wondering what the hell had just happened.

This was a period of teenage rebellion in which I indulged my newly-found freedom from school and adopted a bit of a blithe attitude. I learned to drive at my friend Paul's house where they had a lot of grounds and a couple of old jalopies that we used to race around the place. In the mid-sixties being able to drive a vehicle was a more relevant consideration than whether or not you had a licence, so I thought nothing of waking up my younger brother Mike late at night when our parents were asleep so that he and I could roll the family Mini out of the garage as silently as possible and onto the road before starting it up and zooming off for a bit of a joy ride. We often drove up the newly opened M4 at around sixty miles an hour, which was highly dangerous and of course illegal – not to mention a potential nightmare in prospect for our parents – but we loved every second of it! Amazingly, luckily, we were never discovered by Mum and Dad or caught by the police. And all before I passed my driving test.

Strangely, I have few memories of my mother when all this was going on, but that was a time of great strife for her, so perhaps I simply blocked out the painful stuff. I must have been affected by the growing rift that was occurring in the family at the time, though, because I remember feeling a deep sense of longing to be part of some kind of group or club. This feeling of not belonging caused a significant amount of emotional suffering, and it was the only period in my life when I have had suicidal thoughts. These were never serious enough to act upon, although I did enter a seesaw world of depression and anxiety that lasted until I began to find some independence in my life.

My dad had given me a motorbike for my sixteenth birthday; a Honda 125 Super Sports, which was only a little thing, really, but nevertheless it felt right for me to become a rocker now and try, desperately, to be accepted into a motor cycle gang. I dressed for the part in skin tight jeans, leather jacket and winkle pickers and began to frequent the Cafe Olé in Reading where the bikers met up. I met a guy called Eddie whose bike was a much more powerful 1000cc Ariel Square 4 and for some reason he befriended me – an act which, by good fortune, resulted in my half-acceptance into the Cafe Olé gang. With my posh accent and rather quiet disposition I was hardly a worthy candidate for full membership of a biker's gang consisting of tough rockers, so I think they saw me more as a kind of mascot. These guys were always looking for fights and ways of breaking the law, which wasn't my scene at all, but as it happened I wrote off my bike one afternoon when I took a corner too fast and went headlong into some bushes, an accident which necessitated the removal of a number of sharp thorns from my body, courtesy of Dad.

That whole experience was definitely a wakeup call for me, but even if it hadn't been enough to end my biker days our family was about to uproot again, this time to Harold Wood in Essex. Two things seemed to have prompted the decision to move: the first was to make an attempt to shake off the brooding disquiet in our household by creating a fresh start, and the second was to allow Dad to work in a different GP practice and thereby escape the problems he was having with his current partner who was an alcoholic. This doctor was a real social gadabout whose nickname – for a reason I can't recall – was Fumph!

Despite his own considerable problems, Dad showed me lots of consideration at this time in my life. He was nothing short of amazing in the way he supported me in whatever I chose to do and I suspect, having come to realise the level of suffering I had endured, he was probably trying to make up for sending me to Douai Abbey. I could always rely on getting a lift from him over to friends' houses or to parties now, and he used to give me ten bob every morning to buy my lunch and pay for bus fares, some of which was channelled to the betting shop when I went through a brief phase of gambling.

Around this angst-ridden time Mike and I began to hang out together a lot. It was mostly a matter of convenience as we were both feeling a bit lost and displaced by the sudden move to Harold Wood where we had no real friends. I now owned an old car, though, which meant I could drive us both back to our old haunts in Reading where Mike had just started to enjoy playing music with his friends, so his guitar was always a third passenger in the car. We occasionally visited our sister who was now away living in a house with friends somewhere in Hampshire. Having had a complete change of heart following a very personal awakening experience, Sally left Bristol University where she had been studying English literature and philosophy to explore a completely new direction in music. This was, on the surface, a highly impetuous decision, but history would later vindicate her from any misgivings our parents might have had about it.

∞

By the age of seventeen I started to have lots of girlfriends. Chasing girls became my new way of seeking completeness in a world where something was always missing, and so began a long period of sex addiction when I was desperately trying to compensate for the separation I felt between myself and the world. It was something that at least made me feel connected, if only for brief moments in time. Unfortunately, it also distanced me somewhat from Mike, and I remember on one occasion when I brought home a girlfriend my younger brother was clearly very envious. Coupled with this, his lack of friends in Harold Wood and the feeling that our family was in crisis now saw him divorce himself completely from the unpleasantness around him and retreat into a better, consoling world of music. Now isolated in his room, Mike would play and listen to music for hours on end, developing his intricate guitar instrumentals. Before long, all those solitary hours spent practising combined with his natural musical ability saw him progress to a level where, aged just thirteen, he was already earning a reputation in folk clubs as a decent musician.

My brother and sister now seemed to have found a powerful focus in their individual worlds of music whereas I, in complete contrast, had no clear sense of direction let alone any musical aspirations. What might the future have in store for me? I wondered.

∞

Not long after Mike left school at fifteen, he and Sally joined forces to play together in a few clubs; they even made a studio demo recording at the suggestion of, and assisted by, Mick Jagger of *The Rolling Stones*. This happened as a result of Sally's old school friend, Marianne Faithful, being Mick's girlfriend at the time, not to mention our sister's determination to get a recording deal. Before long, Sally got her wish and she and Mike were signed to make an album with Transatlantic Records. Their folk duo, *The Sallyangie*, was born. Comprising fourteen songs they mostly co-wrote, the album, *Children of the Sun*, was recorded in August 1968 and featured guest appearances by drummer Terry Cox with Ray Warleigh on flute. On this debut album, released the following year, Sally's signature vocals set the sweetly enchanting mood, with Mike's energetic guitar work giving an early glimpse of things to come.

There now came a period when I was a sort of roadie for my brother and sister, driving them around to gigs in an orange minivan; a temporary occupation that would nevertheless portend my more immediate future. Whatever destiny might have had in store for *The Sallyangie* is something over which there will always hang a question mark, since after a few months Mike grew increasingly more disenchanted by the situation. Six years his senior, Sally was always going to be the big sister and, whether intentionally expressed or not, the boss! The fact that the duo was largely her baby didn't help either, and I think my brother felt a bit railroaded into doing things both musically and commercially. The final straw seemed to come when Sally had some colourful hippie clothes made for them for a photo shoot; Mike hated the clothes and the image being moulded for him since his predilection was more towards rock music. Despite having a number of gigs lined up – including one at the Festival Hall – and a second album on the horizon, Mike walked away from *The Sallyangie*.

Regardless of how this may have appeared at the time, my brother's abrupt decision to turn his back on what seemed like a great musical opportunity showed both integrity and a commitment to following his own direction. Ultimately it also lined up a better outcome for both himself and Sally.

When *The Sallyangie* disbanded, Mike and I became closer again. Our musical tastes were more closely matched so, despite the fact that I could only play three chords on guitar and dabbled with a bit of bass, we decided to form a new band called *Barefoot*. We teamed up with a couple of other musicians including a drummer, and Julia Creasey – a lady who had been assistant to *The Sallyangie* manager, Roy Guest – became our manager. Dad provided the cash for us to buy a couple of new amps and upgrade our minivan to a Transit. Throughout our teenage years Dad indulged – and frequently funded – the musical ventures of his offspring, but he always wanted to know when we were going to get 'proper' jobs!

Barefoot performed heavier Rock 'n' Roll oriented songs and instrumentals in various clubs and colleges, but I couldn't really play for toffee and just strummed away on the three guitar chords I knew or plucked a little bit of bass. For me the one enduring piece we played in that period was *Flight of the Eagle*, a song I would record many years later with Mike on guitar on my 2012 album, *Journey into Space*, and a version of which I still perform to this day.

Barefoot turned out to be very short-lived and we only did a few gigs, but it was a fun period and a precious experience with resonance that, like ripples in the pond, resurged throughout my life.

— The Hidden Side —

Now nineteen, I decided I wanted, had to, leave home. Apart from being of an age when most young people want the kind of independence that can only come from flying the nest, the situation with my mum was creating an edgy, unstable atmosphere at home. Mike was feeling it the most, probably because he was the youngest, and music had become his only source of refuge away from all the arguments, sadness and mental instability.

Fortunately, I was offered a share house in Bayswater in the borough of Chelsea and Kensington in West London, and when I took up the offer Mike came with me. We were joined by our girlfriends, so our lives immediately took on a new sense of freedom and increased scope. We listened to music whenever we pleased, often while stoned of an evening, and went to a lot of gigs together. I liked *Donovan, The Incredible String Band, Pink Floyd* and *The Moody Blues*, whereas Mike loved the intricate guitar work of Bert Jansch and John Renbourn, both of whom had had an influence on his own early style of playing. I remember we went to see *The Who* in Reading one night when they were just starting out and being impressed by their stage act where Pete Townsend smashed up his guitar at the end of the concert. I didn't really like *The Rolling Stones, Crosby Stills and Nash* or Neil Young very much, and neither Mike nor I were especially taken by Bob Dylan's music, although sometimes I wonder whether all of them had some kind of collective influence, albeit on a subconscious level.

We also used to go to a music venue in Chalk Farm in London called *The Round House*. This was an old converted railway turning shed that had a great buzz about it – it was also really cheap to get in! At the weekend several bands were on the programme and a lot of the upcoming talent would cut their teeth here, including many of today's megastars. It is quite surreal now for me to recall one evening when Mike and I were sitting there supping a couple of beers and our entertainment consisted of a warm-up act featuring Elton John, followed by *The Who*, then Rod Stewart (who had just exploded onto the scene), and finally, the

2: Lost in The Dream

main event, *Pink Floyd*. All on one bill in a venue with a capacity of around three-hundred people...

You could also just walk up and say hello or have a chat with any of these people who later became so elusive and attained demigod status in the eyes of many. There were no barriers between people in those early days because of course no one knew what was destined to happen; they were all just playing in local pubs and venues around London. It occurs to me now that as I was wandering around these places following the music I was in fact accompanied by a brother who was himself destined to become one such megastar.

∞

While in the house in Bayswater I read a book called *The Hidden Side of Things* by C.W. Leadbeater, a theosophical work based on clairvoyant investigation that examines the hidden aspects of our physical world. This prompted me to begin exploring aspects of the spiritual pathway, and I have come to realise that since then it has been my aim to break free from the conventions of habitual responses and patterns of behaviour imposed upon me by society. The pseudo-religious environment of ritual and mimicry that I was brought up in ironically became the launching pad in that quest. It had provided the necessary level of dissatisfaction to set me moving in search of liberation from the 'Mind-Forged Manacles' that are the source of all suffering in this world.

After a while I moved into a house in Pandora Road in West Hampstead where travelling friends of the occupiers would drop in unannounced. These impromptu visitors often included friends-of-friends from all over the world; back-packers who'd spend a night or two sleeping on the floor and regale us all with tales of their travels. This was the time when the hippie trail to India had just started and, acting in tandem with the existential curiosity that now burned within, these people and their interesting stories really sparked something within me. I began experimenting with my diet, too, after one of the house visitors introduced me to macrobiotic cooking. This really appealed to me, so I started living almost exclusively on brown rice and gomasio (a dry condiment made from sesame seeds and salt) until one day when I was loading music gear into the van I collapsed from exhaustion and had to be brought round by someone who gave me a cheese sandwich!

— 1969. One Small Step... —

In the year that men first landed on the Moon, Mike and I both got jobs involving music. For Mike it was as a bassist with Kevin Ayers' group, *The Whole Earth* (I first learned about this when Kevin came round to rehearse after Mike's successful audition), and in my case a roadie job came up for a band named *Formerly Fat Harry*. The only experience I'd had of this kind of work was driving Mike and Sally around when they were *The Sallyangie*, but luckily the band's previous roadie gave me a little training on how to set up the stage a few days before my first gig with them. I was then handed the keys to a Ford Transit van and left to my own devices. This involved loading the van with all the equipment and picking up – individually – each of the four members of the band before travelling to the gig, unloading the equipment and setting it up on stage and mixing the sound, then doing the same things in reverse at the end of the performance. A one-man, full-time job if ever there was one. But in this baptism of fire I learned a lot about sound and mixing that would serve me well later in my career.

This was still the sixties, of course, so most of the time both me and the band were stoned when all of this was going on. Looking back now this was, bizarrely, something that was not only accepted but *expected*. One of my 'duties' as roadie was actually to ensure the band had a sufficient amount of cannabis available at every gig, so we'd all be doing our thing, setting up stage, performing, travelling to and from gigs, in a haze of drugs.

Mike, Sally and I also took some LSD trips together around that time, and I can remember how the reality of our surroundings would be substituted, invaded, by whatever hallucinations our minds randomly conjured while we were wandering around the streets of London throughout the night. It was a time of stark contrast between drug-induced fantasies and the reality of our young, uncertain worlds.

∞

For the next year or so contact with our parents was sporadic, but I remember one day Mum rang me up unexpectedly and told me flatly, 'I'm going to put my head in the oven and turn on the gas...'

I raced over to the house in Harold Wood as fast as possible only to find Mum just sitting in her armchair in the lounge, calmly smoking a cigarette and watching TV.

After that event I could never take the subsequent episodes or emergencies very seriously, but in any case I don't believe I was especially close to my mother, so I wasn't strongly affected by her illness any longer. I just got on with my life and, for the most part, let it all wash over me.

— A New Platform —

By the time that the swinging sixties' peace signs and love beads had given way to flared trousers and platform shoes in the early 1970s, other than acquiring some helpful knowledge about sound engineering and a bit of cash my roadie job with *Formerly Fat Harry* had offered nothing but a heavy workload. Just at the point when I was starting to think about handing in my notice with them, a very timely piece of good fortune fell into my lap when I was asked to roadie for American rock band *The Byrds* on their European tour in May 1971. It was the same type of job, of course, and still involved some hard work, but it would be a change from my current routine and, more importantly, it promised the excitement of travelling with a famous band. So, I worked my notice with

Formerly Fat Harry and passed on the baton of roadie wisdom to my replacement, Les, before hitting the road with *The Byrds*.

Already with more than half a dozen albums and the hit singles *Mr. Tambourine Man* and *Turn, Turn, Turn,* to their name, *The Byrds* were an auspicious group known for their pioneering exploits in Folk rock, Psychedelia and Country rock styles. This meant that I would now be exposed to more innovative music performed by maverick musicians, but I got more of a different kind of experience during that tour, as well, since there were always groupies lingering around backstage after the concert. These girls were intent on notching up scores on who they slept with, and if all the band was taken then the roadies became fair game.

Being stoned most of the time we'd engage in all the 'Rock 'n' Roll' things you'd typically expect a band to get up to. I can remember going to a red light district one time in **Amsterdam** with all the guys and wandering through the streets looking at all the girls in the windows displaying their wares. I was too shy to be tempted but some of the others would go in and spend some quality time with whoever took their fancy. One of the roadies who indulged later recanted a very amusing story involving two girls and a bubble bath!

Some of the stuff that went on with drugs and alcohol wasn't so funny, and several times I came pretty close to dying on the road. There were virtually no rules about drug or drink driving in those days; we all did it and thought little of it. A tragic and bitterly ironic incident was destined to occur just a couple of years later when guitarist Clarence White was killed by a drunk driver in

California while helping to load the gear after a concert. Looking back I was indeed lucky to have survived those days.

Continuing my run of good fortune, at the end of *The Byrds'* tour I was offered a job as roadie for singer-songwriter and guitarist *Julie Felix. She was a lovely lady who sang folk-influenced songs and gigged a lot in working men's clubs and the like in the north of England; places which were an entirely different world compared to the venues I had been used to working at. I did find it rather strange that she played at Gentleman's Clubs and some other rather strange places on occasion, but she was a strong character and took it all in her stride.

A luxury Julie allowed herself was to be chauffeur-driven to gigs in a Rolls Royce by a neighbour of hers while I followed along with all the gear in her Volvo Estate! However, I used to spend quite a lot of time at her house which was a really nice homely place that she shared with her daughter and female partner, and where she introduced me to healthy foods. We had a good working relationship, but despite being invited to her home on many occasions she nevertheless kept herself a bit aloof from me, and I was very much aware that my position in her life was as someone on the payroll.

∞

* Julie Felix passed away on 22nd March 2020 aged 81, almost at the same time these words were written.

Working as a roadie I gained a lot of experience that would (unknown to me at the time) come in handy later in my career – and of course it paid the bills – but I grew weary and disillusioned by the heavy workload and the stagnancy of the job. Where could it lead? Furthermore, the backpackers I'd been meeting back at the house had kindled a flame of inspiration, a flame constantly being fanned by my spiritual curiosity. I wanted more than was currently on offer in my life.

So, after working with Julie for about a year, I went to a camping shop and bought a sleeping bag and a back pack...

— Take up Thy Bed and Walk! —

Travelling turned out to be my saving grace. It led me to experience the tremendous diversity of life and human nature on this planet within the Great Mystery...

With existential curiosity simmering away within me, and enough money in my pocket saved during my time as a roadie, I began my travels. Fortune would have it that my very first port of call provided the perfect atmospheric surroundings for inner reflection and spiritual enquiry. It was also the place where I had two encounters that would redirect the course of my life.

3. Awakening to The Dream

I think all religion is an attempt to explain the mystery that is life. The rational mind, the problem solver – ego – cannot bear the inexplicable. I have read many books – mystical, practical, esoteric – and taken part in dozens of retreats and courses, and they have always led me back time and again to this point, this living moment in time containing the eternal that these religions profess to seek. As a child, religion for me was just another tedious subject at school, one that had a rather boring practical side that kept me away from important things like football and fishing. The insufferable Latin masses my mother had taken us to every Sunday did nothing to instil any interest, either.

It was only when I came up against some of the unanswerable questions in life that the true spiritual quest began.

— Hydra —

My girlfriend Caroline had always wanted to visit Greece as she was very interested in archaeology. To me it seemed as good a place as any to start, so we motored down through Europe in my Renault 4L (in which I had proudly just fitted a brand new engine), camping as we went, before leaving the car in the port of Piraeus in Athens and, on a whim, catching the ferry across to Hydra.

Located in the Saronic Gulf of the Aegean Sea, the island of Hydra is situated about twenty-seven nautical miles off the Peloponnese on the Greek mainland. Derived from the Greek word for *water*, and in reference to the island's natural springs which unfortunately no longer exist, Hydra has been a popular retreat for tourists and Greek people alike for many decades. To this day, apart from the rubbish truck, no cars are permitted on the island.

The hub of activity was, and still is, focused around a natural crescent-shaped harbour surrounded by steeply sloping stone streets full of small houses, shops, restaurants, cafés, markets and galleries. Like many others before and since my first arrival, visitors and residents enjoy the calm serenity offset by a rich and intimate social and artistic culture where poets, artists and musicians have enjoyed an environment conducive to their respective muses. For some, like me, there is also a hint of something that alludes to the spiritual.

As two young people who had not travelled much before, Caroline and I were naturally awestruck when we arrived at our final destination. The vibrancy of colour all around on land and sea, the intense perpetual blue of the sky, immediately seduced our two impressionable minds and souls. In a state of unsurpassed bliss we explored the terrain by day and the cafés and restaurants by night, always enveloped by Hydra's magical and indefinable atmosphere. It was like a little piece of heaven had been dealt to us in reward for everything unpleasant that had occurred in life thus far.

Caroline only had a few weeks available before her new term at Manchester University resumed, but when the time came all too soon for her to return to England, I decided to stay on in Hydra. I had quite literally fallen in love with the place and for the first time in many years I felt very happy. This was one of those decisions, so frivolous and apparently insignificant at the time, which turn out to be great turning points in life.

3: Awakening to The Dream

∞

After Caroline left I felt a little bit lost but nonetheless very contented. Now sleeping among the rocks on the beach just outside the port because it was summer (and also because it was free!), by day I earned a meagre living making macramé bracelets and selling them to the tourists.

Late one afternoon a small group of young people ambled over to me on the beach. Among them was a pretty girl in high cut shorts whose warm, smiling face immediately caught my eye. Being a shy person I somehow also envied the way she moved about the place with such natural, easy grace, confidently chatting away with her friends. That was something so far beyond my capability when viewed from the space I had created for myself, where I relied more upon a certain interesting aloofness to look appealing to people I longed to have as my friends.

The pretty girl, an Australian called Lynne, was doing some travelling before returning to teach in London that autumn. She bought one of my bracelets and effortlessly engaged me in a conversation like two friends who'd seen each other only yesterday, rather than that of two complete strangers. There was a strong mutual attraction right from the start, and although I had none of her relaxed confidence this was the late '60s and I was a handsome, care-free, long-haired twenty-two year-old with an eye for a pretty girl – and hormones were running high!

We only had a few days together before she had to return to her life in London, but, apart from our fleeting summer island romance in the sunshine and under the stars, before she left Lynne unwittingly gave me a very precious gift. As we were walking along the beach one afternoon she introduced me to a German backpacker she knew. He was sitting on a rock playing the flute. The sound immediately caught my attention. It seemed to surround and communicate with me on an enigmatic yet somehow familiar level. As it turned out, my fellow traveller was not a musician, in fact he could only play one tune, but the sound captivated me nonetheless. I was curious, intrigued. He obviously saw the effect it was having on me and asked, 'Do you want to buy it?'

Reluctantly I had to tell him that I couldn't as I didn't have much money. He seemed to consider this for a little while before saying, 'Alright… you can have it for ten dollars.'

My eyes widened. 'Okay… I can manage that if I sell a few more bracelets today,' I said. 'Thanks!'

And just like that I was the proud owner of a silver flute, an instrument with which I had no experience and, save for their very existence, barely any prior knowledge. It was a completely new thing for me (to this day I can't even recall the make) but, having experienced the sound it made and how this communicated with me, I felt it was perhaps something I could explore and express myself with. As though acting as an agent (or angel) to ensure I continued to be steered safely in the right direction, Lynne was so determined I learn to play the flute that I was carried along on the waves of her enthusiasm at a most crucial point in what was to be my musical life path. For that I owe her a vast debt of gratitude. Strange how the universe plays itself out in seemingly simple ways.

There was no talk between Lynne and I of continuing our relationship, although we wrote to each other until I eventually moved on from Hydra. After that my lack of a fixed address meant that any further contact would have had to be instigated by me. Feeling guilty about what had happened between us, I wrote Caroline a confession letter telling her about the brief affair. As I was penning the words I realised that I was almost certainly ending our three-year relationship, but I couldn't hide the truth from her or live with the guilt hanging over me. A few weeks later I got the letter that confirmed my expectation. It wasn't angry or accusatory, just very calm and very definite. Caroline and I were over.

∞

With no proper idea as to how notes were produced on the instrument, all I could do was experiment with the flute. I discovered that if I removed the mouth piece section it was easier to practise making notes, even though the sound was pretty crude.

From then on I would take my flute into the beautiful solitude of Hydra's pine forests and sit for hours just exploring the instrument and finding my way whilst listening to the wind in the pines, the birdsong and the silence in between. Losing one part of myself and reconnecting with another as gradually, over time, I became more and more familiar with the enigmatic musical tube.

Since Hydra always presented the possibility of a chance encounter with a fellow artisan or a conversation that could easily extend long into the night, it wasn't long before I had a little social circle of friends; people who included local islanders, Greek nationals and of course travellers like myself. With these new friends I often took off to the mainland to visit the remains of some of the old temples and theatres that stand serenely in the ancient landscape, and here I would sometimes play my flute, sensing the energy of the places and expressing my feelings through the magical transformation of breath into music. I had been sad and withdrawn in my teenage years and set off travelling in order to find some sort of meaning in my life, and now, through the flute and my connection with the energies of this ancient Greek world, my own energies again began to flow.

I have come to believe that learning to play the flute in this way – with no formal training or tutor book – provided a great advantage in that it allowed me to develop my own unique style. With no one showing me how to produce the notes or musical phrases, I just regraded the flute as a means of expressing how I was feeling, and thereby, unconsciously, it became a natural extension of 'me'. This later transferred naturally to the Indian bansuri flute, and I now simply use both instruments as an expression of how I'm feeling in the moment. There is a tremendous excitement about not knowing in advance what the next note is going to be, and it is both stimulating and natural to become the conduit for the natural voice of the universe where all I have to do is allow it to flow through me. This seems to extend to listeners, too, who immediately detect the open-hearted honesty, and that they are listening to something that is coming from a place other than just the player's fingers or the composer's mind.

I had found a renewed sense of peace both in the flute and my new surroundings, but I wanted to travel and see more of the world, so this first visit to Hydra only lasted for three or four months. The next destination had been in my mind since the many evenings in Hampstead spent listening to visiting backpackers as they spoke of their adventures in this mysterious land with its promise of spiritual awakening. Exactly what I was looking for.

— India —

With the silver flute a new addition to the contents of my trusty backpack, I left Hydra for Athens to pick up the Renault 4L that Caroline and I had left there when we boarded the ferry to Hydra. Bound for Istanbul and then on to Afghanistan to join the hippie trail through India, I now embarked on a pretty gruelling three-week journey right across Turkey and Iran down to Kabul. Along the way I picked up some hitchhikers who provided company as well as petrol money, and there were lots of stops on the way with cafés and restaurants that catered for western tourists.

When at last the long trip came to an end, I sold the car in Kabul for one hundred and fifty dollars, which would be my funding for the next few months in India. Kabul also happened to yield another bit of serendipity in my spiritual quest when I found a book called *Freedom from the Known* by J. Krishnamurti in a second-hand book stall. As I began reading this in solitude a little while later, something happened inside me. I suddenly found myself unable to formulate a cohesive thought. Somehow I became detached from Terry the character, completely in the present moment, high without any drugs or deliberate attempt to induce the state. I was in fact having my first experience of being 'out of my mind', a lightning-fast response to something in the book that triggered a deep understanding in the way I perceived the exterior world.

When the experience subsided and the world once again came into normal focus, I continued my journey by bus, crossing the border between Pakistan and India on 3rd December 1971, where I was met by a scene of total panic and chaos...

— War —

I had inadvertently chosen the worst possible time to embark on the final leg of my journey as this was the day that war broke out between India and Pakistan and both countries were now shelling each other across the border. The moment my feet touched Indian soil we bus passengers were quickly bedecked with a garland of flowers (presumably for choosing the Indian side) before being whisked away and put on an evacuation train south away from the fighting. Next thing I knew I was in Delhi at night time in a total blackout because of the local fear of air raids. No lights, not even candles, were allowed. I couldn't go anywhere so I just had to lay out my sleeping bag on a railway platform along with about a thousand other people and try to go to sleep!

Sleep, however, wasn't really possible with air raid sirens going off intermittently through the night; an alarm that was particularly frightening since no shelters were available. A fellow traveller also lost all his possessions to robbers who, I quickly learned, were pretty prolific here.

There was no security, no British embassy or government to help; that was just how it was in those days. An accepted part of travelling. Nevertheless, the night spent on that platform taught me a valuable lesson about dealing with adversity. Being in a situation where I had serious concerns for my mortal safety also proved a fertile environment in which to contemplate spiritual matters, fuelled by the re-reading of passages from my book, *Freedom from the Known*.

The long night on the platform passed without further drama and the following morning I was able to move on and book into a seedy little place in Chandi Chowk called the Bell Hotel. Behind the disillusioned-looking little man sitting at the reception desk a bold wall sign informed all patrons:

No responsibility is taken for any guest who attempts to tackle a hooligan on the premises.

Fortunately, the Indo-Pakistan war was a military confrontation that lasted just thirteen days, and therefore also one of the shortest wars in history. The abrupt cessation of conflict immediately rendered me free to spend a year travelling around India, visiting many of the main sites like the Taj Mahal and the Golden Temple, and of course the hippie haven, Goa, which in those days was a very cheap place to live. I travelled there by express train simply because I had become exhausted from sitting on a luggage rack for twelve hours prior to my trip. I was vaguely aware that I hadn't seen any foreigners for some time, then shortly after I exited the train station and was walking past what looked like an old hut in the village a stern voice shouted, 'Stop!' Two policemen then suddenly appeared and led me inside what I now realised was actually the local police station. Both men were armed and, what was somehow even more alarming, pretty drunk. They kept aggressively repeating, 'Where you from?'… 'American?'… 'Why you here?' So I made every effort to be as calm and polite as possible. It was a very threatening situation and I felt highly vulnerable because of course I was alone and, apparently, the only foreigner in the area. Somehow I managed to convince the policemen that I was harmless, after which they offered me a drink from a bottle of cashew fenny, a local hooch brew, and when I accepted and pretended to enjoy it they relaxed and we rapidly became friends. They even found me a place to stay for the night.

After this impromptu initiation, for a period of about three months I travelled around India and stayed on a house boat with a delightful Indian family in Kashmir where I met a lot of interesting people, including the son of the owner of Coutts Bank in London who was travelling for the same reason as me: to see the world and perhaps find some deeper meaning along the way. The only difference was that he had loads of money to do it with!

Necessity dictated that I had to live very frugally as I journeyed through India, and even though it was remarkably cheap I still had to turn to my family back home now and again for a little financial support.

When I reached Madras by train towards the end of 1971 I was almost entirely broke, but I had found a new peace within myself, a contentment that had never really existed previously – except, perhaps, in early childhood.

It was here I met an Australian guy who was on his way to work on an oil rig somewhere. He was a really nice, down-to-earth bloke and we got on tremendously well. One evening we went to see Ravi Shankar and family playing an evening raga on New Year's Eve. It was a wonderful concert, paid for with my last few rupees. I remember walking back to the hostel under a full moon and feeling like nothing could ever be more beautiful than that night, despite the fact that I was now penniless! Anyway, my Australian friend also turned out to be my guardian angel as he lent me enough money to keep me going for another stint on my aimless journey. Strangely, I can't recall his name, but I do remember eventually paying him back when I had the money.

Having now met and reluctantly said goodbye to two Australians, I was already beginning to form a good impression about their distant homeland, a place which was a complete mystery to me.

Financially refreshed, I continued with my travels.

— The Promise of the East —

Travelling only with my backpack, I hopped on a banana boat, deck class, from Madras to Penang, and from there hitchhiked (on two different motor bikes) down to the border between Malaysia and Singapore. When I finally arrived there, limbs stiff from riding pillion on the motorbikes for several hours, I was immediately arrested for being a hippie. It was obvious that the local authorities were feeling very threatened by what they'd heard about the things going on in California with flower power, drugs, free love and the so-called hippie invasion, and they didn't want any of these types coming into Singapore.

The pervading paranoia seemed to be in evidence everywhere. There were even posters dotted around the place featuring a photo fit of a guy sporting long hair and a beard, below which – as though they were a separate and dangerous species to be avoided for one's own safety – was a description of what a hippie *is*. Having been identified as one of these loathsome creatures my passport was confiscated and I wasn't allowed to go through customs until I got a shave and a crew cut after which, under police escort, I was conducted to the nearby harbour and put on another banana boat. This time, entirely at the command of others, I set sail, deck class again, for Palembang on the Indonesian island of Sumatra.

After many more hours of largely uncertain travel, I found myself sitting on a bus now travelling through the island of Java just as the light was beginning to fade, dreamily watching a thunderstorm in the distance lighting up the dark, gathering clouds. By this time I was exhausted from all the travelling and the stress of being treated like a criminal at the border of Singapore, not to mention pretty broke. I was also suffering from a nasty case of impetigo on my face that I had picked up in a Madras swimming pool, but somehow, in spite of it all, those flashes of lightning in the direction I was travelling were like little bursts of joy that gave me hope and a sense of confidence that I was heading in the right direction. Something deep down inside me was having a great adventure and a valuable life experience through not knowing what would happen next, so I just rolled with the dice.

Following another spell of hitchhiking, this time from east Java to Bali (another little haven for travellers in the early 1970s), at last I arrived in what my mind first told me was simply a beautiful, vivid dream. Having fallen asleep on the bus my subconscious had surely dreamed up a heavenly vista by way of compensation for all the recent gruelling travel. It was wishful thinking. Had to be. But it wasn't. It was Bali completely devoid of all the night life and clubs that would spring up there in later years, where expanses of virgin white sand were touched only by sparkling azure ocean stretching for eternity.

I found accommodation here in a little straw hut owned by a family of rice farmers on palm-fringed Kuta beach; meagre living quarters situated right in the middle of paradise that I paid for by helping the family plant new rice in the nearby paddy fields. Every morning the children and I would walk to work holding hands as we crossed sugar white sand in the warming Balinese air, accompanied on the journey by the sound of breaking waves and sea birds delivering a soft serenade. So beautiful.

With surroundings so conducive to improvised expressions of the inner world, my flute playing now became a lot more frequent. Not since my time in Hydra had I spent so many hours outdoors, sitting under the shade of a tree, just letting random melodies flow through me from some mysterious place.

After a couple of months of pure delight on Kuta beach I got to hear about a small charter flight that was leaving shortly for Darwin in Australia, and I wondered whether this might be another 'nudge' in an unplanned direction. Perhaps falling into my lap now was the perfect opportunity to discover the origin country of the two people who had impressed me most on my travels so far. The fact that I'd heard British people referring to Australia as 'the other side of the world' – rendering it the furthest place to which I could possibly travel on planet Earth – only made this distant land even more appealing. So, with most of the money I had left I bought a seat on the charter flight.

— A Land Down Under —

I arrived in Darwin in the Northern Territory of Australia with eight dollars in my pocket. Fortunately, I didn't need a visa or anything, so the first priority was to find any kind of work as soon as possible.

My first impression of the place was nothing like I had anticipated since, in those days, Darwin was very outback and resembled a kind of shanty town where all the houses were built on poles and elevated high above the ground to keep them cool and dry. I was made to feel very welcome by the locals, but I soon discovered that the area was in the middle of a depression so, despite trying very hard for three days, I just couldn't find a job.

I was told there would likely be more opportunities around Alice Springs further south as it was much more populated, so my only option was to start hitchhiking once again. It took another three days, but I finally managed to get a lift in an army truck full of off-duty squaddies bound for a swim in the idyllic Catherine Gorge. The route took us right down through the middle of Australia; hundreds of dusty kilometres on a dead straight road and nothing to see on the trip but ant hills. Our driver had a brick lodged on the accelerator in an early version of cruise control that was apparently common practice among the outback truckers.

Completing my journey south required a second hitchhike, and this time I managed to get a lift on a road train, a huge Mac truck with several trailers. I was of course feeling drained and a bit despondent by this stage, not least of all from the many hours spent on the road, but the driver was friendly and seemed sympathetic to my predicament.

As we were passing through a little town called Tennant Creek, around six hundred kilometres north of Alice Springs, he turned to me and said, 'Look, maybe this'll be a bit of a risk, but there's a mining camp about forty kilometres out from the main road at the crossroads up ahead. If I drop you there you'll see people going to work from Tennant Creek who'll stop and give you a lift to the camp. You might find a job up there.'

So I hedged my bets and was suddenly standing at a deserted crossroads at 4 a.m. in the morning with my pack on my back and two dollars in my pocket, waiting for another stranger to take me to an unknown place for a job that might not exist. I was alone in the middle of nowhere; broke, hungry, thirsty and exhausted.

Two hours later, an aboriginal couple gave me a lift in the back of their old pickup truck beside their dog. The man had a labouring job at the mine and he said he'd show me where to go to ask about work. Rocked by the action of the truck as we cruised along the deserted road, I dozed fitfully on the short journey towards the next cryptic encounter with my immediate future.

∞

The sun was creeping up as I sat perched on the steps of the Peko Mining Camp office waiting for it to open, suddenly thinking, *What the hell am I going to do if I can't get a job here? This is the end of the line.* I look back on that now as the magic moment I gained my true independence because there was no one else to help me, and my only other available option was to become a beggar.

At 8 a.m. a tall, official-looking man turned up wearing khaki shorts and shirt with long socks and (curiously) shiny shoes.

When he caught sight of me sitting on the steps a wistful little grin fell upon his weather-beaten face, as though somehow my story was already familiar to him. 'Where did you spring from, mate?'

'I'm just looking for any kind of job I can get,' I told him through my parched lips.

His smile broadened. 'Don't worry, mate, we'll start you off on the shovel.'

The relief and sense of euphoria I experienced at that moment sends shivers up my spine to this day. It was like I had suddenly come to the end of a very hard endurance course and passed with flying colours. I now knew I had some security.

Next came a pair of boots, a helmet and a meal ticket for the refectory where my khaki-clad saviour, the manager of the camp, ushered me in to breakfast. '**You won't be working today, mate. We'll start you off tomorrow morning.**'

It seemed so improbable that I should experience a similar sense of happiness in this mundane canteen as I had on the day I'd arrived at Kuta beach in Bali, but there it was anyway. Peko Mining Camp would be my home for the next seven months. A place where I would earn every cent of every dollar as I experienced the true meaning of hard work.

∞

As the sun came up next morning in the camp, the first pressing thing I had to do was find the toilets. The savage heat that immediately enveloped me as I exited my tiny accommodation hut stung not just my flesh but my senses. It seemed to contain a mocking disdain, like the camp had its own presence, a personal soul, that recognised the ill-prepared newcomer in its midst. When I found 'the dunny' and opened the main door I was confronted with a large room full of big miners, all with their trousers around their ankles, doing their morning business and chatting away as though it was the local pub. Needless to say, being English I hightailed it out of there pretty sharpish, leaving trails of laughter in my wake. That was my first lesson. In future I would religiously avoid the morning rush.

Before I started work that day I took a little time to have a look around. The camp was entirely surrounded by an arid landscape of red earth stretching as far as the eye could see, with only huge termite mounds breaking up the otherwise featureless view. But I was here to make some money for travelling, not to holiday, so I just took a deep breath and made up my mind to get on with the job.

Starting out as a labourer on the shovel was tough work, especially in the heat of the outback, and had it not been for all the lifting and carrying work I'd done in my previous job as a roadie I might not have been able to keep up. To make more cash I'd also volunteer for any extra shift work whenever possible, which normally entailed pretty awful jobs like unloading sacks of lime from a huge trailer. In the powerful humidity of the day the lime powder would sting like hell when it stuck to damp and sweaty skin, and at the end of those shifts I was literally white and burning. But they paid us double time for that particular job.

I also applied for a job as Cyanide Plant Operator when it became vacant and, probably because of the danger involved, got that straight away without any competition. This made me a surface worker which was physically much easier, although I now had to wear a full body suit and breathing equipment when handling the drums of cyanide used to dissolve the gold in the ore that came out of the mine on conveyor belts. The main products were copper and bismuth, but we produced about three gold bars a day as a by-product!

Typically I worked at night on this job, and because of the complete lack of light pollution in the outback I remember the amazing skies where the eternal cosmos was laid bare, revealing the Milky Way gas cloud and an unfathomable spray of stars and galaxies. This constant and most awe-inspiring scene is also perhaps the one we most commonly take for granted, yet to be still in its presence is to gain perspective on so many levels. One morning I watched the sun coming up just as the full moon was going down on the opposite horizon and there was a perfect balance right there from my point of view on the platform, or 'cakewalk', where I would patrol the giant vats that stirred the ore. Beauty amidst and completely untainted by the enormous plundering of the Earth with great machines.

When not working I spent a great deal of time in my accommodation hut – which had the proportions of a large garden shed – so it was fortunate that I generally like being alone. It contained a very hard single bed and a small table, nothing else, and became so hot that in order to stay cool and sleep at night I had to soak my bed sheet in water from a bucket that I kept nearby.

At first the other mine workers pretty much ignored me as I didn't drink or fight and I kept – somewhat antisocially – to myself. That quickly changed one night when a group of miners who had just come off duty started dancing around my hut, laughing like madmen and shouting 'All Pommies are bastards!' Eventually I poked my head out of the hut's little window and politely asked them all to be quiet. There followed a few seconds of silence that could have indicated anything from bemusement to the calm before a violent storm. It was finally broken, however, by even louder and more raucous laughter. From then on they took me under their wing and treated me with all the kindness and consideration befitting the new Peko Mining Camp mascot.

My only real time off was once a week, if my shift work allowed, when I would get a lift for the forty kilometre trip into Tennant Creek to go to the open air cinema. One evening I saw Zeffirelli's *Romeo and Juliet*, and at the exact moment when Romeo discovered an apparently dead Juliet and said the words, *'Then I defy thee stars',* I happened to look up just as the long tail of a shooting star zipped across the night sky. Life is about moments, some dramatic and others, though seemingly trivial, with equal significance in the annals of memory, and that is one I have never forgotten.

Despite the tremendous heat of the day back at camp, I was fortunate to be there for the rainy season and witness the reawakening of the outback desert when the rains arrived, turning everything green as the dormant seeds awoke to fill the land with colour. I remember the intoxicating scent of fresh rain upon dry red earth when the distant clouds gathered in the Northern Territory to bring new life to the land. Flowers erupted everywhere and birds would arrive in transient flocks, seemingly unafraid of humans since the vast land in which they lived had prevented any previous encounter between both species.

Less extraordinary were the plagues of stink beetles that appeared in numbers so vast that it was quite impossible to walk without crunching scores of them underfoot. When they landed on exposed skin the instinct was to flick them off, but the resulting stench was terrible, like decaying flesh.

Insects of all kinds seemed to be everywhere, the weird and the winged in a tattoo of colour straight from nature's palette. The flies were sometimes so prolific that they blackened my exposed skin, and I soon developed what is known as the *Aussie wave* as I walked along with my hand constantly swiping to and fro across my face to protect eyes and nose from the infernal swarms.

One scary morning I awoke in my hut to discover that a Redback spider had made its web between my pillow and the bedside table. Also known as the Australian black widow, during the night this highly venomous arachnid had been busy spinning its home mere inches from my closed eyes.

— Farewell Tennant Creek —

Having taken an unexpected, though perhaps fortuitous, deviation to the Peko Mine on the road to my intended destination of Alice Springs seven months previously, I had absolutely no idea what was further south of the camp. The only thing I could see around me were termite mounds fashioned from the rust-coloured soil. Of course I was very grateful for the job I had and the security it afforded; simply not having to worry about how I was going to buy my next meal was a great relief, a privilege that so many of us tend to take for granted. It was also very reassuring to be saving money that I knew was going to fund the next part of my journey. Where that might be was unknown to me as yet, but having now been through a rainy season at the mine with its attendant plagues of stink beetles, mosquito swarms and a deadly spider with a penchant for sharing quarters with me, something like an internal alarm clock rang. The time had come to move on.

At that point I was completely unaware of the more civilised areas further south; I only knew that I had had enough of the mine and Australia in general. I now wanted some hard-earned comfort. And more travel.

I handed in my notice and collected my final wage packet – taking my total savings to several hundred dollars (a lot of money in those days) as I had spent very little in the previous months – then got on a bus back to Darwin. From the dusty rear window of the humid bus I watched as Tennant Creek, and another chapter in my life, faded into memory.

— Rome —

When I reached Darwin I bought a ticket to Rome, simply because there happened to be a flight going out there the next day. Deep down I think I was really longing to get back to Hydra, but there were no flights to Greece from Darwin at the time.

I spent my final hours in Australia back in the first little place I arrived at seven months previously. As fate would have it, the town was destined for almost complete destruction on Christmas day 1974 when Cyclone Tracy devastated the area. Remarkable is the ocean that separates hindsight and memory from that which is experienced in the moment.

The journey to Rome involved a stop at Singapore (my hair was short and I was relatively clean shaven, so there were no problems at the border this time) before I was finally flown on to my final destination on an overcast afternoon. To my chagrin, I wasn't particularly impressed by Rome when I arrived there; a first impression that didn't change as time passed. Perhaps it was because the atmosphere was so radically different to anything I'd experienced and found to my liking in the other places I'd visited, but exploring here just wasn't much fun. I didn't feel like I was being enriched in any way, or even having a pleasant experience, which caused me to reflect back even more on my time in Hydra and how much I'd liked it there.

The decision was made there and then.

— Return to Hydra —

After wandering the streets of Rome for only a few days I bought a flight to Athens where I would pick up the ferry across to Hydra.

I began the journey back to Hydra cocooned in a warm sense of anticipation which I hoped wouldn't be thwarted upon my return (as often happens in life) when I would discover that the first visit had been a unique, one-time-only deal. I was not to be disappointed, however, and the moment I first caught sight of the island again I knew it would forever be a little jewel in the crown of my life experience.

I booked into a small hotel this time rather than sleeping rough like before (a little luxury I could now afford), and it wasn't long before I had renewed old acquaintances and made some new friends, including one or two lovely Greek nationals. I also became acquainted with the legendary singer-songwriter Leonard Cohen who had owned a house on Hydra since the early 1960s. On the island he was just one of the guys who hung out with the rest of us at the local Tavernas; sitting at an outdoor table on the balmy evenings talking about music and philosophy or singing a few songs on which he'd accompany himself on guitar. It was all very easy-going and pleasantly untainted by swelled egos or pretence. Just a nice, relaxed life. Absolutely enchanting.

By day I took to walking the mountain tracks or visiting some of the monasteries that are dotted around the island, either alone or with friends, sometimes making the short ferry trip across to the mainland to see the ruined amphitheatres dating back to early Greek times. The semi-circular construction of these open air cultural venues is of such designed-for-purpose architectural precision that each stone resonates sound a split second after the one in front, so that when you stand on what's called the orator's stone in the centre it almost feels like you're wearing headphones!

One day I happened to have my flute in my backpack while we were at the ancient theatre of Epidaurus, so I thought I'd try out the sound for myself. Immediately I was captivated by what I heard. As I expressed how I was feeling at the time through my instrument, simply allowing myself to drift on the waves of the amphitheatre's wonderful acoustics, I began to feel like a hitchhiker on a spontaneous inward journey driven entirely by random musical improvisation. Completely, delightfully, lost. My eyes were closed – probably an unconscious action intended to block out possible visual distraction – and I had no real sense of time passing. I was simply experiencing the moment unfolding. When I finally returned to the here and now I opened my eyes to see that the scene before me had changed in a way that at first I didn't quite comprehend. Around a hundred people were sitting on the stones watching my 'performance'. I hadn't heard these tourists arriving in coaches partly because I was so carried away with my music, but also because when you're on the orator's stone all you can really hear is yourself. As soon as I stopped playing a lady sitting nearby called out, *'C'était Debussy?'* in polite enquiry as to whether my spontaneous music had been a piece by Debussy. High praise indeed.

It seemed that my first public performance had just taken place and I was the last person to know about it!

This spontaneous recital revealed to me the transcendent realm that might be entered if one only becomes entirely open to expressing what exists both within and, at the same time, invisibly, all around. It also served to highlight the enormous chasm between the indescribable peace and euphoria of that realm and the demands imposed by our physical world. Such a stark contrast, such an experience, and all resulting from a random decision to play a few notes in the ruin of an ancient Greek amphitheatre. A chance occurrence, and one that had already instigated a powerful change in my attitude towards flute playing and music in general.

∞

I had now been travelling for almost two years, living and working in several countries with deeply varied cultures. I had learned many things and met lots of interesting people. I had grown up a lot. Moreover, I was much happier now than when I set off in 1971. However, with no reliable source of income or a clear sense of what I was going to do with my life I was also becoming increasingly aware of the ephemeral nature of my current circumstances. I had no career, only temporary roots, and the concern that I should be thinking more seriously about my future began to niggle at me like a persistent, guilty recollection.

3: Awakening to The Dream

The experience at the amphitheatre had planted the seed of an idea that perhaps I could become a musician and do something I now loved – expressing emotion through a musical instrument – and get paid for it. Of course I couldn't do that on the little island I was currently living on. There were no music studios, businesses or contacts that I could approach. Hydra was a wonderful place of inspiration for me, but if I was to carve out any kind of career in music, I knew I would have to return to England to gain perspective and see what might be possible. After all this time I had a desire to catch up with my family and discover what was going on in their lives, too.

∞

In the early 1970s long-distance communication of course wasn't a simple case of selecting 'Home' or 'Mum' in the contacts list of your mobile or even nipping into a public telephone box and punching in the area code for back home followed by the number. Telegrams were the only means of contact, and that involved a trip to the post office and a dictated message for which you paid by the letter. Small wonder, then, why many months had passed in which I hadn't exchanged a single word with my folks or my siblings.

And so one lovely early spring morning on Hydra I wandered down to the Post Restante (post office, basically) in the port and sent a telegraph to my sister – or maybe it was Mike? – to say that I had booked a flight back home and would call when I eventually arrived at Heathrow airport the following week.

— For Whom the Bell Tolls —

When the train came to a standstill at Oxford station and I finally stepped onto the platform, weary from my journeys by air and rail, I let out a long sigh before breathing in the cool, fresh spring air. I was back home. After calling Mike inside the station to let him know that I had arrived, all I had to do now was relax and wait.

About twenty-five minutes later a shiny blue Mercedes 450 SL pulled up outside the station. Sitting behind the wheel was my brother. He was only just about to turn twenty and the last time I heard from him had been many months previously in a letter he sent me in Bombay (now Mumbai), telling me that he was living in a basement flat in London and still playing in Kevin Ayers' band, *The Whole World*. Since then I had absolutely no idea what had been happening in his life, or the situation with our parents in the family home.

I opened the front passenger door and eased into the cosy interior with its lovely new car smell. My brother received a smile from me and, no doubt, a look that surely must have betrayed my questioning incredulity. 'What have you been up to, then, Mike?'

He apparently hadn't lost any of his introversion, looking away from me now as he said, 'Well, I've become a bit of a success story here. Remember that stuff I'd been recording in Harold Wood?' I nodded, only vaguely recalling him mentioning something about making a demo in his letter a few months previously. 'A guy named Richard Branson liked my demo tape. He's just started a little company called Virgin Records and he gave me some free time in his studio to record an album. I've only just finished it.' Mike finally looked up at me, a little spark in his eye this time, and with complete innocence added, 'Maybe I'll be able to afford somewhere nice and quiet to live one day.'

∞

As it happened we were actually on our way to the Virgin Records home base at that very moment; Mike had been living there whilst recording his album and I was now invited to stay with him for the time being. *The Manor* was a large country house in the village of Shipton-on-Cherwell, near Oxford, that had recently been converted into a purpose-built recording studio.

Speeding along, my brother and I chatted at a more restrained pace, somewhat reservedly catching up on each other's news. Things were not good at home. Mike had spent Christmas there with our parents and Sally a few months previously when Mum, now in a constant state of alcohol and prescription drug induced numbness, had been in a pretty bad way. Her disintegrating condition was apparently punctuated intermittently by suicidal moods which had prompted Sally to return home and provide support.

I had so much to tell about my travels, but this news doused any sense of excited anticipation I may have had about sharing it. To lift the mood in the car a little I changed the subject. 'So, tell me more about your album, Mike. Do you sing on it?'

'No. There's no singing. Everyone wanted me to put vocals on it but that's not what the music is about. It's all instrumental. At the start Richard tried to get me a deal with some other record companies but they all turned it down because it doesn't have any songs. That's when he decided to take a chance and release it himself as Virgin's first ever record.'

My brother's lack of willingness to make compromises and alter his work, even at the expense of securing his first recording deal, seemed a bit stubborn, but this single-mindedness was part of Mike's character, especially when it came to music, and I admired him for it.

'What's it called?' I asked. Doing my best to sound up-beat.

Mike didn't answer straight away, as though there was some embarrassing or ironic aspect behind the album title to which only he was privy at that moment. Then I heard its name for the first time. 'Tubular Bells.'

— A New Motivation —

Having spent my first night back in England at, of all places, a country manor in which my brother had just recorded his debut forty-minute instrumental album, the following morning I awoke with the mindset that absolutely anything could happen next. Later that day I met my brother's would-be mentor, a man who turned out to be younger, jollier, shyer and altogether less businessman-like than I had expected. Turning up in well-worn jeans and a dark sweater, the wiry-haired and bespectacled Richard Branson more resembled a student – and not a particularly studious one at that – than an entrepreneur. Yet this guy who was almost a year younger than me had started a student magazine after leaving school, followed by a mail order record company and then – aided by a generous loan of £20,000 from his magistrate father – the purchase of this large country house with a barn that he'd just converted into a recording studio. I wasn't sure whether he was highly ambitious, reckless or just a tiny bit mad. Maybe even a blend of all three.

The Manor was only the third residential recording studio in the UK at the time, the others being Tittenhurst Park Mansion – owned by John Lennon and used to record his album, *Imagine* – and Ascot Sound Studios, built just a couple of years previously.

Branson's manor was a very easy-going place and the handful of guys who ran it were all relaxed and friendly. As well as being given a nice place to live and sleep I was immediately accepted as Mike's brother and treated like I belonged in this designed-for-purpose residential recording studio where all sorts of colourful characters turned up (some of whom would later become superstars), all just milling around smoking and chatting away.

As soon as *Tubular Bells* had been produced, Richard Branson wasted no time in launching an advertising campaign to promote this first release on Virgin Records, an integral part of which was a premiere performance of the piece at London's Queen Elizabeth Hall. The only trouble was that my brother, with his introverted personality, flatly refused to play live. The prospect of performing *Tubular Bells* live in front of a large audience was so unthinkable to Mike that he dismissed it as something of an impossibility.

Richard had already made arrangements at the prestigious venue, and the 25th May concert date was only weeks away. But Mike wasn't budging. Everyone tried to coax and encourage him but nothing was working – until Richard, in a desperate last-ditch attempt, tried a bribe. On top of everything else that had so far failed to act as an enticement to Mike – money, promotion, elevated status – the keys to Richard's Bentley would be added. But only if my introverted brother agreed to perform.

All we could do now was wait and see how Mike responded.

While this significant life event was unfolding in my brother's life, another suddenly began to blossom in mine, too.

It had been more than a year since Lynne and I parted company after our brief and intense romance during my first visit to Hydra. For a time we had remained in touch by letter so I knew that she now worked as a teacher in London where she shared a flat with another girl. I had thought about her a lot since coming home, especially as the distance between us had now been reduced to just a few miles where previously it was one and a half thousand. So one day I plucked up a little courage and called the number written on the last letter she sent me in Australia. After only a couple of rings Lynne's familiar voice answered. She seemed delighted to hear that

3: Awakening to The Dream

I was in London and invited me to come around to her flat that same evening. Thereby, our relationship was rekindled almost at once.

∞

When Mike finally agreed to do the concert the relief was palpable all around The Manor. Shortly after making the announcement he marched up to me and said, 'You can play flute at the concert if you like.'

I chuckled. 'Mike, don't be daft. I can't play well enough yet for that kind of thing.'

With the same tenacity that we had badgered him about doing the concert, Mike persisted with me, explaining that there would be another, more experienced flute player performing alongside me, and therefore I'd have a professional guide. That immediately gave me a bit more confidence and eventually I agreed.

The next few weeks for me were spent in a haze of intense practice and nervous anticipation of performing live at a major London concert venue. Just as well I was oblivious to the fact that I had actually been given a part in the world premiere of what was destined to become one of the biggest selling instrumental albums of all time! And, truth be told, I couldn't even play reliably in tune. During practice sessions with the other flautist I had to pitch to him and hope it was sounding okay. On the positive side, being part of the group gave me some focus as well as a bit of cash. There was no financial distinction between any of us either; regardless of experience we were all paid standard Musicians' Union fees, even though other musicians taking part in the premiere included David Bedford, Steve Hillage, Pierre Moerlen, Tom Newman and, thanks to Richard Branson's influence, Mick Taylor of *The Rolling Stones*. Mike had also secured the services of our sister, Sally, as a performer in the 'Girlie chorus' section, and Kevin Ayers on bass guitar. So the scene was set. There was just one problem: as the concert drew closer Mike's confidence decreased exponentially and he started to suffer from panic attacks.

3: Awakening to The Dream

— Baptism of Fire —

Tubular Bells

Live Premiere Performance

The Queen Elizabeth Hall, 25th June 1973

With Terry Oldfield on Flute

These were the words on the huge billboard outside the box office of the Queen Elizabeth Hall on the evening of the concert. It had been the patient handiwork of insatiable practical joker, Richard Branson, a prank that only served to put a bit more pressure on me – as if the prospect of making a live debut performance wasn't already making me nervous enough.

Fortunately, Richard had used his other considerable entrepreneurial skills to set up the perfect launching pad for *Tubular Bells* that night, inviting figures from the music industry, businessmen, celebrity figures and musicians alike. Among the guest list was Mick Jagger, who came into the dressing room to wish Mike well as we were all waiting to go on stage. This seemed to give my brother a little boost of much-needed confidence as, at that point, he looked as though he might panic at any moment and refuse to come out of the Green Room. And I knew precisely how he felt.

Suddenly the call came for us to go on stage and we all marched into the corridor of the theatre to whatever fate awaited us. My heart was pounding. I can only imagine how Mike must have been feeling.

David Bedford who was conducting as well as performing started us off too slowly, which of course set the tempo for the rest of the music, and I had the impression that the music was trudging along in places. Some of the instruments weren't properly in tune, either, and I knew both of these factors would be troubling Mike. I genuinely feared the worst.

When the entire forty-minute piece reached its conclusion and the last bars of *The Sailor's Hornpipe* were being played I had the feeling that the audience might be bored, or that they'd be less than impressed by such an unusual and extended piece of music. Then they all got on their feet and applauded loudly. Some were cheering. It was an unexpected reaction that surprised most of us and absolutely stunned Mike who later said that he was very unhappy with the performance and thought he was going to get booed off the stage, perhaps even under a hail of projectiles thrown at him by a disgruntled audience. But they just kept on cheering and applauding and Mike stood there in dumbfounded silence. Richard made a few attempts to hoist him up onto his shoulders so that he could carry him aloft for a quick lap of honour around the stage, but Mike resisted, desperate to get away from all the focused attention. With *Tubular Bells* now having been successfully revealed in concert and released as an album, my brother was puzzled, dumbstruck and relieved. He was also on the brink of becoming very famous.

∞

Life now became somewhat surreal and dream-like. On one hand spending a great deal of time with Mike at The Manor, watching as he was swept along on the euphoric first wave of Virgin Records' beginnings, made me starry-eyed about the future possibilities looming beneath my own rather naive and hopeful gaze, but on the other my flourishing relationship with Lynne was adding a very different dimension, one that fanned the flames of an underlying inhibition.

I was almost twenty-five years old with no fixed abode and suffering deep pangs of insecurity about lack of money and direction, an insecurity which, I knew, was trying to resolve itself by latching onto Mike's looming success and his ascending record company. Now penniless and in a rather beggarly situation where my younger brother had effectively began to look after me, I saw the possibility of becoming part of his success story. This belief helped to placate my worries a little, but the insecurity ran deeper than financial difficulty. There was also a sense of not knowing where to be or where to go, what I could possibly *do*. This was an emotional hole that seemed to have originated in childhood when my mother's illness began and I was sent off to boarding school.

From that time the stability of my family – and particularly my mother – had dissolved, leaving behind shadows of the parents I had once known; two adults no longer capable of giving me the love and support I so needed as a child. That wound had left a lingering insecurity that was now undoubtedly seeking to be pacified by a mother figure who would address this vacuous need and fill the enormous gap left by difficult circumstances in our family.

I had now entered the very beginnings of a dark night of the soul in which the 'I' as the separate self was craving certainty in direction and, above all, security in a relationship.

Of the many scenarios that would exemplify my unstable emotions at this time, perhaps the most fickle took place one day whilst Lynne and I were sitting in a car parked outside Harrods. Out of the blue, Lynne instigated a conversation about the possibility of having a baby together, a prospect that fitted in so well with my desperate need to cement something in place for the future and alleviate the suffering of my own insecurity that I agreed immediately. No in-depth discussion, no consideration of our circumstances. Just the quick fix. Or so it seemed at the time.

— Family Ties —

When Lynne eventually announced that I was going to be a father I wasn't quite sure how I felt, or even how I *should* be feeling, about this news. It certainly came as no particular surprise, and I had certainly fallen for the idea of being in a steady relationship with the possibility of becoming a Dad but, as ever, there were my circumstances. Having now moved out of The Manor and back into the family home with my parents, my status had advanced no further since my student days. Not a stable foundation for starting a family. Nevertheless, Lynne and I decided to seal our own family unit by getting married a couple of weeks later. The ceremony was a low-key event, attended only by family and a few close friends, but it nevertheless ushered a huge change into my life. I was now a husband and soon-to-be father, with all the attendant responsibilities of that position. I had a wife, and in about eight months I would also have a son or a daughter. That particular gap had now been filled, giving a sense of contentment and completion. My days of spontaneity and care-free explorations in travel when I only had to think about myself had come to an abrupt end.

    Probably.

∞

In between all of the activity and concerns in our lives, Mike and I did let off a bit of steam whenever we could. I recall one day in autumn 1973, shortly before the BBC Second House recording of *Tubular Bells* (in which I'd also be performing again), Mike, Richard and I decided to head down to Cornwall. We often did things like that just for the hell of it, acting completely on a whim.

    A few more Virgin record shops had recently opened here and there in various towns around England, so on our way to Cornwall Richard got us to stop in Exeter as he wanted to make a surprise visit to the newly opened Virgin store there. The three of us just casually walked in, pretending to be customers having a general look around. No one recognised Richard and he didn't make them wise to the fact that he owned the place; that was just the kind of thing he liked to do.

We had no particular plans thereafter so, following our impromptu visit to the store we booked into a small hotel in one of those lovely little fishing villages dotted along the Cornish coast and had a wander around. Richard suddenly came up with the idea to hire a small boat and go out fishing in the estuary, so we rented the boat and a few fishing rods, got some bait and motored out. We weren't really expecting to catch anything as it was all just about having a bit of a lark.

We anchored in the river mouth, cast out our lines and put our feet up, settling back to enjoy the sea air. There was no talk about *Tubular Bells*, concerts, performing or business. Just three young fellas enjoying the moment.

Suddenly, one of the rods began nodding then doubled over as an obviously large fish took one of our baits. Richard jumped up and grabbed the rod just before it was wrenched into the water and, after a lot of excited puffing, gasping and winding on the reel handle, he lifted a huge bass into the boat. Richard was very pleased with himself as he and I admired the lovely big bar of silver that now lay bucking and flapping its tail on the bottom of the boat.

Then we heard a rather sad voice saying, 'Put it back... poor thing.' In his fragile emotional state, Mike was seeing things from a very different perspective. 'Put it back,' he insisted.

3: Awakening to The Dream

Still basking in the glory of his wonderful and unexpected catch, Richard was not at all keen to put the fish back, and in protest he referred to the current price of locally caught fish! The look on Mike's face was enough for him to relent, however, and so, with some ceremony and much reluctance, the prize catch of the Virgin boss was returned to the water.

∞

Sales of *Tubular Bells* were slow initially, but as the months went by they gradually increased, presumably as word began to spread. The opening piano section on the album was also taken up as the main theme for what was to become a classic horror movie, *The Exorcist*, released towards the end of 1973 in America. Shortly after that, popularity of Mike's enigmatic instrumental piece soared, but that only created more anxiety for my brother as the phone now rang more often with people seeking him out for media events, concerts, public appearances and the like.

It is well documented that Mike had trouble coping with the success of *Tubular Bells*. The album's explosive popularity was something which took many of us – perhaps Mike most of all – by surprise. Naturally, Richard Branson wanted him to build on the album's notoriety by doing more live concerts, interviews and such, but my brother remained a very introverted young man going through emotional issues. *Tubular Bells* was forged in a turbulent cauldron of angst, stress and themes woven to create a musical balm for his pain, and now that it had been recorded Mike felt it was something that had finally been ejected from his system. The last thing he wanted to do was appear in public to reawaken the process by performing or talking about his masterpiece. His only desire now was to retreat further away from the public eye, but unfortunately people couldn't understand this. To them it was incomprehensible why such a young and talented musician wouldn't want to bask in the glory of his success just at the point when his work had opened the door to stardom. But of course, few people understood what was going on inside my brother at the time.

The only way to escape public attention, Mike felt, was to retreat into solitude. This he found in the remoteness of the Welsh hills where, conceding to contractual demands, he started work on his second album for Virgin Records.

∞

Life wasn't easy for any of us at this time. Mike was having his problems, my mum's condition was not good, and I was struggling to make a living with my first child on the way, which naturally created some friction between my new wife and I. Feeling the weight of responsibility – and inspired when *Tubular Bells* reached number one in the album charts – I began to practice the flute diligently, turning my full attention to becoming a musician now in an attempt to navigate a way out of poverty.

— Rachel Oldfield, Welcome to the World —

My first child was born on 11th April 1974 in Queen Charlotte's Hospital in London. Mother and baby Rachel had a comfortable ride home in the now rather beaten up old Bentley that Richard Branson had given Mike as an inducement to do the Queen Elizabeth Hall concert.

Although having a new baby girl was a wonderful experience, bringing her and Lynne back to my childhood home in Harold Wood where we now lived with my parents was uncomfortable for me. Sally was also coming and going at the time, which meant that there were sometimes five of us sharing the house, and there was increasing pressure on me to step up as a provider. Now was the time when traditionally the male would begin his duties of creating security around his family – make a living, so to speak. Unfortunately I could not imagine getting a job and being able to keep it; somehow that simply didn't seem to be in my genetics, and although I considered various options I just couldn't bring myself to do it. Consequently, my thoughts kept turning to Mike's success and the possibility of me and my family being included in that equation. I was driving Mike's cars, Richard Branson was taking us out to dinner and regularly inviting us to stay over at his house in London, so Lynne and I had already tasted the trappings of success epitomised by my own brother's new life. But with no obvious way of earning money of my own we were effectively dining out on borrowed glory, and this, combined with the fact that we were living with my parents, slowly began to take its toll and create further tension between Lynne and I.

By an incredible stroke of fortune, and just in the nick of time, an opportunity arose for us to move into a friend's flat in Portobello Road in London, close to where Virgin had their offices and main record store. Naturally, we leapt at this, only too relieved to move out of my parents' house in Harold Wood. Our change of residence relieved certain domestic issues, but the cloud of unfulfilled responsibility still hung low over my shoulders. Determined to rectify the situation, I really went for it with the flute playing in our new place and spent many hours practising in the basement amongst all the old furniture and stuff, teaching the fingers to do the walking while my lungs developed enough stamina to blow and my lip muscles evolved an embouchure.

Now living close to the Virgin 'nerve centre' I was always made welcome to drop in for a chat with Simon Draper (a sort of 'second in command' at Virgin) and the other guys. Richard and I had also become quite good friends by this point and the same atmosphere of informality existed in his house, which was just around the corner. I'd often pop around there for a cuppa or to discuss the current situation with myself, my brother and music in general.

One evening we all went out to a posh restaurant in Hampstead at Richard's invitation and at the end of the meal our kind benefactor suddenly disappeared, leaving the rest of us to foot the bill. When we went outside Richard came around the corner laughing his head off at yet another practical joke he'd played on us. We all thought it quite funny, too, until we realised there wasn't going to be any kind of financial reimbursement.

Outside of his business ventures, Richard seemed to live for practical jokes. I vividly recall when he dressed up as a clown to visit Robert Wyatt (from *Soft Machine*) in hospital after the drummer/singer fell from a fourth-floor window at a birthday party. This was of course an attempt to cheer up Wyatt who was now paralysed from the waist down, and just the type of well-meaning thing Richard would do, but I think the gag amused 'the clown' even more.

That sense of dualism in Richard – the erudite and imaginative businessman on one hand, and the practical joker on the other – seems to have stuck with him throughout his life.

I stayed in the guest room at the top of Richard's house rather a lot in those days and I recall how one afternoon he suddenly asked me if I would like to meet the actress Julie Christie as he wanted to take her out but thought it would be good if I came along too. It turned out that Richard and I spent a lovely evening at a club in Hampstead having dinner with this beautiful, iconic and very sweet British actress. At the end of the evening we dropped Julie off at her flat in Notting Hill Gate and that was that. I have no idea if Richard ever saw her again.

Another time he asked me to come along with him to an antique shop in Westbourne Grove called *Dodo* as there was a girl working there he rather fancied. This time, presumably just to give him a little confidence, Richard wanted me there in the shop pretending to be an interested browser while he chatted her up.

The shop assistant's name was Joan, a girl who eventually became Richard's second wife.

So I can happily say that I played a very small role in helping to bring Richard and Joan together!

— Different Outlooks —

Mike and his girlfriend Maggie had moved into an isolated little house in Herefordshire called *The Beacon*, situated high up on Bradnor Hill overlooking Hergest Ridge on the border between England and Wales. It was a bit run down, but he'd bought the place for its remote location, surrounded as it was only by vast fields of bracken and wandering sheep, with expansive views that looked down on Kington in Herefordshire below and the Black Mountains far off in the distance.

Whenever he came to London with Maggie, Mike used to pick up Lynne and I in his Mercedes and take us out to a pub for a meal. This was very nice of course, but, rather like a carrot dangling in front of a donkey's nose, on one level these visits only served to make visible that which for me remained just out-of-reach.

To make a bit of money at this time I took on the job of driving Julie Felix to her gigs again, and now that I had learned to play a bit of flute she would occasionally ask me to come onstage and accompany her on a few songs, and that was always enjoyable. It also gave me a bit of a taste of what it might be like to be a working musician.

My roadie job involved being away from home quite a lot of the time, which unfortunately only aggravated Lynne's feelings of discontent about living in London, so when she heard that one of our friends from Hydra, Fiona, had rented a farmhouse in Wales, she went down with Rachel to visit her for a few days.

This was a time of unrest and deep struggle for both of us. One day I hit rock bottom and went for a walk to escape the house and try to think, only to end up going into a phone box up the lane and calling my brother to ask if I could borrow a fiver. I could see absolutely no way of making a living, and although I was persevering with the flute practice my hopes in that area were also diminishing. Mike told me that he would send the fiver but I had to get my act together and stop asking him for money. He also said that he'd been talking to Sally and they both felt that I had acted irresponsibly by having a child without first securing some means of support. This took me into the very depths of despair and at that point I suddenly realised that Mike's success wasn't going to overflow into my own life. At least not at this time. But despite it all, there still remained the tiniest vestige of hope in my troubled mind.

Not long after this desperate phone call, perhaps a week or so, Mike rang to say that he had finished things with Maggie and could he come to see me. I think he always regarded me as a kind of anchor point or refuge in troubled times, whereas if things were going well, emotionally speaking, I wouldn't hear from him for ages. I suppose it was a kind of 'Big Brother' syndrome that naturally evolved in childhood and flowed on for some years after that.

Mike was in a very bad way indeed. Now suffering from anxiety and panic attacks, he had retreated into a reclusive shell, not answering the phone and generally struggling to hold everything together. *The Beacon* was his sanctuary, a refuge from the world where he could escape media attention from the ever-increasing popularity of *Tubular Bells* and Richard Branson's frequent pleas to take a more active role in promoting the record. It was also obvious that Richard wanted him to get a move on with the second album that he'd started, but Mike just wanted to be left alone. He was mentally exhausted after completing *Tubular Bells*, recorded as it was under stressful, time-sensitive conditions and representing – as Mike put it – his whole life poured into one piece of music. He felt there simply wasn't anything left in the tank for the time being.

We often took long walks together at this time and, perhaps in the interest of my own sanity as much as my brother's, we'd do a lot of spontaneous things just to break free from the current circumstances in our lives. One day when we were wandering through Knightsbridge on a trip to London Mike decided to buy a Range Rover for cash and, completely on a whim, suggested that we go to Ireland in his new car to try it out. Though essentially indulging Mike, his impulsiveness was exhilarating to my own free-spirited and travel-hungry nature, so a few days later Lynne, little Rachel and I set off with Mike for the Emerald Isle.

3: Awakening to The Dream

We sped off down the motorway to catch the ferry for Dublin and from there drove all the way down to Cork in the south, the city of our mother's birth, although at that time we weren't particularly drawn to explore the family history. Instead, we visited a lot of pubs where there was music playing; we loved that and Mike especially enjoyed the Guinness! In the end, though, that turned out to be a rather difficult trip, what with Mike feeling insecure about having moved into solo mode combined with the weight of his new found wealth and my contrasting poverty hanging over us. I remember one moment when Lynne, who was sitting in the back of the Range Rover with Rachel on her lap, suddenly blurted out to Mike, 'Why don't you just give your brother a job?' Mike didn't respond, and after that things became very frosty between them.

Shortly after that trip to Ireland my family and I moved into *The Beacon* with Mike when he continued to have trouble adapting to being alone, which really suited Lynne as it meant we were now living outside London. Not surprisingly, though, it was a disastrous move, what with all the mismatched tension going on between us, and one day I told Mike that we were packing up and leaving. We didn't even have a car at the time so I had to swallow my pride and ask my brother to give us a lift to the bus stop.

Just as we were about to leave *The Beacon* the most amazing and unexpected thing happened: Mike's phone started ringing and, after a few seconds of hesitation (he often ignored phone calls at that time), he picked it up. 'Hello… Yes… Yes, he is… Okay,' Mike responded to the caller before passing me the handset. 'It's Richard. He wants to talk to you.'

In the next few moments I went from staring a desperate situation square in the face to being an employee of Virgin Records. Frustrated at how my brother's painful introversion was rendering him constantly out-of-reach, Richard asked if I would liaise between himself and Mike, a job that would hopefully help to reconnect the flow of communication. Richard explained how things had become extremely difficult between them as Mike's struggle to deal with life in general had reached a point where he was now unavailable, so the Virgin Records boss was keen to have someone close to Mike who could act as a middle man. Being the person closest to Mike at this time I was the best and most obvious candidate for the task, and just to sweeten the deal in case I felt the wage wasn't sufficient, Richard added, 'By the way, the job comes with a company car... of your choice.'

And just like that, the stress of poverty and its accompanying sense of guilt vanished. I had a 'proper' job on Virgin's payroll as a minder and go-between. In today's parlance that would probably be translated into an overblown description like *Personal Security Officer and Communications Facilitator*, but minder and go-between was what I was – and all just to ensure that a level of communication could be maintained between Richard Branson and my reclusive brother.

Just as important as the twenty quid a week (equivalent to about £200 today), the new job also removed the 'Sword of Damocles' that had been hanging over my brother and I, immediately improving our respective situations. Money pressures between Lynne and I relaxed, Rachel was thriving and, with

Richard's blessing, I chose a gold Saab from the local car dealer to assume my role as intermediary between artist and manager. One phone call had made everything much better. My wage wasn't a lot, but it was an income that snatched me from the clutches of penury and that seemed like more than enough for the present.

— Terry Oldfield, Shop Assistant —

By putting me on the Virgin payroll Richard had thrown me a lifeline. Whether this had been a purely altruistic act or because he genuinely saw me as the best possible person to act as intermediary between himself and Mike (it could well have been a mix of both) is something only Richard knew for sure, but in any case I now had a regular job, one which soon extended to the position of shopkeeper in Virgin's first record store in Notting Hill Gate. Doing this second job only seemed fair, since helping to keep communication open between Richard and Mike in his tender state didn't take up all that much time. So I ended up selling vinyl records and occasionally washing windows and doing odd jobs. I had certainly had dirtier, tougher jobs, so I couldn't really complain. That was just the way it was with Virgin; if you worked with them you did whatever you were asked. There were no job interviews, CVs, job descriptions or politics. In fact, that's how people who weren't qualified or particularly well trained got into high powered jobs in the company later on. They had started off, like me, with no references or degrees at a time when we were all 'qualifying' and there was no real hierarchy among employees.

Everybody, regardless of their job, got paid twenty pounds a week, and whilst being employed again really mattered to me, living on that amount with a family to support wasn't all that easy. It was frustrating, too, how there was so much money floating about all around me, yet I had no way to access it. I began to feel rather jealous of Mike's success and couldn't understand why, even with his emotional problems, he didn't seem to appreciate the magnitude of what had happened to him. He had effectively just won the lottery and Virgin was beginning to fly on the wings of *Tubular Bells*, their ground-breaking first release which, as though to twist the knife of irony, I was now selling abundantly in my new job. Another irony arose in the fact that both Virgin Music and my brother now had accounts at Coutts Bank, which made me recall my time on the house boat in India when my path had crossed with that of the son of this bank's founder, a young man who had simply been a fellow traveller at the time. It wasn't too long before I, too, opened an account there for a short time, and I couldn't help feeling that there may be some kind of deeply-hidden synchronicity at work within all of this, as opposed to mere random coincidence.

∞

Back in isolation on Bradnor Hill, Mike was still using music as a means of escaping anxiety and the threat of panic attacks, but had little interest in returning to the process of recording what would be anticipated as the follow-up to *Tubular Bells*. Nevertheless, he was now under contract to produce a series of further albums for Virgin – and in a sense he didn't really know what else he was 'supposed' to do – so in the basic little recording studio he'd set up in a downstairs room of *The Beacon*, Mike resumed work on his next musical offering for the world. Much of the process would be a little unpleasant for him, but at least now he had his brother alongside to offer some support.

The wild rural surroundings strongly influenced the music of what would become his second studio album, with some expansive, free-floating melodies and haunting whistles wistfully describing a spacious pastoral scene. Its title even adopted the name of the geographic feature that lay in front of the house in which it was created: *Hergest Ridge*.

The album took shape in trying circumstances for both Mike and myself as we each had personal struggles to endure. For Mike it was mainly the demands of overnight success on his withdrawn personality, whilst I was struggling with long-term financial worries and what was beginning to look like a crumbling marriage. We also shared the lingering residue of unpleasant childhood memories stemming from our mother's prolonged illness, and I now became a bit closer to my brother because of this.

At Mike's request I played some flute on the final recording of *Hergest Ridge* at The Manor studio, but because of my preoccupied state of mind at the time I don't actually recall the session. In the end I think my passage of music was used on the remix of *Hergest Ridge* which took place at a later date, hence I wasn't credited on the first pressings of the album.

By the time this second album was released later that year, things had begun to improve a little for Mike – something that was in no small measure due to his exploration of the local music scene and the discovery of Penrhos Court, a nearby Elizabethan manor house that had been converted to a restaurant. Long before *Hergest Ridge* was completed the place became a haven for Mike when he met folk musician Les Penning there, after which he frequently sought refuge playing music with Les (in return for wine) when the recording of *Hergest Ridge* became a bit of a struggle. I remember being invited over to Penrhos to help with the treading of the grapes for the new wine that was to be made there... We all ended up a very merry little bunch that day!

My brother's friend William Murray, a drummer, had also moved into *The Beacon* as housemate, which meant that Mike was no longer living in isolation. The two had shared a certain rapport with each other since their days working with Kevin Ayers, and Mike seemed relatively happy with the way everything had turned out.

That Christmas our family congregated at *The Beacon* where we all got tipsy and sang carols. Sally also brought along her new boyfriend, Rosie (a nickname he got because of the huge rose tattoo on his chest), who was a bit of a rough diamond but with a sweet and engaging character. What was to become especially poignant about this gathering was Mum's recitation of *The Little Match Girl*, a Christmas poem she knew by heart, since this would be the last time any of us would hear her recite this old favourite of hers.

— Changes —

Not long after January 1975 had been toasted in, I had a sensing that things, lives, were somehow about to alter their course. Ever since Willy Murray moved into *The Beacon* a few months previously he had gradually begun to undertake many of the liaison duties between Mike and Richard that would normally have been my responsibility, so there was the ominous feeling that my job was gradually being taken over. Around this time, our friend Fiona introduced Lynne and I to some of her friends who had started a commune called *Hayden Farm* in Gloucestershire, so when we discovered that there was an opening at the farm for me and my family, Lynne and I decided to take the plunge and start packing.

That turned out to be a very insightful decision since not long afterwards Richard rang to officially fire me and thereby allow Willy to take over liaison duties with Mike. Thankfully, he also offered a deal for me to buy the company car, my lovely Saab, at a very low price - which was a pretty nice gesture from him.

One afternoon the phone rang. It was Mike. When I heard his voice on the other end of the line I registered how long it had been since he'd called. I also detected something unusual in his tone. 'It's me,' he said very flatly, followed by a curiously long pause. Then, 'How are you doing with the news?'

He hadn't offered any explanation as to what 'news' he was referring to, and I had just taken a breath to tell him that when the realisation struck me with the force of a truck.

Without a further word being exchanged between Mike and I, and by whatever means – the intonation of my brother's voice? Intuition? A strange familial telepathy? – I just knew what had happened. I burst into tears.

Our mum was dead.

∞

For some reason, probably his own shock and grief, Mike had assumed I already knew that Mum died earlier that day. After my initial emotional outburst on the telephone I had regained my composure almost as quickly as I lost it, and soon afterwards began to feel better. On some level I think there was a feeling of relief for my mum's sake that came from knowing she had at last found peace from many years of emotional suffering. I also think that Sally and I, being the eldest, had been less affected by the domestic situation than Mike since we were able to get out of the house earlier. In the previous year, however, my sister had borne much more of the brunt when things became really bad in Harold Wood and Dad moved out for good. Sally lived there right up until Mum died, and that must have been a difficult time for her. She has tremendous spirit, though, and I always remember her undertaking everything with a happy and enthusiastic attitude.

A few days later, Mum's funeral ended a significant chapter in all our lives, and thereby heralded a new era for each of us. Apart from a few Christmas gatherings I don't really recall any other memorable times when we were all together again after that.

Now free from the emotional responsibilities upon her, Sally turned her undivided attention towards a career in music, marked a few months later when she recorded some vocals for *Genesis* star Steve Hackett on his album, *Shadow of the Hierophant*. It would be followed by many more solo albums and song collaborations.

Mike's third big instrumental composition was already underway. He was putting a lot into this new work partly in reaction to criticism meted out to the previous album. Despite the healthy sales of *Hergest Ridge*, this album did not enjoy anything like the reception of its predecessor, even though it replaced *Tubular Bells* on the number one position in the album charts. Reviews were not kind, nor were they particularly fair. Everyone seemed to have expected *Tubular Bells 2* and instead they got a more sedate and introspective work with a pastoral character; entirely worthy if considered on its own musical merits, but of course it was always destined to be compared with the innovative forerunner. Mike was naturally despondent, but also determined to readdress the balance next time around.

A lot had passed in each of our lives up to that point, and yet we were only really starting out on our respective journeys. There was much, much more still to come. In my case the next step into the future was taken at Hayden Farm which was to be an important foothold for my little family during the next year or so. Light years away from the mania of London, this tranquil setting provided a lovely environment for eight-month-old Rachel to live and grow, surrounded by good people and nature.

∞

With Mum no longer around to act as a sort of catalyst for the family, we each seemed to scatter ourselves to live very independent and separate lives where chunks of time passed in which we didn't communicate with each other. I still travelled back to *The Beacon* occasionally to do a few things for Mike, which included playing a short section of music on pan pipes for *Ommadawn* as it neared completion. This album would vindicate him from the harsh criticism of *Hergest Ridge*, and go on to become one of the most celebrated compositions of his career, but again it had been created in a cauldron of emotional trauma exacerbated by grief. It was begun when our mum was still alive and contains lots of Celtic and Irish themed music, including a passage with uilleann pipes (sometimes called Irish bagpipes) played by Paddy Moloney of *The Chieftains* and a section that concludes the first part of the album with Clodagh Simonds singing a repetitive chant concocted from Irish Gaelic. Mike performs an emotionally charged electric guitar solo in this section which he later recalled as a primal scream in a time of absolute catharsis. But the album ends, poignantly, on a most peaceful mood, a calm resolution, with the song, *On Horseback*.

3: Awakening to The Dream

Around the time that Mike was finishing off *Ommadawn*, in tribute to our mum he also recorded his own arrangement of her favourite Christmas carol, *In Dulce Jubilo*. This upbeat version of the traditional carol was later released as a single (which had the simple testimonial, '*For Maureen*') with *On Horseback* on the B side. The record peaked at number four in the UK charts and has remained a favourite on Christmas music compilations ever since. One day my brother would even perform an abbreviated version of it to a global audience of millions at the opening ceremony of the London Olympic Games in 2012.

— Sacred Geometry —

By 1976 Mike was on the lookout for a new house. He had purchased *The Beacon* in a dash to escape the spotlight, and whilst the house offered the solitude he had craved after the release of *Tubular Bells*, it was cold, cramped and the neighbours had complained about the noise levels produced when he was working on *Ommadawn*. He now desperately needed a place where he could work without disturbing or being disturbed, but this time around he was fussy about what he wanted – and, with *Ommadawn* having already sold more than 100,000 copies and reached gold certification by the British Phonographic Industry, he could afford to be.

Mike had been scouting around looking for a suitable location, but the search was proving unsuccessful and his time was rather limited so, knowing that I was strapped for cash, he offered me a commission if I could find him a new house as soon as possible. When I eventually managed to locate a piece of land in Herefordshire with a nice aspect, Mike had the idea to ask maverick architect, Keith Critchlow (whom he had heard of recently), if he would consider designing a house. Keith had just started his own company, *Essential Designs*, and seemed the perfect person to create a home that would suit Mike's needs. The land hadn't yet been purchased since that would depend on the house design and whether we could get planning permission, so we arranged for Keith to come down from London and take a look at the site.

When I went to pick him up at Hereford train station I just got there in time for the arrival of the London train. Back then we all dressed pretty casually in jeans and a sweat shirt, maybe a donkey jacket if it was cold, so I was surprised to see Keith step off the train in a pin stripe suit and looking rather like a city banker. When he spotted me waving at him he swiftly came over and said, 'Don't worry about my appearance, one has to dress right for each occasion and I was allowing for a planning officer or two from the council and, well, this makes things easier.'

For a man accredited with having one of the rarest and finest conceptual minds in architecture he was also a very humble individual, and certainly not without humour!

On the journey back to *The Beacon* to meet Mike we stopped off at an old prehistoric dolmen at Keith's request, and I was very impressed with his knowledge of the way it was built. We also spoke about the I Ching and he was delighted to tell me that he had some ideas based around that for Mike's house design.

Predictably, Keith had some stunning and innovative ideas for what would have been my brother's perfect house, but unfortunately in the end we didn't get planning permission and so, reluctantly, it was back to the proverbial drawing board – for me, in any case. This time around, though, I just placed an advertisement in *Country Life Magazine* to see whether that would yield anything. On the plus side, even though plans for a specially designed house for Mike had fallen through, we got to spend some invaluable hours with the truly remarkable Keith, and it wouldn't be the only time, either. We met socially on a few other occasions and I came to regard him as one of the most inspiring scholar-teachers I have had the privilege to know. I had no idea that the tendrils of this connection with Keith were also destined to reach out towards my own as-yet unevolved career.

Much to our surprise, my ad in *Country Life Magazine* sparked an almost immediate response and before long Mike was moving into a large sixteenth century manor house named *Througham Slad*, which had previously been owned by the Cadbury family. Crucially for my financial situation, Mike paid me a decent finder's fee that allowed some leeway with money for a few months, which was a great relief.

While Lynne and I continued to live with Rachel on the commune at Hayden Farm, Mike moved into *Througham Slad* with big plans to construct a purpose-built music studio and make full use of the property's several out buildings. Willy Murray moved in with him for a time, and I did a few odd jobs like moving his equipment and generally helping out with the transition to the new place. I didn't mind that this work was taking me away from home as things were not going at all well with Lynne. It was at this time that I reconnected with my old girlfriend Caroline, and although I felt guilty about seeing her, sometimes the need to love is greater than the need to be loved, and I was drawn to the uncomplicated warmth of her presence. Ironically, I soon came across a letter between Lynne and another man which revealed that she had been doing the same thing as me. As soon as I confronted her about it everything that had been occurring on both sides came out and we voiced the many things that needed to be said. After this purging we made a big effort to come together again. We had a beautiful daughter and needed to try to make things work for her sake as much as our own.

While helping my brother with his new place I came across a tiny, almost derelict cottage for sale nearby called *Woodlands* in Bismore Bottom, a valley in Eastcombe. It was going pretty cheap and, only half-serious, I rang Richard Branson to ask his advice on where someone like me could borrow money. He told me to leave it with him and he'd look into it. Within an hour the phone rang again and I hardly had time to get the handset up to my ear before Richard excitedly blurted out the question, 'Guess how much I got the cottage for?' He had made a ridiculously low offer of £7,500 which had somehow been accepted. It seemed that some people are born to business and negotiation just as others are to creativity or sport.

After obtaining a valuation that came out much higher than the offer, Lynne and I were able to get a loan through Lloyds bank and, during the second hottest UK summer since records began, we bought the cottage and continued on in a state of denial regarding our relationship.

With a home of our own there came a renewed sense of purpose and I threw all my energy into renovating the place. It wasn't easy to live there at first as it was so small and damp, but we made the best of it and soon had the cottage in a liveable condition. Lynne and I shared the common bond of loving Rachel very deeply, but the uncomfortable feeling between us hung stubbornly in the air, a miasma rendered fouler by the fact that I had no obvious way of earning a living. Nothing was coming up for me, and I even briefly, desperately, tried to make a living as an estate agent, having been inspired by my success in finding Mike a new place so quickly. Of course, I soon learned that I had just been lucky in my brother's case, and didn't, in fact, have any hidden talent for selling homes.

Invariably we respond to failure with negative thoughts about our performance or capability that make us question our self-worth when in fact the universe may simply be pointing the way towards something else. Something more appropriate for us. Something better. Only with hindsight are we likely to recognise this, and it was certainly the case with me, but at the time I only had the brooding notion that something was preventing me from becoming involved in anything normal, like a proper job.

As though to counteract the effect of all the employment doors that were being slammed shut in my face, Mike came to the rescue one day and paid off the mortgage on *Woodlands Cottage*, immediately relieving a lot of the financial pressure. Around the same time he gifted *The Beacon* to Sally and turned up on my birthday with a new mixer for the little studio I had set up in my attic. My brother knew what I had in mind now that there were fewer financial concerns to gnaw at me; I was going to have a go at making a music demo of my own.

∞

Keith Critchlow had brought his family down to *Througham Slad* to spend Christmas with daughter Louise who was now living there in a relationship with Mike. My brother had also recently worked on the music for *Reflections*, a short film by Keith about the relationship between nature and humans and how we emulate nature's patterns in our creations, often in religious architecture.

One evening we were all sitting by the log fire in *The Bear* at Bisley when the conversation turned to the subject of ghosts and Keith told us a fascinating story of how he discovered that he could 'See'. He asked us if we knew the paintings of El Greco, declaring that this sixteenth-century Greek artist must also have been able to 'See' since ghosts look much like the figures with elongated faces that he painted. Some years previously Keith had developed an interest in Kirlian photography (photos that reveal the auras around people) and went to see an expert to find out more about it. When he walked into the room the man sitting behind his desk said to Keith, 'I suppose you've come to me to find out if you can See?' At first Keith was taken aback by the remarkable insight, then the man held his hands in front of a flowery tie he was wearing and Keith saw colours flashing between his fingertips. From that moment on, he told us, the hidden or occult world opened up for him and he could 'See'.

It took some time, to say the least, for the genius architect to get used to this newfound ability, and it was only his wife and children who kept him from losing his grip on reality until he could integrate the expanded way of viewing things into his life.

Lynne very kindly prepared Christmas stockings for everyone that year when Dad, too, joined us at *Througham Slad* where he looked happier, or at least less troubled, than I'd seen him in many years. After Mum died he seemed to have obtained a freedom that gave him a new lease of life. Without the responsibility of looking after her he literally flourished and began doing all sorts of wonderful and very unusual things; real adventures like trekking in the Himalayas with only a guide and ponies! He played squash, tennis and golf, started writing, listening to music and even bought himself a sports car. Poor Mum's illness had taken its toll on all of us over the years, but on Christmas night 1976, while I watched Dad dance the night away as he steadily got drunk – something that was most unusual for him – we all enjoyed a brief hiatus from our individual troubles.

∞

The considerable respite afforded by having our mortgage paid off by Mike was making it apparent that neither financial nor domiciliary issues were essentially at the root of the problems between Lynne and I – a reality that our frequent moves had probably been an unconscious attempt to outrun.

Lynne was beginning to lose all confidence in me as far as music was concerned, added to which she now felt isolated in our remote little cottage in the woods. Being naturally more socially-oriented than me, the effect of the location on her personality was inevitable, but this was another reality that had been overlooked in our state of denial. We were both making a big effort to improve our relationship, but it was not looking or feeling good at all. We had been ignoring the signs, the ominous feelings – in fact, the *obvious* – far too long, motivated to do so largely for the sake of our little girl. Rachel had brought a lot of love with her into this world and for a time Lynne and I thought, as many couples do, that this alone could sustain our relationship. But things were much worse than we realised, or could openly admit, as we treaded water in our loveless ocean, until finally one evening around dusk I went out for my usual walk up the valley and didn't return to the cottage. I just couldn't.

I hadn't set out with any intention to leave my family, especially not my gorgeous little innocent child, but it was one of those unplanned and somehow irrevocable moments when we feel incapable of doing anything to counteract the way things are happening once they start flowing.

Close to tears, I found myself knocking on the door of a friend in Bisley and immediately confessing, offloading everything to her, revealing all my pent-up woes and sense of despair. She allowed me to spend the night there and I later rang Lynne to tell her that we had only been pretending to ourselves that we could make things work, that we could somehow fix the broken situation. I told her it was irreparable, and that I wouldn't be coming back.

Of course, all hell then broke loose, and I knew I could do nothing but weather the ensuing storm. Having taken the bold and inevitable step to end the relationship, I was aware that I had fashioned an almost unbearable path that both Lynne and I would have to walk for the foreseeable future. There was no going back. No way around it. The only way was through the pain. Yet with this realisation came an immediate sense of relief that I had been moved out and away from a relationship that was causing a great deal of suffering for both of us, coupled with a conviction that what I had done would ultimately be in our best interests. I was of course devastated about leaving Rachel, and my strongest regret was that she would innocently become embroiled in whatever would follow.

The tiny glimmer of hope on the horizon was that, just as new shoots emerge from a land seemingly dead after the ravages of fire, nature would, over time, eventually clear the emotional devastation that lay in store for my family.

Lynne and Rachel returned to the security of Hayden Farm and I rented a cottage in Bisley where I lived alone. Everyone had been told that I had run off with a local floozy because the first person I had turned to happened to be a female friend, but that simply wasn't true. On the evening I knocked on her door I felt I couldn't survive the experience alone, and her house was nearby. I hadn't been thinking at all clearly about anything, merely reacting. There certainly hadn't been any amorous intentions on my part, but people naturally respond to what appears to be rather than what is or could be, preferring to believe the juiciest, most gossip-worthy scenario. So the poisonous whispers flowed freely and all blame for the break-up was fully apportioned to me. Being vilified in this way nevertheless helped to assuage the terrible feelings of guilt I was feeling about little Rachel, so I didn't say a single word in my own defence. In any case I simply didn't have the energy to fight for my corner.

We immediately sold the cottage that had for a brief time seemed such a serendipitous find, one that promised the possibility of a fresh start, a 'cure', for our failing relationship, and I gave all the proceeds to Lynne to buy another place of her choice. I didn't want anything at all, again partly because of my sense of guilt, but of course the need for Lynne and Rachel to have a stable home was of paramount importance, and certainly far exceeded my own considerations. My turbulent teenage years had taught me that somehow I would always find a way to look after myself.

— Moving On —

After *Woodlands Cottage* was sold I entered an abyss of solitude and emotional pain in which I felt deeply lonely and, strangely, betrayed. To this day that period in my life is still a bit of a surreal blur where I lived on my own in rented cottages in Bisley, then later at *Througham Slad* with Mike after his relationship with Louise also broke down. I began to spend a lot of time with my brother again as we were now both living in our own worlds of unhappiness and could support each other to some extent, even if only for the fact that we shared a common burden. We would often pop out to *The Daneway* Pub in Sapperton for a couple of pints, and after a while I started going there on my own to play darts with the locals just to chase away the desperate loneliness. This happened a lot after Lynne accepted an invitation to work in Boston where she took little Rachel, thereby separating me indefinitely from my daughter. Again I didn't raise any protest to this as I'd felt I had caused enough disruption to Lynne's life without instigating any action that could actuate further distress or unhappiness. But, whilst the demise of my relationship with Lynne had been an inevitability evolved over time, being unable to see my daughter created a feeling of loss that felt like a hole had been burned in the very core of my being.

— Spiral —

Towards the end of the previous year Sally had recorded some songs on an album for Finnish bass player, Pekka Pohjola, in Mike's new studio at *Througham Slad* which at the time was being put through its paces. *Keesojen Lehto* (The Grove of Keesos) would be considered her first truly collaborative mainstream album, due for release early in 1977 and co-produced by Mike who had also contributed some guitar playing.

My own aspirations of making a demo recording had so far been inhibited by domestic circumstances and the resulting stress, but now something seemed to be pointing the way for me to follow in Mike and Sally's footsteps. I just had to get a decent demo out there.

With no mortgage and fewer familial demands now hanging over me – and a brand new mixer to boot – my efforts to create a music demo went up a gear. Perhaps taking a leaf out of Mike's book, for the remainder of that winter I rented a cottage in Llanrhaedr Ym Mochnant in Wales – a quiet little place in a remote country setting famous for its beautiful waterfall – and transferred my studio equipment there where I could focus my full attention on making the demo. Such a scenario would never have been possible in the rather cramped conditions of *Woodlands Cottage* where my wife and daughter couldn't avoid generating constant distractions. Ironically it was still as much for them that I wanted to get something recorded and out there quick, to see whether I too could create a piece of music that would spark off a career and, ultimately, better long-term security for them.

Mike lent me two stereo TEAC reel-to-reel tape recorders – a four-track and a two-track – and I taught myself how to cut and splice and edit the music, partly from what I remembered from watching others, but mainly through learning on the job. Of course I also got some sound mixing experience while working as a roadie, so I felt I had enough technical knowledge to produce a decent demo. Now I just wanted to know if I could compose something.

Inspired by many long walks around the Welsh countryside, often in the frost and snow, over the next few months I composed a twenty-minute demo piece which I called *Spiral*. The title came from a notion I'd always had that music often behaves like a spiral in the way it rises and descends in octaves. Every time it completes the circle of an ascending octave it spirals on upwards, the coils becoming smaller and smaller as the pitch increases until the notes eventually disappear from human hearing.

When the demo was complete the next job was to get it out there to see if I could secure a record deal. The obvious first choice was of course Virgin Records. Much to my delight, when I popped around to Richard's house one day and played *Spiral*, he loved it and took it off to Simon Draper who also liked it very much. My heart soared as already everything seemed to be falling into place. The scene was set.

Shortly afterwards, Richard came to see me with one of those big trademark grins on his face. 'I have a surprise for you. Come around to the office later and Simon and I will tell you what it is.'

That was all Richard would tell me, but of course it had to be positive news about my demo, and that inevitably meant a record deal. First Mike, now me. This was turning into a real family affair. I felt sure that Sally would soon be next.

The three of us, Richard, Simon and I, sat in the office listening to *Spiral*. My heart rate was elevated slightly above its normal rested beat for most of the play through. The excitement seemed to be present in the very air as both Richard and Simon were smiling, offering occasional appreciate comments as the music played out. The enthusiasm was a palpable energy in the room.

'We want to offer a deal,' Richard suddenly said. Although I had been fully expecting these words, the affirmation was enough to fire a bolt of joy through me. 'And here it is…' he continued. 'We'd love you, Mike and Sally to do a family album together.'

I was thrown a little, but my joy didn't wane. Then it reached new heights. Perhaps bringing our combined talents together would forge a tremendous result. Yes. Of course it would. Simon and Richard had had another sage idea and at that moment I felt that I was present at the very beginning of what could be Virgin's next big album release.

I couldn't wait to tell Mike and Sally the exciting news.

— A Beginning —

'Absolutely no…'

Mike's response to the suggestion of a family album was both immediate and emphatic. I was rendered speechless. And yet, deep down his words weren't so surprising to me, considering how he'd previously felt so musically and commercially coerced in *The Sallyangie*. With that in mind, it seemed obvious that he was bound to reject any possibility of repeating such a scenario. I also knew that leaving Sally in the lurch had affected him quite strongly. I remember our sister having to turn up on her own to do the Festival Hall gig in 1968 where *The Sallyangie* had been booked to appear as the warm-up act to *The Incredible String Band*. That officially signalled the end of the duo and Sally must have been very disappointed, especially as things had been looking so promising for them.

Another reason for Mike's flat rejection was likely because his previous experiences with groups over the years (*Gong, The Whole World, Barefoot*) had demonstrated that solo work was the only way he could express himself fully and effectively. And creating *Tubular Bells*, painful process though it was, had confirmed this. Going his own way rather than following the money in a way that didn't feel right to him also said a lot about Mike's character and, unfortunately for me, the strength of his conviction.

Nevertheless, I was hugely disappointed. Not only did I feel sure that the album would have been a great success, but it would probably have gone a long way towards launching my career ambitions, too, not to mention resolving my financial issues. Certainly, that had been the hope.

The light at the end of the tunnel switched on by Richard and Simon had now been extinguished by my brother.

However...

An interesting, perhaps vital thing now happened. This latest disappointment combined with Mike and Sally's successes – and undoubtedly the weight of financial instability – all lined up and ignited a fire inside me. I now felt more determined than ever to forge a successful musical career of my own.

I made about twenty-five cassette copies of *Spiral* and sent them off to various places including, of course, all the big record companies and waited for their responses. My thinking was, if Richard Branson and Simon Draper had been so enthusiastic about *Spiral*, at least a few others were bound to feel the same.

All I could do now was wait and see if that was true.

∞

Several weeks passed. No reply came. Not one. Yet another disappointment, and a rather surprising one, too, as I felt sure that my music had something to say. Perhaps it was all just wishful thinking on my part, and Richard and Simon's enthusiasm had been inspired more by my familial association with *Tubular Bells* than my music. Was it Mike's next album rather than my first that had been on their minds? Perhaps the universe hadn't after all been guiding me towards a music career, but was instead leading me down a path that would demonstrate categorically that I wasn't destined to follow in my brother's footsteps, and that something else was out there waiting for me. It certainly wasn't marital bliss, as Lynne and I had already begun divorce proceedings.

The harsh reality seemed to be that nobody wanted the music I was offering, and maybe the harsher reality was that I just wasn't good enough. Whatever the truth happened to be, I had now all but written off any hope of becoming a musician.

3: Awakening to The Dream

    How stunning, and cruel, the rapid transition from the place of hope and euphoria I had been propelled into that day in Richard Branson's office, to this dungeon of sadness and despair that bordered on self-loathing.

∞

We had some vague understanding, or suspicion, that Dad had been seeing someone he'd met on his recent travels and adventures, but we were all genuinely stunned when he announced his impending marriage to a German lady named Helga. The prospect of having a new stepmother must bring a pile of mixed emotional baggage to children of any age, but perhaps even more so when those children – who may already be adults themselves – have had many years with the mother the 'new woman' is in some sense about to replace. Coupled with that was the complete unexpectedness of Dad's announcement, and we worried that his decision to marry again barely two years after Mum's passing was more an impetuous psychological reaction than a considered decision born from genuine love. The fact that he'd been introduced to this lady while on a ski trip only gave us further reason to be concerned that, in combination with his newfound sense of freedom, maybe Dad had been seduced by the allure of an exotic romance with a lady outside of his English culture.

    He seemed to be happy, though, so we could only hope that he would find lasting love and happiness in this new relationship.

Helga could never replace our mum, of course, but if Dad liked – loved – her then how could we resent that? If she suited Dad then she had to be a nice person with whom, in time, my siblings and I could come to form a pleasant relationship. Time would tell.

∞

My attentions were, for the time being at least, immediately diverted from Dad, Helga and my inert financial situation on the day I was contacted by Lawrence Moore at Vortex films. Lawrence, who had produced Keith Critchlow's film *Reflections*, had somehow got to hear my demo, *Spiral*, which he liked. With little preamble he asked if I would be prepared to compose the music for his next project, *Mystery in the Plain*, a film about Stonehenge that would go out in cinemas as the short movie to a main feature called *Breaker Morant*, starring Edward Woodward.

And so came the next almost surreal blow I received that year. This time, however, rather than leaving me perplexed and disgruntled, I was catapulted into a realm of absolute joy that spawned a whole new sense of hope. It seemed that all my efforts with *Spiral* hadn't been in vain after all, and my first ever foray into professional composing, my first commission, was going to end up on the big screen!

Right after saying yes, I thanked Lawrence for giving me the opportunity, for liking my music, and probably for a few other things (whether spoken or simply felt), and as soon as our conversation ended I got straight to work.

I turned up at the studio in East London to record the music for *Mystery in the Plain* with my flute and a bag full of percussion instruments and a few whistles that I had mostly borrowed from Mike's studio at *Througham Slad*. I kind of busked the whole moody recording whilst watching the film and getting inspiration from each scene as it went along, a strategy which suited the instinctive sense of playing I had developed since my first days of playing the flute. Luckily, everyone was happy with the result of this spontaneous recording technique which meant the film was now 'in the bag'. It would not be screened until the following year when the main feature it had been made to accompany, *Breaker Morant*, would become a box office hit.

— Travels with my Brother —

Mike's studio at *Througham Slad* was built to his own specific design and no expense had been spared in getting it right. The end result was spectacular and he seemed to have finally fulfilled his dream. The cottage that came with the property also allowed a full-time studio engineer named Paul Lyndsay to move in there with his wife, Barbara. Like all large, top facilities it was a high maintenance site, so Mike – who had now begun work on his fourth album, *Incantations*, in the new purpose-built studio – couldn't really do everything on his own this time. Mike's enthusiasm for his latest album had begun to wane, largely as a result of the advent of punk music and what he saw as Richard Branson and Virgin's new allegiance to this rebellious music that had just exploded onto the scene. He felt both he and his music were being left behind by the fickle commercialism of music in general and Virgin in particular. Consequently, my brother shrank further into personal withdrawal and began drinking too much. I visited him and tried to help as much as I could, staying at his house on many occasions, but it often seemed impossible to pull him out of his disconsolate state of mind.

In complete contrast, Sally was offered a contract with Bronze records to make an album of her own songs. Titled *Water Bearer*, her first solo album would include *Mirrors*, the song with which she would perhaps become most associated throughout her career. I'll never forget the day she turned up at Mike's place to tell us the glorious news. It was a lovely summer's day and within minutes she was outside in the garden and on the Olympic size trampoline that sat on the lawn there, bouncing so high that at one point I feared for her safety. She was, in every sense, high as a kite!

As though to maintain the pattern of seesawing extreme fortunes that seemed to haunt our family, around the time that Sally was jumping with joy and Mike was once again in a very dark place, I was teetering between the renewed optimism that my own musical career seemed poised to take off and the despondency of finalising a divorce. Then Dad announced his marriage to Helga, and my two siblings and I suddenly had a stepmother we hardly knew at all. It wouldn't be too long, though, before we discovered that she was in fact the archetypal wicked stepmother.

3: Awakening to The Dream

∞

Partly for diversion, but mainly in an attempt to help my brother get over a fear of travelling, Mike and I made a couple of trips to Europe. On each occasion our destinations were determined by a specific purpose, the first of which was to enable a meeting between Mike and his publisher at Disci Ricordi in Italy, a trip we made in his Alfa Romeo Montreal with me mostly at the wheel because my brother was feeling very fragile at the time. For some reason, though, he didn't seem to mind at all when I took the car up to speeds in excess of a hundred and fifty miles an hour!

The other trip was to Crete to look for a Phaistos Disc – a decorative clay artefact reputedly dating back to the Minoan Bronze Age, first discovered on the island's Palace of Phaistos – as a gift for a girl Mike knew. Bearing in mind that there has only ever been one such disc found, this trip was a pretty nebulous affair. Yes, these were strange times indeed...

While we were in Greece a friend of mine, Roger, who I knew from my time on Hydra, took us on a guided tour of some of the ancient sites including Delphi, where we illegally climbed into the site at dawn to watch the sunrise over the Temple of Apollo. Roger told us the legend of how the rising sun was regarded by the ancient Greeks as the God of Light entering Apollo's temple on midsummer's day, and promised that it would be a truly awesome sight to behold. He was right. Watching the sun slowly emerge and flood the temple ruin, witnessing something that had such significance to the ancient people, was an experience beyond explanation that became permanently etched in our minds. Mike and I still reminisce about it to this day.

The trips were good for both of us, but when we returned to England Mike's demons were still there waiting for him as of course the problems hadn't gone anywhere. It was becoming a real cause for concern. With musical fashion in the middle of a revolution that seemed poised to leave my brother's art behind in the dust, both his career and sanity were under threat. Then, a chance conversation one afternoon between Mike and his resident studio engineer's wife, Barbara, altered the course of everything.

— Exegesis —

It seems travelling the full length of the path is entirely necessary in order to reach the end and the realisation that you're back where you started. Understanding that the only thing to 'get' there is that NOW *is what you get suddenly transforms the ordinary into extraordinary and we awaken, or become enlightened, because now we are fully present in the moment. That is when the subliminal barriers come tumbling down and we realise that we are living on the leading edge of creation where each one of us has infinite potential.*

My sister Sally and I were astounded by the change in our brother. The withdrawn, troubled young man that we had grown accustomed to as 'Mike' had been transformed overnight into an outgoing, confident and generally happier person. The transformation seemed unlikely in the extreme, if not miraculous, which at first made us a bit suspicious as to what was going on. Here was a young man who had shunned all contact with the public and most forms of publicity to live in solitude now instigating social situations and interacting with people on a whole new level – he was even talking about doing live concerts and taking his music on tour, for heaven's sake. It was like he had literally been reborn. And no drug, prescribed or otherwise, was responsible.

It turned out that the new Mike was the result of a weekend seminar called *Exegesis* that he had attended after Barbara told him about the amazing experience she and husband Paul had had at this event. She had been so enthusiastic about the seminar, and so convinced that Mike would benefit from it, that she arranged for the event organiser's sister to come and speak to him about it. Her name was Diana.

Mike was impressed by what he heard, and by the 'living proof' change he'd apparently seen in Paul's attitude to life, so he decided to give it a try himself.

The word *Exegesis*, though having come to be specifically associated with the critical interpretation or explanation of a sacred text, originates from an ancient Greek word meaning to *interpret, guide* or *lead*. Apart from this, I knew very little except that the seminar comprised a series of processes and discussions that were 'enlightenment intensive'. It seemed very intriguing, not least of all because of the profound effect it had had on Mike, so Sally and I decided to sign up for the next event which was due to be held in Bristol.

The seminar took place in a large hotel conference room and was attended by a throng of different types of people who, judging by their excited chatter and facial expressions, like me were expecting fireworks, emotion and lots of drama. There was an unmistakable buzz in the air, a sense of expectancy that we all might be on the cusp of receiving the gift of some ancient and little-known secret that would induce sudden enlightenment. The last thing we were expecting to get from the event was what we ultimately ended up with, which was, actually, nothing. Nothing other than what we already had in that moment. But we weren't ripped-off by an organisation that promised the whole Earth and instead delivered a rock; on the contrary, the point of the seminar was to awaken us in precisely the way we had been. To expect something wonderful and enlightening and then come to realise that there is no hidden secret to enlightenment requiring a dramatic experience in order to be attained. Now is what you get. Now is what has to be experienced. Searching for it, trying to attain it, believing there is something to be mastered, is a delusion that creates the resistance which prevents it from manifesting. Stop seeking. Stop expecting. Tune in to and experience the present moment.

The nothing we got was that there is nothing *to* get. And that indeed turned out to be a truly wonderful gift. So simple. And so priceless.

At the start of the seminar we were encouraged to get in touch with our feelings, make a *true* connection with them. This is the crux of the whole thing, really, because it's not until we are able to relax into who, what, we are – something ultimately mysterious incarnate in a human body – can we be truly here on Earth, fully open to experience the totality of living. Several other 'processes' followed, one of the most important of which was to go out front as individuals and share what we were feeling with the group. Bearing in mind there were over five hundred people on the seminar this was the ultimate confrontation for many of us, because the main thing we had been taught by our parents and society throughout our lives was to avoid our feelings. Laying them bare by making them public pulled the plug and unleashed the pressure of all the pent up emotion. Releasing in such a way before others was completely overwhelming for some people, and there were reactions that included anything from low sobbing to high-pitched, almost feral wailing and screaming. My brother has written about his Exegesis experience being a cathartic re-enactment of his birth into this world, a dramatic ordeal which ultimately culminated in a great sense of relief and emotional purging. It certainly changed his life for the better.

    This wasn't the case for everyone, however, and I remember there were some who simply could not face the increased flow and left the seminar in a hurry. Unfortunately my dad turned out to be one of these individuals. We managed to convince him to go along to a seminar in the hope that it might help him release all the long-repressed emotions linked to his own childhood, as well as those associated with the more recent trauma involving my mum, but sadly he could not face his feelings and later told me that the whole thing was a dreadful and embarrassing experience. So many of us are simply not quite ready yet to open our arms and embrace life.

By the end of the seminar I felt that a profound change had definitely taken place within me which was, essentially, the realisation that what I had been looking for was already there, inside all along, provided I put up no resistance.

And in that moment something stopped.

The next thing I experienced was an enormous surge of vitality as all the energy that had previously been bound up in repetitive patterns and responses (which were using up that energy just to enable me to survive as a separate character) was released into my system. This suddenly available resource – accompanied, curiously, by the same inability to think that I had first experienced after reading Krishnamurti's book in India – was both exhilarating and disarming. I realised that I had been living in automation, *'Reacting to stimuli based upon past experience',* and that nothing really new had been happening at all. I was simply living in a series of behavioural loops or patterns that were running most things in my life. This is only how it's meant to be on the physical level, where automation has an essential part to play in running things like heartbeat, breathing and reactions to danger etc.; background processes designed to dial the number, not actually speak.

The relief was enormous and I remember subsequently waking up each morning hoping that the feeling would still be there. This time around I was able to integrate the 'new way' of living into my life more effectively, as though the message itself now had stronger resonance and the sense of living differently was destined to continue. For some weeks after the Exegesis seminar I couldn't take myself far from being in the present moment. Something really had clicked.

In order to gain more insight into the background of how the Exegesis weekend self-awareness intensives were run, I offered to assist on some of the seminars and then got involved in the movement for a year or two, as did Sally who I'm sure, as well as being quite profoundly moved by the whole experience, also found it helpful in cementing together her future career. This was one of the important things about the seminar; it often helped people to move forward in any areas that were being blocked by a dam of repressed feelings through eventually reaching a point where all that residue is expressed or expunged, leaving them free to move with the flow of experience without accumulating new stuff. This process liberates so much energy and makes us available to face and fully experience life. And music.

I believe that, just as in that condensed Exegesis experience, the whole spiritual path – which for some may take a lifetime, if it even happens at all – leads to this. It did for me, at least. All the courses, practices, effort, striving, travelling and expectations all led me to arrive right back here, because here is not a static thing; it's a constantly moving flow yet always the present moment.

This is what guides my creativity because music comes from that flow of creation, so inspiration is only here when it's here and to get that inspiration I have to be here, or present in that moment. When I feel taken over (literally) in the moment by inspiration, or the so-called muse, I will be carried along in a flow that may become many hours of creation, all unfolding in the now, where I have no awareness of time passing or even that I am the musician. I only have to allow myself to be empty, receptive, for the inspiration to flow through in the form of music, since inspiration itself comes from the Great Mystery that is beyond description or definition. Flow can only happen in the continuity of the moment. To be moved by the universe in this way is rather like being 'lived', since you are no longer making conscious decisions in the same way as someone who has a fixed intention, ambition or a goal, just as those who have a fixed idea about what awakening is won't experience it until they drop the expectations and therefore the resistance.

That's why, for me, 'trying' to write music seems impossible. You only meet inspiration here, now, and if you're not here you **simply** won't get it.

∞

Mike was now pouring all of his newfound energy and attitude to life into the recording of *Incantations* (which is evident in most of the composition), working flat out to fine-tune the mix. With its many confident and jubilant themes, this album – his longest ever – would truly reflect the post-Exegesis Mike. In the middle of this frenetic activity, he asked me if I would record some flute passages on the album. He was very fussy about getting it just right and the end result was pretty good, however there were far too many notes for me on some parts (lots of double tonguing etc.), so he had to use another professional flautist for those bits. I certainly could never have played it all live!

No longer concerned about the apparent threat to his style of music posed by the new wave of punk rock, Mike was forging ahead with unshakable confidence in what he had to offer. As though to confound everyone further, when his latest album was completed and its official release date set for December 1st 1978, Mike did the one thing no one expected. He announced that he was going to take *Incantations* on tour the following year.

Where he had previously run away from all self-promotion, my brother was now boldly stepping forward to present himself and his live music to the world. This time it was he, not Richard Branson, who instigated the tour and plugged the music, funding much of it himself in an unprecedented and highly ambitious musical project that would include a large band, female choir, percussion section and a small string orchestra.

One bizarrely spontaneous thing Mike did at this time was marry Diana D'Aubigny, the sister of the Exegesis seminar leader, Robert D'Aubigny, but he soon realised the folly of this rash move and the marriage only lasted a few months.

By the end of 1978 both my brother and sister had new album releases. Mike's *Incantations* seemed poised for success, especially with the upcoming European promotional concert tour, and Sally's debut album, *Water Bearer*, was already enjoying a positive reception. Her song *Mirrors* from this album had climbed up the UK singles charts, earning my sister an appearance on Top Of The Pops.

Now, what, if anything, might the future have in store for me, I wondered...

— Paddling to Success —

One of the biggest (of the relatively few) fans I had at this time happened to be an editor at HTV called Dennis Pratt. After receiving one of my cassette copies of *Spiral*, Dennis invited me down to his cutting room in Cardiff to discuss the possibility of writing some music for a new series about a team of canoeists travelling around the Aleutian Islands in Alaska. (It seems I had been heading in the direction of wildlife films almost from the start.)

    Dennis and I got on very well and he showed a lot of faith in me and my music, and it wasn't long before I was making a start on the score for *Canoeing into the Past.* The music was recorded in Hackney, East London, as I was still using commercial studios at the time (on a very controlled budget), but the finished result went down really well, which led to the promise of future work with HTV. I was absolutely delighted. A year had passed since I'd worked on *Mystery in the Plain* and nothing had happened in between, but I hoped that maybe now things were about to start moving for me and my career.

∞

When the local air base at Fairford began making their air strip available for the transit of USAF super tankers, the noise levels produced by these low-flying aircraft were such that they filtered into Mike's recording studio at *Througham Slad*. Despite the formal protests (of Mike and other locals) and lobbying against allowing these particular planes to fly in and out of the base, and thereby pollute the area with high noise levels, their cries went unheeded. Reluctantly, then, Mike was forced to put *Througham Slad* up for sale. As all of this coincided with his *Incantations* tour that year, Mike asked me to sell the house for him and I managed to find a buyer quite easily. The price was set and, as he was away at the time and couldn't sign a contract, Mike made a Gentleman's Agreement with the buyer. When Richard Branson got to hear about the sale he actually put in a much higher offer for the place, but Mike wasn't tempted to break his agreement and the sale went ahead as planned. This was one of those little unpublicised things that revealed my brother's integrity even when few people would have blamed him for taking the higher offer.

∞

As 1979 progressed and I was still waiting patiently, hopefully, for another commission, or even just a lead to some kind of musical project, despondency began to re-emerge. In contrast, my siblings were thriving. Sally's career seemed to be gathering momentum with her second successful solo album, *Easy*, and Mike was literally flying after the release of his hit single, *Guilty*, and the live album, *Exposed* – compiled from his tour that year – with another album, *Platinum*, due for release that November. Topping it all off for him, my little brother's personal life was also in the ascendancy as his relationship with girlfriend, Sally Cooper, whom he had met through Virgin, was positively flourishing.

For me it began to seem as though something was cruelly teasing me. Having already had my musical capability affirmed on two successful film projects, and therefore been given tempting glimpses of what *might* be, it was frustrating that things were moving so sluggishly. It felt like I was in a state of limbo with absolutely no guarantee that the condition would ever change.

The same could not be said about my home base, on the other hand. Since the split with Lynne I had lived alone in three rented cottages, then briefly with a friend in Sussex, followed by a flat share in Kingston, in between which I'd stayed on and off with Mike at *Througham Slad*. I wasn't entirely sure whether all of these moves had been an attempt to inject some kind of action into my life or were simply a reflection of its instability. I also began to consider that they were perhaps a reawakening of my innate desire for travel triggered, as before, by unhappiness and the stagnation of my circumstances.

I listened to my heart. And my feet. Within a week I was on the magic bus to India again where I was destined to live on a houseboat on Daal Lake in Kashmir for the next six months.

3: Awakening to The Dream

— A Hard Realisation —

By 1980 I was back in England and sharing a flat in Notting Hill Gate with my sister. My extended trip to India had been followed by another visit to Hydra, an island I had come to regard as a sort of spiritual home, but now I had returned to the land of my birth to see whether I could make something happen musically. (And speaking of birth, my brother and his girlfriend had just had their first child together, Molly; making me 'Uncle Terry'.)

Whereas Sally was working on her next album, *Celebration*, and Mike busy with his sixth, *QE2*, no offers or opportunities were coming my way. Not even a single potential avenue of exploration presented itself, and already I was feeling lost. The sense that my life completely lacked direction was once again in evidence.

I eventually came to understand that, since my return to England from Hydra seven years previously, I had effectively been following in my brother's huge shadow. I was grateful for the unexpected steady job with Virgin that had come out of it at the time, of course, but I now realised that trying to emulate his particular pathway to success was probably holding me back from pursuing my own career. In the end it was actually Mike himself who helped me to move on by gradually creating a kind of distance between us. This had nothing to do with Mike adopting a position of superiority or anything like that; he was simply being whisked up, albeit reluctantly at times, in the music business whirlwind. At the time I did interpret this as a kind of arrogance, but that was coming from my own insecurity. I see that quite clearly now. I can also admit that I was a bit jealous of my brother's success – not that I wasn't genuinely pleased for him, but I was likely seeing things from the perspective of an elder sibling and thinking, *'This is my baby brother, still so young, and even he's put together something that's achieved tremendous success. He's done it. Why can't I?'*

Mike – and perhaps Sally, too – had suddenly made it seem that making an album was something I could do, or at least attempt, for myself. But my sorely anticipated career path had been something of a non-starter, despite some tantalising portents with the two film commissions. I could only console myself with the knowledge that I had given it my best shot and it hadn't worked out. The doors of my musical ambitions, like my marriage, were now firmly closed. I decided the best thing, the only thing, to do now was return to the place I felt most at home and perhaps find that elusive sense of direction in my life.

I packed up, said the necessary one or two goodbyes, and got on a plane bound for Greece; on my way to Hydra again, but this time with no more thought of music.

— A New Start in an Old Place —

I rented a house high up on the hill above Hydra's busy port and, like so many on that rocky island full of poets and painters, writers and philosophers – an 'artist colony' as it was dubbed in the guide books – I began to spend a great deal of time alone. During the summer season tourists would come to spot the creative people as though they were a separate, rare species, and I was often asked if I was a 'member' of the artist colony.

One evening I was out on the town with my friend Rick when he pointed out a pretty girl across the street. He told me she was an Australian working on the island as an Au Pair. I thought nothing more about this until later that evening when the girl suddenly appeared near where I was sitting with a group of friends watching the sunset. I strolled over to sit on the wall next to her and we struck up a conversation. Her name was Rhonda. She had a lovely, bubbly personality and had come to Hydra from Victoria to work for a family who lived on the island. We chatted easily together, partly because I could share my backpacking experiences of Australia, but there was also an immediate mutual attraction and ultimately we ended up spending the night together at my place. Despite the fireworks of an obvious shared magnetism, however, I wasn't really expecting anything else to happen after that. Since Lynne and I split up I had grown accustomed to moving on before any relationship had time to develop. Much of that was undoubtedly due to residual feelings of guilt, but I just wasn't in the right space for commitment at the time – at least, that's what I believed. As usual, of course, the universe seemed to have other plans.

Rhonda and I made a vague arrangement to meet in the port the following evening but, convinced that this was little more than a 'morning after' courtesy, when some friends invited me to dinner later that day I joined them instead. That night when I returned to my house I found Rhonda sitting on the wall by my gate. When I first saw her I thought I might be about to receive a rebuttal for standing her up, but instead there was the same relaxed warmth of the previous evening, and an unspoken understanding of how rendezvous plans made in these times and on this island were always somewhat tenuous. I was very pleased to see her; she could see that and so we naturally ended up spending another night together.

Hydra is a small island with a very close community so, although Rhonda and I made few official 'dates' after that, our paths kept crossing wherever we went and we began to spend more and more time together. After just a few weeks we moved into a house-sit for the annual winter sojourn when the tourist trade dries up and all the local Greeks come out to rekindle the old ways of island life. Hydra really was very different when it reverted to being traditionally Greek again after the madness of the summer months when boatloads of tourists were coming and going at all hours of the day. For a time we lived quite blissfully where my concerns about career and future were all but dissolved and I stopped trying to force things into place. I put faith in the moment, in love, and allowed everything to unfold as it may.

A few weeks later when Rhonda announced that she was expecting a baby we were both genuinely delighted. With me now doing odd jobs on the island our joint financial resources were enough to support a simple, contented life in Hydra's beautiful surroundings. I also think that babies and their pending arrival bring with them a unique kind of support for parents, perhaps because the joy they instil generates the belief that any obstacle can be overcome. Yet again I had been rapidly transported from a place of aimless uncertainty and low self-esteem to a plateau of joy and purpose. My life suddenly had direction. Meaning.

As time wore on Rhonda grew concerned about living on a comparatively primitive Greek island while she was pregnant, especially regarding safety issues around the delivery, so we decided to do a house swap with a friend in Chelsea back in the UK until after the baby was born. I was pretty much open to anything at that time; happy, and willing to just go along with the flow.

— Survival of the Fittest —

As though to confirm that my life was finally on the right heading, not long after Rhonda and I returned to England I got a job composing the incidental music for *Survival of the Fittest*, a series about a sort of triathlon that took place in the wilds of nature. It was largely through the influence of HTV editor Dennis Pratt (who had previously commissioned the music for *Canoeing into the Past*) that I got this project, and my spirits soared when he contacted me with the offer. In order to get ideas for matching the musical score to the film I would have to make many trips to the recording studio in Cardiff, but since our London flat came with a Mercedes sports car this turned out to be an absolute pleasure – in fact it was difficult not to feel a bit like a celebrity whizzing along the M4 bound for the TV studio!

∞

By uncanny coincidence, as I awaited the arrival of my second child my brother and his wife Sally announced that they, too, were to become parents for the second time at the start of the following year. It seemed that a period of new beginnings was blossoming within our family, something that was also being reflected in our creativity. Sally was working on yet another album, *Playing in the Flame*, and Mike – currently on a sixty-one date tour of Europe – had entered what would become his most successful era. He also achieved a long-term ambition of obtaining a private pilot licence and bought himself a single prop Beechcraft Sierra aeroplane – as you do when you've just passed your flying test!

Adding fuel to whatever engine was powering this meteoric period, I was asked to write a new theme for the HTV Welsh evening news, *Wales at Six*, a commission arising from the fact that the TV studio news team loved the music I had written for *Survival of the Fittest* so much that they plugged for me to score the new theme. I was absolutely thrilled to get this so soon after the previous job, not least of all because the music was to be played every day for over a year and the royalties would provide a sorely needed income. This time around the timing seemed more like a gift from God than a fortunate coincidence.

Though I hardly **dared** believe it, it looked as though, at last, work was starting to come in for me and more things were looking possible all the time. Rhonda and I could not have been more

3: Awakening to The Dream

delighted with the timing combination of this new prospect and the pending arrival of our new baby, and we were already discussing the necessity, sooner or later, of having to set up a more permanent base in England if indeed the musical tide had started turning for me.

Did these positive signs portend a more settled, happy future for us all, or were we just experiencing another peak in the great undulating roller-coaster of dizzying ascents inevitably proceeded by alarming falls back down to earth? Of course there was no way of knowing – and perhaps no real *desire* to know, since sometimes ignorance really can be bliss. But I had every reason to feel positive about the rekindled possibility of a music career, and every right to savour each moment of excited expectancy inspired by the impending birth of my second child.

∞

In the third week of October 1980, with our baby now expected any day, Rhonda and I prepared for the home birth we had planned. It was an intense time of great anticipation that we dearly wanted to share together in the private and homely atmosphere of our apartment but, as with so many plans, there is 'Oft a slip twixt cup and lip', and after twenty-four hours of difficult labour we ended up in a hospital in Chelsea. Suddenly Rhonda's concerns about safety several months previously on Hydra now took on a more poignant and somehow precognitive significance.

In the distressed state of her later years my mum had come to formulate the belief that giving birth to a child with Downs Syndrome was a punishment from God for having strayed from the tenets of her strict Catholic upbringing, and whilst I didn't share her indoctrinated negative outlook, as I sat in the 'fathers room' of the maternity ward waiting, hoping, even praying, for a happy outcome, I could clearly understand how the mind can project all sorts of improbable and terrifying scenarios in situations of mortal vulnerability.

After a few more hours of helpless and agonised waiting, a nurse appeared to tell me that Rhonda had safely given birth to my first son.

— Island of the Soul —

Looking back now I see that I was in the early stages of discovering the amazing truth that harmony exists in every corner of the universe and that this awesome discovery, once integrated into my being, would later be expressed in music. The whole idea of the randomness of creation had begun to dissipate with the emergence of the Big Bang theory, and over time I began to see and feel the unfathomable intelligence that orchestrates and conducts the music of the spheres.

We returned to Hydra a couple of weeks later with our new son, Matthew, and resumed our insular island lifestyle, wilfully confined to shores whose only connection with the outside world was through the ships that transited the harbour; the main hub of commerce and social interaction among the islanders. Here the writers, poets, painters and musicians would gravitate to shop, have a meal or meet friends for a leisurely drink, before retreating back into their own worlds and the creativity that thrived in the atmosphere of this magical colony. On showing me his basement room one calm winter afternoon, Leonard Cohen once remarked, 'This room has been kind to me,' meaning that many of his greatest inspirations for songs came through there.

With Rhonda unable to work for the time being, things became a bit challenging for us, financially speaking, for the next few months. The royalties on the jobs I had done for HTV were keeping us afloat, barely, but I still wasn't making enough money from music to live on, so that winter I had to take on more odd jobs around the island to bolster our income. Fortunately, having previously laid down some social foundations on the island, finding work wasn't a problem, so I was soon back to white washing walls and looking after properties mostly owner-occupied during the summer months, which meant that over winter it was easy for us to find a place to live.

Despite having very little in the way of spare cash, Rhonda and I enjoyed our simple life on Hydra with our new baby. We were very close as a family unit and I was feeling entirely committed to the relationship. I still had no idea what might come next for me as far as music was concerned; when I looked to this aspect of my future there was still only a blank canvas, possibly ripe with potential to be worked into something impressive, or simply destined to remain blank, with countless variations in between those extreme possibilities. All I could do for the moment was live each day as it unfolded.

We were now house sitting for a painter friend, American artist **Bryce** Marden. Described as both an abstract and minimalist artist, **Bryce** was just one of the many creative individuals for whom Hydra provided a great source of inspiration. His *Souvenir de Grèce* works on paper and the five *Grove Group* paintings are examples, and he also made thirty-one oil paintings on fragments of marble at various locations on the island.

Prompted perhaps by the abstract paintings that adorned the walls of Bryce's house, there now followed a period lasting about six months when I drew endless diagrams illustrating how music, numbers, I Ching and geometry all relate together. Sacred Geometry and the concept of infinite circles had resonated with me for some time, and I recalled the Christmas evening in *The Bear* at Bisley with Keith Critchlow a few years earlier when he had drawn a diagram (on a beer mat!) showing me how to square a circle using numbers. He explained that this was something of a forgotten ancient secret after I had enthusiastically shown him one of my own conceptual diagrams (also scribbled on a beer mat).

The diagrams that were now coming through from me in Hydra also related to the idea that, in order to experience itself, consciousness requires a circle of perception to be drawn (or formed) upon the apparent cosmic chaos as a kind of aperture to perceive or 'see through'. This is the porthole or window of perception through which consciousness, in sentient beings like us, gazes upon its own reflection. My feeling is that we as Oneness are all looking through this window of perception at the same time, as if seeing through a prism at myriad reflections of ourselves; an apparent 8.7 billion of us each on different facets.

— A Trip Back in Time —

I had not particularly enjoyed living in the hectic environment of London for Matthew's delivery, so now that we had returned to Hydra with our new baby I was enjoying having some space once again. Through friends I heard about a mysterious place called Mount Athos, a peninsula in Northern Greece dedicated to the Holy Mother where (somewhat ironically) no female has been allowed to set foot in hundreds of years. It sounded like an intriguing place to visit, especially when I learnt that the monasteries there held a number of ancient Byzantine music manuscripts. So, feeling well up for an adventure at the time, I made the necessary application to the Greek Orthodox Church in Athens for permission to visit Mount Athos and examine these manuscripts which I understood were kept securely under lock and key.

Accompanied by fellow resident islander and poet Kevin McGrath, the expedition began with an overnight stay in a small guest house on the Grecian coast before taking the Kaiki (traditional Greek fishing boat) over to Athos the following day. When we arrived we were to present ourselves before the Holy See with my letter granting permission to spend seven days walking the ancient footpaths and staying in various monasteries.

Though one might conjure up any number of mental images as to what such a place may be like, nothing is ever likely to match the actual living experience, and this was certainly the case with Mount Athos. To begin with, Byzantine time is observed there, meaning daytime (or 00.00 hour) begins at sunset rather than midnight, so arriving there literally involves stepping into another time. The absence of any form of motorised transport also lends a special kind of tranquility, an atmosphere that focuses the senses on everything nature itself has provided.

Travel is undertaken along steep forested slopes that form a link between the twenty monasteries there; ancient pathways worn into existence over the centuries from the activity of monks and pilgrims travelling by mule or on foot. Along these time slip highways we saw some of the hermit caves where individual monks still live in absolute solitude; lone supplicants who are brought meagre provisions by fellow members of their order. There are also rest places on the way where sustenance such as bread, cheese and olives are placed for travellers in a wooden box, safe from foraging animals, and the tradition is that each walker leaves some food for those who will follow. As this was winter the landscape at higher altitude was covered in a layer of snow which betrayed the presence of various kinds of wildlife (most notably lynx) by their tracks in the virgin white carpet.

We took time to visit several of the monasteries including Lavra, the first to be built on the peninsula, where I was permitted to look at some of the ancient Byzantine music manuscripts. Just looking at these age-yellowed texts, musing on their history as some of the first examples of music actually being written down, was a sublime privilege.

Staying overnight in a monastery was in itself something of a retreat, the perfect environment for inward reflection or meditation. We attended mass at every monastery visited, but of course observing Byzantine time meant that these religious celebrations took place very late at night (to our body clocks), so we were asleep for the first part of each day.

As well as the monasteries, we also visited some of the *skitis* or villages where monks from other orders lived and worked in a more open, less austere environment. There was much serenity in these places; a palpable contentment where people lived simple and untroubled lives, and my only regret was that Rhonda hadn't been with me on such a special trip.

As the Kaiki motored slowly back across a gentle sea on the return journey, I was grateful to have had the opportunity to visit Mount Athos and take away with me an indelible memory of the peace surrounding this unique and sacred place.

— Message in a Bottle – By Telegram —

The Post **Restante** on Hydra was a genuine lifeline (the only one) for retaining contact with the outside world, and during my extended stays on the island over the years I had sent and received many letters at this little building. It was here that I recently discovered I had become an uncle again with the birth of Mike's second son, Dougal, and kept up-to-date with Sally's healthy song-writing and recording career. Her fourth album, *Playing in the Flame*, was already set for release.

I had sent the odd telegram, too, but the only time I actually received one was some considerable time ago when Richard Branson got in touch to ask if I could find him a rental house to stay in as he had a girlfriend he wanted to bring here for a holiday. Shortly after I got a place for him he arrived with a French girl called Virginie whom he had met, ironically, in the Rue De La Vierge – *Street of the Virgin* – in Paris. I really think he had a bit of a fixation with the word *Virgin* for some reason.

Richard fell in love with Hydra – if not Virginie – and later bought a sizeable bit of land on the island with a view to building a house. As a result, for a while I became unpopular with the locals who felt that I had introduced a tycoon to the island who would surely now spoil it with developers. Fortunately for me, and perhaps also the island, Richard changed his mind and built his dream house in the Virgin Islands. (Where else?!)

The memory of that occasion was recalled to mind when, on a routine mail check to the Post Restante one morning while Rhonda and Matthew were still asleep, I discovered a telegram waiting for me. Initially I had a sinking feeling in my stomach since a telegram could easily bring bad news from back home. The curious way in which the telegram had been addressed, however, suggested otherwise…

Terry Oldfield. Poste Restante. Hydra. Greece.

No one in my family would have been responsible for such a vague mailing address.

It was from a man called Gerry Troyna, but I knew no one of that name. The opening line of the telegram read:

I am a producer at the BBC. Would you be interested in composing the music for an upcoming TV series called Great Railway Journeys of the World?

I had to read the words twice just to confirm I had neither misread them nor projected an illusory wish onto the flimsy piece of paper in my hand. Somehow Gerry Troyna had obtained one of my cassette recordings of *Spiral* and thought that this style of music would be a perfect accompaniment to his almost completed TV series. He'd immediately set about trying to get hold of me and, luckily, someone knew where I was and how I might be contacted. In the remainder of the telegram Gerry told me that he'd really like to work with me and if I was interested I should come and see him at the BBC where the cost of my flight to England would be reimbursed.

Needless to say, this wasn't something Rhonda and I had to think through for very long, but rather than accompany me back to England yet again, this time she decided to remain on Hydra with Matthew. We had a rather close circle of friends on the island who would gladly offer their support, and even though I'd have to commute between London and Greece for a while to visit my family, this was a golden opportunity in which I had Rhonda's full blessing.

As I prepared to embark on my third, and largest, composing commission for a film project, it occurred to me that I had been so focused on securing a deal with a record company at the start that I hadn't even considered sending my demo to film or TV companies. Distracted by the recording success of Mike and Sally, it seemed I had overlooked this as a possibility despite the two previous score commissions. Maybe a part of me hadn't regarded this field of music production to be as 'real' or prestigious as releasing an album, but even though I still passionately wanted to get a record deal, I now realised that perhaps my natural composing style was ideally suited to this type of work. Considering also how this was now another occasion where one of my demo cassettes had ended up on the desk of just the right person at just the right time in a broadcasting company I hadn't even approached, maybe it was time to start taking the hint from the universe.

— The Journey Begins —

The music for *Great Railway Journeys of the World* was recorded in a studio in Hackney, and Gerry Troyna, a very pleasant man with a natural infectious energy, came down from Manchester for all of the sessions. At our first meeting I reminded him that I'd never done anything like the composing project he was proposing, but he told me not to worry, that he'd guide me through it. Gerry was a real angel, and I don't mean that entirely figuratively; he really did seem like a guardian angel whose sole purpose was to help me out of the career and financial stagnancy in my life. I had no problem with the musical side of things, but without his guidance on the technical aspects of production I would not have had the necessary experience to do the job properly.

 I learnt fast, though, and took on board all the technology I needed as I went along. I'd be given a fine cut of the film and from that put together some basic themes (one of which was based on a section from my demo, *Spiral*, that Gerry liked), followed by the complicated task of fitting it all to picture – a process which is straightforward in today's computer assisted, cut-and-paste world, but wasn't so easy in those days. I remember that I had to stripe the audio tape with a 60Hz tone in order to sync the music to the film, whereas nowadays all that is done using computer software where the film can be advanced frame by frame onscreen and all music, edits, tempo changes etc. inserted at any point. This is why so many people are making music for TV and films these days; it is literally a musical world of sound loops and easy editing where the computer instantly takes care of all the processes that previously would have demanded days of hands-on production by the composer or sound engineer.

 And so together Gerry and I worked enthusiastically to create the music for the series, a project in which I acquired a great deal of knowledge and experience that would stand me in good stead for the future – providing, of course, this time my composing career really had begun to take flight. I had learned to be cautious about celebrating success prematurely, but it was difficult to restrain the sense of optimism now, especially when a few people at the BBC expressed confidence for my future potential. With this in mind, and because the commute between London and Greece had been pretty exhausting, Rhonda and I decided to return to England just before spring of 1981 so that I could better pursue a potential career in music. This time we got a place in Newnham on Severn, mutually buoyant with hopes for the future.

As though to vindicate our blossoming confidence, within weeks of arriving back in England I received a second BBC commission, this time for *Great Little Railways*, a follow-up series to *Great Railway Journeys of the World*. The new programmes had a different producer, but luckily I was beginning to find my footing with the film composing process so this second project only consolidated everything I had learnt whilst working with Gerry Troyna. Just as well, because two further commissions came in that year which meant that, to my utter amazement, I was working flat out as a professional composer for the duration of 1981.

The first of these commissions was *Lady with the Llamas*, a little HTV film produced by Don Llewellyn (with whom I would later work quite a lot) that followed the life of a woman living in Patagonia who was breeding llamas from Peru. This TV film gave me the perfect opportunity to play my pan pipes and create music with a spontaneous, improvised feel, and consequently I really enjoyed working on it.

I can't recall very much about the second commission, *Bangor Lads*, except that it was an endearing film set in Ireland that gave me cause to seek some inspiration from deep inside where my own Celtic roots reside.

My spirits, my confidence, began to soar to uncharted heights. Finally, it seemed as though things were on their way up for Rhonda and I and we had some decent money coming in at last. Our lucrative and optimistic year was capped off perfectly one afternoon in early December when Rhonda walked into my little study area and declared that she was pregnant.

— And Baby Makes Four —

As though to test our resolve – or perhaps satisfy some karmic necessity – Rhonda's happy announcement coincided with an abrupt hiatus in new composing commissions. The money I had made from the four TV commissions had comfortably sustained us for twelve months, but it wasn't sufficient to sustain us through an extended period of unemployment. Consequently, with a young family to support and now another child on the way, after a few months I found myself staring adversity in the face once again. I took some odd jobs as a builder's labourer, but eventually had to seek help from the government who put me on Family Income Supplement. This was the one and only time in my life that I ever had to apply for that kind of help, and it did nothing for my peace of mind or self-respect to find myself in such a situation, especially so soon after tasting solvency and an apparently blossoming musical career.

I decided that I had to keep working on my music, not least of all because it seemed the only way to climb out of the slump we were in once and for all. At least now there were film and TV producers who knew me and liked my work, and that I could deliver the goods, so as far as that musical avenue was concerned all I could do was wait until another commission came in. My attention therefore turned again towards getting a record deal, and that meant composing more demo music. Fortunately, there was a recording studio in Bristol called *Sounds in Motion* where I managed to secure a time-in-lieu-of-points deal; this was a common term which simply meant that the studio got a share of the royalties if the finished work led to a record deal. So, most days I would drive from Newnham on Severn to the studio and lay down as much new music as I could, some of it related to *Spiral*, that first piece that had spawned such good fortune. Perhaps I was subconsciously seeking to give history a fighting chance to repeat itself, but I had done it before and I knew I could do it again. I just had to keep motoring on with the music whilst doing whatever else was necessary to make ends meet for my family.

As I once more began to roll with the punches administered by dramatically altering fortunes in my life, the career progress of my two siblings on the other hand continued to experience a more stable ascent. Mike was preparing for the one hundred and three date 1982 world tour to promote the release of his new album, *Five Miles Out*, due for release in March that year, whilst Sally was continuing a one-album-a-year average with the pending release of her fifth record, *In Concert*.

3: Awakening to The Dream

∞

Bringing with him a joyful respite amid the domestic challenges, our second son Oliver was born in Gloucester hospital on 13th August 1982, just one day after my own birthday.

When we brought little Oliver back from the hospital Rhonda's mother – who was over from Australia staying with us at the time – on first seeing the baby's face immediately commented in a typically proud mother-in-law tone, 'He's definitely a Preston, alright!' This reference to her side of the family was in fact pretty accurate; Oliver's features did indeed bear a greater resemblance to Rhonda's family members than mine.

It is remarkable how grounding a newborn child can be; bringing not only love but a sense of perspective, a reminder of what is most important in life. And so for many weeks our baby formed a sort of cosy bubble within which Rhonda and I could avoid facing certain unpleasant domestic realities, the most pressing of which, apart from financial security, was where we were living.

Being in the UK had had a great advantage as far as proximity to my work was concerned, but that was the *only* real advantage for us, and now that the music commissions had halted (for how long nobody knew) we were already beginning to feel the strain of living in an environment which wasn't at all suited to our personalities. I was also prone to mood swings and bouts of depression that I assumed stemmed from the stressful experiences of my teenage years combined with more recent familial responsibilities, and this too caused friction between me and my wife. Many years later I would discover that there had been a physical cause contributing to these mood swings, but at the time I could only assume the issue was purely psychological.

Rhonda and I came to realise that we were both just accepting a state of mutual discontent for the sake of making a living, enduring our location whilst missing the island we both loved. Things soon became so stressful that we knew we had to find a way to escape this unpleasant way of life without dragging ourselves into a financial quagmire in the process. Surely we could make *something* work...

The decision was sort of inevitable. We would take the bold step of having one more try at living on Hydra. I would find a workable compromise between composing in my home studio there and commuting to the UK for any necessary professional recording sessions. To a casual observer this may have seemed like an insane decision, but for the sake of our mental health and our relationship there was little alternative. We had to give it a go. So we bundled everything we could into our old Volkswagen Estate and drove down through Europe to Italy en route to Greece.

— An Experience Out Of Body —

I had recently started to experience an alarming phenomenon usually at the point of dropping off to sleep where a curious buzzing vibration would envelop my whole body; a physical sensation that increased in intensity until it became a roaring buzz in my ears. I assumed this was the product of recent emotional strain, nothing more, but it always took an enormous effort for me to stop the unnerving experience by rousing my half-asleep body enough to quieten the vibrations.

    On the night we took the ferry over to Greece from Italy and settled down for the night in our family cabin, the buzzing sensation began to manifest just as I was drifting off to sleep. Perhaps because I had reached the point of frustration at being at the mercy of this recurring incident, perhaps partly out of curiosity, this time I made the decision to allow the experience to unfold as it would and see what might happen…

    When the roaring sound evolved from the buzzing in my entire body I just went with it, steeling my resolve against the rising anxiety of the unknown. Suddenly I found myself no longer in my body but on the floor next to the tiny wardrobe across the room. From this vantage point I began to hear what sounded like a deep, guttural growling that seemed to be emanating from every direction, surrounding me with invisible threat. It was so terrifying that I actually feared for my life as I looked up to the top bunk where my body lay sleeping, apparently separated from the other part of 'me' that was now longing for this terrible thing to end. If only these sounds from hell would stop.

    After a period that could have been seconds or hours – there was no awareness of time in this outlandish realm – they did stop, and I was abruptly reunited with my physical body where I became fully awake at once, sitting bolt upright in the bunk and reflecting on what in the hell (literally) had just happened. In the cabin my family were sleeping peacefully, oblivious to the drama that had just taken place.

This was my first and most extreme Out-Of-Body Experience (OOBE), one that led me to investigate the phenomenon further. In one of Robert Monroe's fascinating early books I read descriptions of the sensation of vibration and the buzzing and roaring sounds that preceded his own OOBEs, which he claimed he had learned to instigate at will, and I got goose bumps! The similarity with my own experiences was uncanny. Furthermore the experience, I learned, was not at all uncommon, merely something of a taboo area that experiencers were understandably reluctant to talk about for fear of ridicule or accusations of mental instability. But with such an experience occurring so uniformly among a wide and varied section of the population, surely there had to be something in it? Even from my cursory research it seemed to be an as-yet unexplained aspect of human consciousness (perhaps even the true nature of consciousness itself), the existence of which was largely dismissed because of its conflicting position with accepted scientific models.

These findings tempted me to explore the Out-Of-Body Experience path in the months and years that followed, despite my initial terrifying encounter with the phenomenon. Several times I repeated the experiment of allowing the roaring buzz to develop, which resulted in a few more Out-Of-Body Experiences, but none of them, fortunately, accompanied by the hellish growling. These milder experiences never led to anything of particular note, so eventually I gave up on the exploration. One thing that did result from that metaphysical probing, however, was a long period of lucid dreaming when I would literally 'wake up' in the dream state to a realm that seemed as real as any worldly experience, always accompanied by the vibration and audible buzzing sound. One of these was so powerful that it heralded a major change in my life and later inspired the song, *Dreamer* (in 2001), written as a sort of memoir of those lucid dreaming experiences.

    Another connection I made with my vacillating emotions occurred much later after reading Eckhart Tolle's book, *The Power of Now*, in which he refers to a thing called *The pain body* which is basically emotional suffering produced from the residue of incomplete experience. It became obvious to me that a major shift in my overall approach to living would be required if I was ever to deal effectively with this 'pain body' that was rising and falling in me from time to time. And so, rather than trying to smother the onslaught of fatalistic emotions or allow them to provoke outward cynical reactions, I began to allow my body to accept these feelings and live with less resistance to them in order to fully experience the natural flow of things. I learnt the importance of noticing the early warning signs of an oncoming negative emotional episode through bodily sensations such as a tingling in the back of my neck and shoulders, or a change in breathing or pulse rate. With this growing awareness and the embodiment of real *feeling* came a noticeable lessening of anger and fear resulting from my basic willingness to be with 'What Is'. I eventually came to understand that this is the secret to inner calm and a much happier life and, as with so many other significant realisations and experiences in my life, it inspired a piece of music; a song called *No Resistance*.

∞

Watching Hydra growing ever-larger from our vantage point on the deck of the little ferry from mainland Greece was enough to restore the mental energy that had recently been lacking in me and Rhonda. The unabashed joy screamed silently in the surrounding air, filling us with a contented sense of homecoming.

Upon docking, we took our two children up to their big new house on the hill that looms above the port of Hydra and began unpacking almost immediately. I set up my porta-studio in one of the rooms while Rhonda got the kids sorted out, each of us silently absorbed in our individual tasks. There was no humming or random singing as we went about the job of setting up home, the initial relief at being back on our island retreat having already dispersed. Apparently. But there was something else. This time, something was different. Missing. And as we busied ourselves with getting organised and settling the kids into their new home, it was obvious that we were both experiencing this dreadfully ominous feeling. The exchanged smiles between us now as we flitted from room to room were considerate props adorned for each other's benefit, affectations that nevertheless failed to silence the unanimous, dejected little voice inside that whispered, *This isn't going to work after all, is it..?*

From that moment on, in a valiant state of denial Rhonda and I battled to create a life on Hydra for our family, doing what we each could to generate enough extra money to attain the happiness we had once known here together, this time with our two sons. The crucial difference, though, was that this time we *had* two children; two dependents that brought the kind of responsibility that would not permit the freedoms previously known to youth and new, flourishing love. And whilst the adventurous and unpretentious spirits of Rhonda and I could more easily endure poverty on a peaceful island paradise than financial comfort in London, there were now four people in the equation.

With neither odd-jobs on the island nor my music work abundant enough to provide adequate support, before long it was obvious that, although we had tried very hard to make a go of it, Rhonda and I could no longer sustain living on Hydra with two kids to support.

The prospect of returning to precisely the same living situation we had left in England was repugnant to both of us, so, as a compromise, I arranged for an advertisement to be placed in a local newspaper in Stroud, one of the few other places I had been contented in my life. It read something like, *'Composer and family seek cottage to rent in the Stroud area'.*

I believed that life in Stroud might also appeal more to Rhonda, and it was a great environment to bring up young children, so when the newspaper ad got several replies at least we knew we were heading somewhere that wasn't going to make us dread our return to England.

And so we closed our chapter on Hydra forever.

— All is Not Lost —

The journey back to Britain in the Volkswagen was fraught with troubles. We broke down on the motorway in Germany and had to spend every remaining penny on hotels and car repairs, an inconvenience that became a nightmare when travelling with two very young children. Eventually we limped our way back to Stroud and *Well Cottage*, the long-term rental we had secured in the small hamlet of Wallow Green, just outside Nailsworth.

In complete contrast to the house on Hydra and our previous places in England, the feeling in the cottage was at once welcoming and curiously familiar, giving us a sense that this would be our home for the foreseeable future. As I set up the components of my porta-studio in one of the cottage's little rooms, all I could really do now was hope and pray for the best, but a wondrous omen came in the form of my little girl, Rachel, who had recently returned permanently to the UK. Better still, she was living nearby with Lynne, which meant that my now nine-year-old daughter could come over and visit us and get to know her half-brothers. Rachel was of course warmly welcomed into the family and from then on we saw each other quite regularly. She was attending the local Steiner school and for a while stayed with us at weekends when she developed a close relationship with the two boys.

∞

Whether my prayer was being answered or *Well Cottage* had brought us luck, shortly after we'd settled into the new place I received a score commission for a BBC wildlife production about cuttlefish called *Aliens from Inner Space*. Despite the limitations of my home studio I set about putting together all the main ideas that would be recorded later in a professional studio (my future goal was to upgrade to equipment that would make me as independent as possible) and, inspired by the title, I composed some music with a science fiction flavour. This in itself was a bit of a diversion for me, and one that turned out to be a lot of fun.

To my astonishment, on the heels of this came a larger BBC commission to create a soundtrack for *Great River Journeys*, yet another spin-off series from *Great Railway Journeys of the World*. The music was pretty easy to compose as I was feeling particularly inspired at the time – mainly, I think, because the visuals on these programmes were so stunning, but also because the production team got on extremely well together and this always makes a big difference on a project.

Bearing in mind that twice before I'd been in a highly promising position such as this in recent years, only to be disappointed later by a lengthy period of inactivity, I dared not get my hopes up at this point. But it was beginning to look as though I had finally gained sufficient reputation to maintain a momentum in the music career I wanted so badly.

Indeed, I hardly had time to catch my breath after *Great River Journeys* before the next job came in; a soundtrack for another BBC wildlife film called *The Sisterhood*, which chronicled the behaviours of a pack of hyenas. Unlike the previous film there wasn't so much in the way of inspirational visuals, so the project was treated as a straightforward professional venture.

In between all of this, incredibly, ITV asked permission for some of my music to be used in the background of a new children's TV series called *Storybook International*. Each half hour episode featured a folk tale or fairy story dramatised in the global location of its origin (including Czechoslovakia, Romania, England, Turkey, Wales, Africa and India) and read by one of three narrators. I can't even recall the particular excerpts they used, but a total of sixty-five episodes were made and the series ran for three years from 1983-86.

Needless to say, steering my way towards making music a lucrative source of income and stability for my family relieved a lot of the tension that had existed between Rhonda and I, thereby improving our relationship. And as my composing work expanded and our boys grew into toddlers we all settled down to a happy family life together in Stroud.

— My Turn in the Recording Studio —

I had now entered a prolific and successful period in my life, a time when all the stars just seemed to line up and bring about the most successful outcome – something which my brother and sister had been experiencing for years. In 1983 Sally released yet another successful album, *Strange Day in Berlin*, and Mike was touring Europe to promote *Crises*, the album that would become his most successful of the 1980s, partly due to the success of one of its songs, *Moonlight Shadow*, which reached the number one position in nine countries.

In between touring my brother occasionally invited me over to his neck of the woods to go for a beer or play squash, which was always nice, although sometimes a bit of an effort. He was pretty stressed out at this time and it surprised me to discover that he had taken up having an afternoon siesta on the advice of his doctor, a habit he retains to this day. I was a good squash player back then and I often wondered later whether, under the circumstances, it was prudent of me to beat him so often!

One night we went out to a pub called *The Tunnel House* which was full of rowdy Hell's Angels. I immediately felt uncomfortable walking in the door but Mike was completely unfazed and just went in and sat down like he was in his local pub. This was around the time when he had been exploring elements of heavy metal music – best exemplified in the song, *Shadow on the Wall*, featuring the earthy vocals of Roger Chapman – so I think Mike had grown accustomed to having these guys around the various stages he played while on tour. I, on the other hand, didn't feel at ease again until we eventually left the pub.

A commercial project I instigated myself in 1983 was a collaboration with my friend from London, David Pash, whom I invited to play some guitar parts in a piece that eventually became a BBC library album called *Sunshine Holidays*. I also used some contemporary '80s synth sounds on this project with the intention of making the music appealing to contemporary producers and the like who would pay to use excerpts for background or 'jingle' music.

Working with Dave was great fun, and importantly rekindled a friendship that would lead to further collaborations together on later projects. I had known Dave since the time I'd been living with Lynne and baby Rachel in Portobello Road when I'd call into the shop he had inherited from his parents. *Pash Music* was an Aladdin's cave stacked full of ancient paraphernalia and musical instruments that I loved trying out. One day I got my eye on an old wooden flute and, seeing how much I loved its sound, Dave ended up selling it to me for a song. Much later on I discovered that the instrument was in fact a famous early Ritterhausen flute and worth a considerable amount of money!

— 1984 —

In the year that George Orwell, some thirty-five years previously, had chosen as the futuristic setting for his novel featuring the infamous global super computer, Big Brother, my career reached undreamed of plateaus. Commissions literally began to line up and I entered a period of dizzying, almost surreal success accompanied by some pretty hard work.

In Search of the Trojan War was the next six-part BBC documentary series I worked on. Written and presented by Michael Wood (the presenter of my first BBC commission, *Great Railway*

Journeys of the World), the series was essentially an investigative analysis of how much the story of the Trojan War as told by Homer in *The Iliad* could be supported by historical and archaeological evidence.

This time the production team were looking for a more orchestral sound so, still rather inexperienced with certain aspects of score writing at the time, particularly orchestral parts, I enlisted my friend David Pash to co-write and arrange some of the music. Dave, who had had a lot of classical training, became an integral part of this project and even conducted the recording sessions we had with the BBC Northern singers in Manchester.

The music we did for this series really seems to have hit the spot with a lot of people, and to this day I still receive so much positive feedback on it. BBC Records released the soundtrack on vinyl and one of the tracks also appeared on a *Telly Hits* album – which, incidentally, paid really well as it got into the charts for a time!

Dave and I worked really well together, and this second successful venture cemented a collaborative partnership – where he arranged and played on a lot of my film music – that would last for many years.

∞

In response to the increasing workload (and a healthier income), I now upgraded my attic music studio in order to improve the overall quality of film and personal demo recordings. I had had to travel up to Manchester by train to work on *In Search of the Trojan War* (where, in addition to the BBC Northern singers, I was given access to any soloists I needed... those really were the days!), and whenever possible I was also commuting to the Bristol studio to professionally record my own non-commissioned compositions, but at least now I always had a studio on-hand to get material down in decent quality as and when it came to me. The new equipment proved invaluable, paying for itself many times over as the commissions continued to roll in...

— Bears, Tigers, Rabbits, a Bit of Silence and Some Climbing —

Kingdom of the Ice Bear was a stunningly filmed documentary in the BBC's Natural World series that tracked the daily survival struggle of the Arctic animals, in particular that of a mother polar bear and her cubs. Produced by Hugh Miles (a fellow angler) and Mike Salisbury who was high up in the echelons of the BBC at the time, the film, perfectly narrated by Hywel Bennett, also turned out to be a pivotal music commission for me, one which led to many other projects.

The opening theme was unique in that I used some recordings of Inuit chanting mixed with a big orchestral sound that really stood out on the screen as something very different. The score also contained a theme which was actually part of a previous attempt I'd made to compose a viola concerto whilst living on Hydra before my music career had even begun! This was the first time the segment had been performed or recorded, and the haunting theme, now actually played on Cor Anglais, worked very well as an accompaniment to a scene in which the cameras floated over the snowy wastes and icebergs. The music came together pretty quickly for me and the whole soundtrack was beautifully recorded with a group of orchestral players at the BBC studios in London.

Almost overlapping *Kingdom of the Ice Bear* another BBC wildlife film project came in, this time for an hour-long programme called *Run, Rabbit Run*. Once again I called in Dave Pash to work on this simple and endearing little production, and we recorded all the music in a single afternoon session in the studio. Our work on this was well-received and, literally, short and sweet.

Coupled with the BBC work I also received two commissions from HTV. *Images of Wales* was made by Don Llewellyn (*Lady with the Llamas* producer) and was an interesting piece to work on because the only audio it contained was music and sound effects. Since the images largely spoke for themselves and literally begged the music to come along, there were fewer restrictions concerning musical entry points and mood etc., which gave me considerable scope and freedom to experiment.

The second HTV film, *The Only Genuine Jones*, was in contrast more of a composing challenge. Documenting the life of famous nineteenth-century rock climber, Owen Glynne Jones, it contained a lot of history which didn't need so much music, but the climbing sequences, all portrayed by actors, were quite dramatic and required just the right kind of music to generate and maintain a level of tension. For that very reason, though, composing the music was in itself something of an adrenalin rush!

With no time to come down from the musical high, I was catapulted into the next production, *Land of the Tiger*, which brought several new experiences my way – not least of which would be an EMMY award nomination. For this, my first score commission for The National Geographic Society, I was invited to Los Angeles to view the footage and discuss a way forward with the music. When I arrived at the airport there was a limousine waiting for me with a driver who showed me around town before taking me to the editing rooms; this was a little surprise that the production company had very kindly laid on for me. Then, a few days later when all the music business had been sewn up, I got another surprise at LA airport when I discovered that my return Pan Am flight to London had been upgraded to first class. Absolute bliss. And, so far, the only time in my life that I have travelled first class on a flight.

The music for *Land of the Tiger* had to reflect moments of majesty and danger in almost equal measure, yet somehow also be suffused with a grace and beauty that reflected the character of these magnificent animals. I think I managed to achieve this quite successfully whilst also learning a few new things along the way that added to my rapidly accumulating experience, and the end result seemed to satisfy all concerned. No sooner had I rounded off this commission when Rhonda came up to my attic studio one day and gifted me one more little surprise.

— High as a Kite and Still Rising —

Life had turned around so quickly and so very positively for me in recent times that it almost felt like I was now being rewarded for my endurance, that all the little deposits of happiness that should have been distributed to me over the years were finally being paid off in a lump sum. Although this was the least likely explanation for the sudden change of **fortune** in my life, the news that I was about to become a father for the fourth time only served to endorse it. By way of a celebration, Rhonda and I did two things: we got married and bought our first home together. The flood of recent commissions (which showed no sign of drying up any time soon) had ensured that both of these steps were financially within our reach, and I had at last got to a point where I was earning enough to focus solely on the music.

Our marriage was a low-key event with just a few friends and family members, after which we soon managed to find a nice property on Coronation Road in the village of Rodborough near Stroud. The new house, like *Well Cottage,* had a really nice feeling about it, and of course it was located in an area that I loved, so from the outset Rhonda and I felt confident about the purchase. Once more, then, the still-expanding Oldfield family, not known for allowing the grass to grow under their feet, were packing up and moving on.

— The Wicked Stepmother —

It's interesting how much a new player coming onto the world stage can affect the whole scenario, particularly if they are somehow linked with your own life. Such it was with my stepmother, Helga, whose negative influence on all our lives cannot be overstated. She was one of those unfortunate people who never seem to give others any consideration whatsoever and, with apparently no filter control over how to verbalise their thoughts, often say things that are rude, condescending or just downright mean. Typically she would do things like point at people and call them idiots whilst walking through a shopping mall or make crass comments about their misfortunes, often cracking loud and totally inappropriate jokes in the process.

One morning Dad called me from a hotel in Heathrow. 'I've left Helga,' he said, rather like a child owning up to a transgression. At last it seemed he had come to his senses and made a desperate bid for freedom, I thought. Apparently Hell Girl (our nickname for her) had been cussing and swearing at the neighbours from the balcony of her house in Germany and had even thrown a big pot of flowers at them. This was the final straw for Dad who was naturally polite and well-mannered, and he quickly drove off for the airport and hopped on a plane to London, grabbing all the money he could from their joint account on the way. He came to stay with us in our new place in Rodborough and we were encouraged by his newfound determination not to go back to Helga. After a few weeks Dad went to visit some Irish cousins who were living in Spain, apparently now set on enjoying his freedom once again, and we all breathed a great sigh of relief. Not too long afterwards, and much to everyone's disappointment, however, we heard that he had returned to the hell realms in Stuttgart. The pull – or, more likely, his sense of duty – must have become too great, and I suspect also that he couldn't face up to his own solitude. If Dad had a character flaw it lay in his propensity towards pleasing others and maintaining harmony where possible. He later told us that Helga had been devastated by his leaving and had promised all sorts of changes, so he went back to her. 'I couldn't bear to upset her,' he reasoned with me on the telephone weeks later, but I told him I thought he had made a very bad decision, even though he was adamant that things were going to change.

Somewhat ironically, around the time all this was going on Sally relocated to Germany to pursue her musical career, a move that was triggered largely by the demise of her UK label, Bronze Records. Here she would go on to find success working with producers including Candy DeRouge and Gunther Mende, recording several more albums as well as appearing regularly on national TV and radio stations. Now living close to their home, Sally visited Dad and Helga in Stuttgart from time to time, whereas I now only saw them on occasions such as Christmas. Mike, who was currently living in Switzerland, really had little tolerance for Helga; he had tried to put up with her a few times for Dad's sake, but in the end cut himself off from all but the most essential family contact. His all-consuming working life at the time only made this emphatic decision easier to justify, since that year he released two albums, *Discovery* and *The Killing Fields*, the latter of which, a soundtrack, was his one and only commission for film music.

There was something oddly ironic about the fact that my music career was behaving like a mirror image of my brother's in that my soundtracks were in popular demand yet so far I hadn't released a single solo album!

— Pirating —

The first music commission I received after setting up my studio in the new house – and one which took up a large chunk of the first part of 1985 for me – was *Return to Treasure Island*, a swashbuckling HTV TV series starring Brian Blessed as Long John Silver. There is always a lot of music required in drama and this was a bit of an epic one for me involving a great deal of work, but I learnt so much from the project as it was recorded in Hans Zimmer and Stanley Myers' Lillie Yard studio in Chelsea which was specifically set up for film scoring. Being surrounded by highly experienced film composers and music producers who were on hand to offer advice (and thereby indirectly teach) also really helped me to focus more on the music itself.

Tom McGuinness from Manfred Mann's *Earth Band* was also involved in the music production on this film (with whom I spent many happy days recording), and once again I called in David Pash to conduct the string orchestra for the opening titles. Two versions of this main theme (released as a music EP) together with a full soundtrack album were later released by HTV.

3: Awakening to The Dream

— An Unexpected Call —

The potential impact a simple phone call can have on a person's life is a long-established aspect of living. Although most of us don't dwell on it, this communication mode that has attained unprecedented presence in most of our lives has the power to send us into a state of euphoria or abject misery, depending on the nature of the call. The majority of calls we receive will be made by relatives and friends sharing twee information or checking on our well-being, and consequently that is kind of what we expect when we hear the sound of that ring tone or favourite preselected jingle. Then there are the others. The calls that can be life-changing or completely devastating. The sombre voice of a sibling struggling to compose themselves long enough to tell you about an unexpected death in the family. Or the same sibling giddily announcing that the arrival of their first baby ten minutes previously has just made you an uncle. That *unknown* number that flashes on your mobile screen will probably be an annoying marketing call, or someone who's misdialed and destined to be as confused to hear your voice as you are theirs. But there is always the chance that the voice you hear will be that of a sympathetic stranger calling from a hospital or police station to impart some shocking news. Because we know that tragedies are always sudden. That they can happen any time. Consequently, in the first seconds when we hear that stranger on the other end of the line, our brows furrow and our minds are immediately sent into frantic search mode... Who could this person be? Is their voice tone suggesting benign professionalism or a scam? Which family member could possibly have been involved in an accident? Has anyone we know been ill lately?

Such it was when I answered the phone that morning to hear the formally pleasant yet unfamiliar voice of a young woman. After establishing that she was speaking to Terry Oldfield, she introduced herself as a representative from the British Film and Television Academy (BAFTA) association and informed me that I had been nominated for an award for my music on *Kingdom of the Ice Bear*. Prior to the official televised event at The Hilton Hotel in London's Park Lane, nominees were invited to attend a special private ceremony at which we would receive our certificates of nomination. So, two ceremonies would be involved, the second of which would reveal the BAFTA winners in each category. I was warmly congratulated for my achievement and assured that a letter formally inviting me to the main ceremony would follow shortly.

Initially I was stunned by the information. It was of course a total surprise, one for which I hadn't had even the slightest indication beforehand, and it wasn't really until I had replayed the conversation in my head for a third time that it began to sink in.

Whatever you do in life, it's always nice to have your work acknowledged in a manner beyond and unrelated to financial remuneration, especially those of us involved in creative activities who necessarily dig that bit deeper and give that bit more of ourselves, usually with fewer expectations of exponential reward. I hadn't actually won anything yet, but just to be nominated for such a prestigious award, shortlisted from so many other potential composers, was a true vindication for all the years of hope turned to disappointment that I'd experienced. The vacillating fortunes had tempted and deflated me as I'd engaged in a musical quest that often seemed to be little more than a futile pursuit of someone else's dream, but I'd carried on, never knowing whether I was being tenacious or foolish. And here, it seemed, was my answer. My true reward. Whatever came now would just be varnish.

When I told Rhonda the news her eruption of delight somehow confirmed the absolute reality of the situation, thereby giving the seal of approval for my own expressions of delight to unfold. It was then I realised that all of this was for both of us.

∞

The nomination ceremony at the BAFTA Centre in Piccadilly was in itself quite an experience. Full of association members, many of whom I recognised, the room was peppered with well-known British actors, among them the brothers James and Edward Fox – who made light-hearted fun of the Nehru style Indian jacket I was wearing; a proudly-worn garment that had been tailor-made for me years previously in Delhi.

We were officially presented with our nomination certificates individually, and just as I was stepping up to receive mine, composer and conductor Carl Davis – who was coming off the stage – stopped to shake my hand and congratulate me on the music for *Kingdom of the Ice Bear* which he said was 'brilliant'. I remember feeling both astounded and absolutely chuffed with this compliment.

Being treated a bit like a hero that day was something of an honour, but I was still in a state of innocence really, believing that all of this ceremony was actually just a sort of official run-of-the-mill occurrence. Consequently, I didn't become overawed or overly nervous. In fact, I felt strangely at home. (Writing this, I've just glanced over at the nomination certificate which hangs on my wall here in Australia to this day.)

When I received notification of a second award nomination soon afterwards for my work on *Land of the Tiger* – this time it was an American EMMY award – complete astonishment more than delight overwhelmed me. Surely I wasn't sufficiently experienced or good enough yet to be in the running for such prestigious awards – especially two of them in such close succession? I was highly appreciative of this second acknowledgement of my work, of course, if not overly excited yet as the whole thing seemed so surreal and far away. As with the BAFTA nomination, I had no clear understanding of the position I found myself in at the time.

And so, bizarrely, I was soon on my way to New York for the EMMY awards ceremony at the Grand Hyatt hotel – which I remember had a fifty foot tree growing in the lobby! It was my first time in New York and, being a person who generally prefers tranquil surroundings, I wasn't quite sure how I'd react to being in such a lively city. Sure enough, when I first ventured out of the hotel for a look around I immediately felt like I had been caught up in a rip tide of manic activity. So many people, all somehow displaying their social background, ethnicity and financial status in their clothing, stature, behaviour... all with purposeful and preoccupied expressions, many engaged in animated and over-loud conversations that nevertheless projected insincerity, the impersonal... yellow cabs, car horns, street vendors, police horse hooves and thousands of shoes treading upon the pavement (here known as the sidewalk), every nuance contributing to the mechanical and organic cacophony of noise. The odours of fast food blended with car exhaust fumes and the ever-present and indefinable street smell that can be experienced in any city on the planet. *Walk. Don't Walk.* Illuminated commands issued at pedestrians who could be fined – get a 'ticket' – for disobeying the relentlessly alternating couplet. Consequently, no jaywalking here.

New York is certainly unique, yet in one sense only in how it processes innate facets of human nature within a peerless cauldron of cultural, historical and environmental influences.

I began to feel quite unsafe walking around this frenetic and unfamiliar territory, and my sense of foreboding wasn't appeased any by the periodic wail of police sirens echoing around various parts of the city. This was a recurring noise that would also stir me from sleep throughout that night. Given enough time, no doubt these sounds of the city would have paled into the background just as the nocturnal activity of the insects and wildlife in the Australian jungle have for me, but, unlike any call from the natural world, the man-made alarms carried unsettling suggestions of threat and human suffering.

The following evening I took my place at one of the big round tables that had been set up in the hotel's main conference room in preparation for the awards ceremony. The room sparkled with ostentatious decoration and buzzed with the promise of overblown pageantry. Organisers and TV cameras seemed to be scooting around everywhere in a sort of microcosmic rendition of the activity I had experienced on the streets of New York the previous day. When the ceremony got underway and it finally came to the nominations for my category, three TV cameras suddenly zoomed in on my face, right on cue, in order to capture my reaction to the announcement of the winner. I had been prepped beforehand to look at each one in turn, which I didn't feel comfortable with at all as it felt so fake and staged. But I graciously complied, smiling and doing my best to look pensive until the winner (who, it turned out, wasn't me) was announced and the cameras finally swung away in perfect unison, making me almost glad the award and its associated attention had gone to someone else.

All in all, that whole experience wasn't great and, to be honest, I couldn't wait to get on the plane home.

∞

On 23rd December 1985 my second beautiful daughter, Allegra, was born at our house in Rodborough after a relatively easy birth carried out by the visiting midwife. Our doctor had been expected to attend, but somehow he got detained along the way and arrived just after little Allegra Jean Oldfield entered the world. A short while later I tenderly cradled and carried the tiny bundle downstairs to show her off to Rhonda's mother and stepfather who were over from Australia and waiting anxiously in the sitting room.

Although I was already riding high on musical success at the time, nothing could compare to the joy and light this baby girl brought into my life.

— A New Age —

I remember a strong feeling of inevitability about the whole thing and the presence of a different kind of energy. There was an inner knowing that this direction would be supported, although I had no idea how. I was learning fast that the feelings associated with this kind of decision-making – the sort that requires what I now call the Just Do It *approach – are pretty intense, and the willingness to be present with whatever happens, even if it is uncomfortable, is a prerequisite to actually being in the natural flow of creation. This is where true support or grace comes into play and the miracles can happen.*

With my fourth child safely delivered and my music career now definitely on the up, I took on the purchase and renovation of a large house in Chalford, a village four miles outside Stroud. *The Old Mission Hall* was a large, mostly derelict four-storey building originally developed from two cottages built up against a cliff overlooking the Chalford canal in Stroud. I could offer no logical explanation for why I had made a purchase that was not only financially irrational (I was not yet earning quite enough to pay for such a big undertaking), but also brought with it a lot of hard work. Our budget meant that I would have to be fully hands-on with all the renovation work, and whilst I had had various labouring jobs in my life and was no stranger to physically demanding jobs, using my hands for chiselling work and shifting rubble was certainly not conducive with my 'real job' as a musician and composer whose instrument demanded very subtle and articulate finger movements. Fortunately, a friend also offered to work on the building with me on a pay-as-you-go basis and he turned out to be the perfect man for the job as he was also at a place in his life that required some trust in the flow of things.

All I can say about this impetuous act of madness is that I had been overwhelmed by a powerful sensing that it was the right, strangely inevitable, thing to do, and I, Terry Oldfield, was merely carrying out my role in a well-established play in which I was both director and subservient actor. I could enjoy every moment of the production, perhaps suffer various forms of performance anxiety, but I had no business altering the script, or choosing another play. Besides, navy blue boiler suits were quite fashionable at the time and I was now to be seen wearing one most days.

As though to support my newly adopted *Just Do It* approach and thereby fulfil a prophecy about which I only had a tenuous sensing, the commissions kept on pouring in. One of these was a BBC *Wildlife on One* production presented by David Attenborough that followed the antics of a gang of meerkats in

Southern Africa. The wonderful cinematography on *Meerkats United* revealed the naturally entertaining group behaviour of these animals, humorously likening it to a football team working together for a common goal. Consequently, my music was very jolly with an African flavour running all the way through to reflect the geographical location. This documentary, one of the first to portray the lives of these often amusing creatures, was voted 'Best wildlife film of all time' in a national television poll. The only sad occurrence associated with the film was that its producer, Marion Zunz, died in a skiing accident not long after her landmark film was made.

Two other contrasting commissions that came in around this time presented their own unique compositional demands. The first was for a main opening theme for Russell Harty's popular ITV talk show, *Harty*, which was recorded in a studio in Taunton, Somerset where the producer was based at the time. I think my music was only used for one season, something which wasn't uncommon in those days where a new TV season or series was often heralded with new or newly-arranged music.

Next came *Portrait of Newton*, a documentary about physicist, mathematician, astronomer and theologian Isaac Newton in which I renewed my acquaintance with producer Lawrence Moore, the man behind my first experience of film scoring with *Mystery in the Plain*. Working on this project I learnt rather a lot about Newton and how he thought – which was a necessity since the character of the music had to reflect the logical and mathematical mind processes of this seventeenth century genius.

Consequently, I put together music that I hoped was Bach-like (another genius born forty-three years after Newton); something that was quite challenging for me as a budding tunesmith now being asked to work in so many different styles. Whilst it paid the bills, and I was grateful to be an 'official' professional composer, this aspect of having to write music to a highly specific brief on certain projects was not ultimately fulfilling, and already causing me to feel restrained by the demands it imposed. With so many back-to-back commissions I no longer had any time for my own personal musical creation, and as time wore on I yearned for, needed, the freedom to focus on my own flow and style.

I could only hope that one day the tide would turn in that direction.

∞

Rhonda and I sat in the huge room amid an atmosphere charged with the fluctuating babble and laughter of exhilarated guests accompanied by sweetly tinkling crystal champagne glasses.

The surrealism had begun with the chauffeur-driven limousine journey from Rodborough to The Hilton Hotel and the ostentatious banqueting hall where we were now seated up front at a nominee table with actress Dame Peggy Ashcroft and various other people (whom I didn't recognise). I have never been one for small talk and really don't recall the content of any conversations at the table, but I do remember receiving brief handshakes and well wishes from passing actors including John Hurt and Sir John Mills.

3: Awakening to The Dream

There had also been an embarrassing moment as I was coming into the hall when I stepped on the trailing dress of a lady whose head instantly snapped around as she shot me a stare that might have proved fatal if indeed looks could kill!

Master of Ceremonies that evening was Bob Geldof who himself received quite an accolade after presenting a BAFTA for Best Actress to Peggy Ashcroft when the first thing she said was, 'I just want to say that I am honoured to be standing on the podium with this man.' This was of course in recognition of Geldof's involvement in the hugely successful *Live Aid* concert the previous year.

The names of all the BAFTA nominees hadn't been published until well after the nomination ceremony, so not until presentation night did I discover that Richard Rodney Bennett, Carl Davis and Eric Clapton were the other three shortlisted in my category for Best Original Television Music. To be shortlisted alongside such big names was in itself a pinnacle event of this dreamlike interlude in my life, especially when not so long ago I was having doubts about making a living by composing music. Now here I was, fast-tracked it seemed, into a world where my work was being reckoned among that of some of the most renowned musician/composers.

Happily accepting that I had precious little chance against such icons, there was absolutely no expectation of going all the way and actually winning the BAFTA – unless, perhaps, there was indeed some cosmic manipulation taking place here to ensure that outcome – so it came as no surprise when Bob Geldof announced that Eric Clapton and Michael Kamen had secured the award for their incidental music on a series called *Edge of Darkness*. Rather than feeling disappointed, I was actually amazed that I had been pipped at the post by none other than Eric Clapton. Not so bad at all, really.

Not long after my own night of theatre, a real-life drama unfolded in my family when Mike announced that his seven-year relationship with Sally Cooper had broken down and the couple had decided to split up. Despite the amicable nature of their parting, they had three children together; Molly, Dougal and, only recently, Luke, so unfortunately there were some uncomfortable times ahead for all of them.

∞

With BAFTA and EMMY nominations now to my credit, I was settling into working very productively on TV music when the BBC forwarded a letter from John Hitchens, a well-known English painter. John had been recording my music from the TV and using it as an inspirational background for his work, and now asked if I could possibly make him a cassette recording of my music so that he would have something of better quality to listen to while working on his landscapes for a big upcoming exhibition in London. Rather flattered that my music was of such help and inspiration to him, I happily compiled a tape mostly comprising film cues that I was working on at the time and sent this off to John. I thought no more about it until a few weeks later when I got a letter from Colin and Carmen Wilcox, a young couple in Grenada in the Caribbean who were moving to London to set up their new mail order music company, *New World Cassettes*. Having recently heard and been impressed by a sample of my music, they wondered if I'd like to do a similar album to launch their new label.

It turned out that John had been sending copies of the tape I gave him to various companies because he thought that my music should be 'out there'. Being a creative person himself and familiar with the often difficult commercial side of things, I think he found it a bit of a travesty that few people had heard of me and I'd never made an album.

Apart from the way in which my music had once again found its own curiously serendipitous path, one of the first things that flashed into my mind was how *Tubular Bells* had launched a fledgling record company. I also considered how John Hitchens had turned out to be something of an angel helping me.

Thrilled that my long-standing ambition to release a solo album was finally about to be realised, I immediately added this new project to my other recording commitments and began putting together an instrumental album. I had accumulated a sizeable library of rejected or unused film music over the last few years and it was from this stockpile that I pieced together my first ambient album, *Cascade*, without the need for a professional standard home studio. I sent off the completed work to Colin and Carmen in truth with no big expectations; they were, after all, two people (whom I had never met) with an unproven track record and therefore presumably limited advertising clout. I had at least responded to their request, so all I could do now was wait and see what transpired and in the meantime get on with other things like my house renovation project.

I was almost knocked over when, several months later, I received my first royalty statement from *New World Cassettes* informing me that *Cascade* had sold over seventy thousand copies! Back then in the mid-eighties the recording deals were fair and, unlike today's tiny percentages, a sixty-forty split wasn't uncommon, so the attached cheque was very healthy indeed.

And that was how my album recording era began – as swiftly and unexpectedly as my film and TV music scoring career – together with a long-term relationship with a new company whose promotional by-line was *'Music for a New Age'*.

My life was certainly entering something of a new age, a time of complete consolidation between family and career. My uncharacteristically cavalier act of buying *The Old Mission Hall* had now been completely vindicated by the new secondary recording career. All it had taken was a bold plunge into the unknown with only faith in my instincts as a guide. This untypical (for me) way of living was oddly thrilling, not so scary after all; rather like in fairy stories where the dreaded monster turns out to be a pussy cat when confronted face-to-face.

It would be some time before we could all move into the new place as a family, but at this point in my life the house was every bit a physical representation, or 'proof', of the growing confidence I had in myself and the future. Hindsight might reveal this – at least on some level – to be an act of self-delusion, but with the building work now well underway all I could see was that Rhonda and I were getting on well, the kids were doing great and my music career was soaring.

∞

New World Cassettes were already talking about a follow-up to *Cascade*. I was absolutely thrilled about this explosive start to my album recording career, but the professional standard home studio I planned to install in the new house was still quite a long way off, so I would have to use external studios for all of the final recording and mixing. To be recording solo albums was something I'd dreamt of since I produced *Spiral*, my first demo tape, but in addition to my TV commissions – which of course had to take priority – I was now right in the middle of renovation work on the house, so time was in short supply for the creation of my second piece of music. Nevertheless, I loosely agreed on a delivery date for the album (that would become *Reverence*) with my new recording label and began putting ideas together whenever I could.

Not surprisingly, months evaporated as I simultaneously juggled these musical and construction projects, and before long I came to the stressful realisation that making the second album my lowest priority could well affect my chances of becoming a solo artist. With the due delivery date for *Reverence* now having come and gone, necessity colluded with my new *Just Do It* approach to life and I took the rather drastic step of booking time in a small studio in the nearby village of Avebury to record the album for which I only had a series of musical ideas. I managed to secure an affordable three-day deal at the studio where I decided I would 'wing it' and do the whole album in that time with absolutely nothing written down beforehand. My only real preparation was the intention to be fully available to the muse if she happened along.

And so I arrived at the studio in Avebury early one morning with all my flutes and pan pipes together with some whale recordings that I had inherited from my BBC work. I told the engineer that this was going to be an entirely improvised affair, a comment I expected was going to stun or maybe even irritate him, but fortunately he was the perfect person for the project and we managed to put together the whole album in the available three days. The completely spontaneous approach of putting myself on the spot with the universe paid off not only with the recording but also the album's popularity as *Reverence* went on to sell over two hundred thousand copies. The Gold Disc Award still hangs on my studio wall here in Australia.

∞

For Christmas that year we all joined Mike and his new partner, Norwegian singer Anita Hegerland, in Gstaad, Switzerland. The couple had invited me and my family, together with Sally, Dad and

Helga, to spend a few days with them in a huge chalet they had rented for the occasion. It was actually a wonderful white Christmas and Anita had arranged for candles to be placed in every conceivable spot indoors and around the garden. To begin with, a bit of a shadow hung over the occasion as Dad hadn't come to terms with the fact that Mike had left Sally Cooper and the kids, creating an atmosphere which at one stage nearly evolved into a fracas, but Mike was determined for the Christmas spirit to remain intact and managed to calm the situation down. So we all went out to dinner in a restaurant where we were seated next to none other than Michael Caine and Roger Moore! Sally sweet-talked the two gentlemen into autographing some menus for the kids, shortly after which I believe that ex-James Bond actor Mr. Moore asked my sister to join him later for a drink.

    Mike was at his most social during this festive period and went out of his way to hire skis for everyone so we could all go up on the slopes and have a great time together. I was a novice back then but, thanks to this outing and a bit of decent coaching, I soon caught the skiing bug. One evening after drinking a few (too many) shots of the local schnapps Mike and I also went sledging, but that occasion didn't turn out so well as I ended up cracking a rib… My brother was once again happy and in love, though, and it was nice to see him like that.

— A Fresh Mission —

1987 began in Southern England with one of the coldest winters since records began. Described as a little Ice Age, the temperatures for the days around mid-January went as low as minus twenty-six degrees and are logged as the coldest since January 1740. There were ice floes on the river Severn for the first time in living memory and our village was completely cut off by heavy snowdrifts for two weeks. As is often the case in such situations, the local community rallied together to help each other however they could, and every morning during this weather-enforced lockdown our local farmer delivered milk in churns with his tractor. When the snow finally began to thaw around the third week of the month, all the water pipes started bursting from the change in temperature and the plumbers were inundated with work. As is also typical in times of crisis, one person's misfortune is another's pay day.

Work on the house renovation naturally slowed down during this period, but by that point the interior was in a reasonably liveable condition (for me if not yet Rhonda and the kids), and I had set up my new studio on the top level. The top two storeys of the house must have experienced a fire at some point as these levels were partly built on the burnt eaves of the two cottages and partly on the top of the cliff, a process which effectively doubled the size of the house. Up on the fourth floor my studio had a great view of the Chalford canal, once used to transport coal up the River Severn in horse drawn barges. Not far up the canal in the valley near Chalford was *The Daneway*, originally a bargees pub that also happened to be a favourite of my brother and I when he lived at *Througham Slad*. It was a real old-world type pub with oak beams and a log fire where you could happily spend an afternoon lost in thought or conversation, as I often did with Mike. We occasionally saw the now legendary Steve Winwood in there, too, who had set up his home nearby.

Installed up in my 'proper' studio I spent hours happily experimenting with the new recording equipment which included a cutting edge 8-track Tascam Portastudio, one of the first all-in-one-studios to come onto the market and simply perfect for me. The upgraded equipment abolished the need to use external studios as I could now produce a professional quality finished product at home, which was exciting as well as highly convenient since I could create new sounds and record final ideas whenever I chose, no longer restricted by office hours and the pressure of having to keep one eye on the studio clock.

Because of this my third album, *In the Presence of Light*, was recorded in a very short time and is rather unique for me in that it contains hardly any real instruments as I'd become fascinated by all the big string sounds, washes and pads that were now magically available at my fingertips. I was mesmerised, completely drawn into all of that for a while – which I supposed was part of the learning process of a developing composer, but it also gave me real insight into how we can all be sucked in and taken over by new technology, rather like little magpie musicians fascinated by glitter rather than true substance. Consequently, the album was never a favourite of mine and I still don't really like it so much.

Greatly facilitated by the new studio, however, were my TV commissions which just kept on coming...

One of the first commercial projects I recorded at *The Old Mission Hall* was *Ancient Alliance*, a BBC documentary about the relationship between wolves and buffalo co-existing in Wood Buffalo National Park in Northern Canada, the only remaining place on Earth where wolves hunt buffalo. The abundance of new sounds available to me now meant that as well as having greater creative scope I also experienced a renewed enthusiasm for these TV commissions, so working life began to tick over pretty smoothly.

Two other BBC productions that I worked on in close succession that year were *Night Hunters* and *World of the Unborn*. The first was a wildlife documentary about owls which presented me with an opportunity to try mimicking owl cries with various wind instruments. In the end I mainly used flute and pan pipes, getting some nice effects by blowing into the flute with the head joint removed and recording the pans with a very breathy, almost toneless sound.

The footage of *World of the Unborn*, a fascinating film about the life of a fetus inside the womb, on the other hand allowed me to represent through music that sense of wonder that is so important for us in life. This project was, not surprisingly, highly immersive for me – a joy, really – and the result worked very well. The film won many awards in its field and led to my working on

The Second Imperative with the same production team later on, but unfortunately my experiences with this second film would be better likened to a nightmare.

In between the larger and frequently demanding scores were the little ones; those commissions which not only helped with living costs but, by virtue of the lack of challenge and pressure they presented, were also a lot of fun. Such a project was *A Winter Sleep*, a short film about hibernating ground squirrels that David Pash and I recorded in a single session. To those in the recording studio we acted as though we were well prepared, but the flute and classical guitar music we produced was mostly busked as we went along. It worked well, though, and nobody in the studio was any the wiser to what was going on. As though to compound the banality of the whole endeavour, the score for this documentary went on to win the Best Music Award at the Chicago International Film Festival!

— Rekindling an Old Passion —

My daughter Rachel, now thirteen, continued to visit us regularly at weekends and sometimes also on her way home from school. That year the school had arranged a ski trip to Austria which I was fortunately able to take with her as one of the small group of year eight parents who would be accompanying the kids on their adventure. This was a great father and daughter bonding experience and I also got on very well with Graeme Whiting, Rachel's class teacher and the trip leader. It had been a very long time since I'd been fishing and I was delighted to discover that Graeme was a keen angler who had recently taken up fly fishing and was now tying his own flies. As we developed our acquaintance he soon showed me the basics of fly tying, and it wasn't long before I had two desks up in my studio; one for music and one for tying flies. When I ran out of inspiration for the music I would simply scoot my chair across to the fly tying bench and create a new pattern or two.

My first forays back into fishing were at Tewkesbury weir where I would often go now to spin for pike, the great freshwater predator. It was a wonderful balance to the many hours I was spending in the studio and it helped me relax and just 'Be' in nature. While fishing I have always spent much of the time sitting on a rock or a grassy bank just staring at the water whose hypnotic power always beguiles me. It seems to draw me to connect strongly with the whirling flow of feelings and emotions that lie unexpressed there, to get a sense of the undercurrents and hidden secrets beneath the surface, sometimes appearing as a little whirlpool on the surface, sometimes as bubbles drifting up from mud disturbed, perhaps, by a foraging tench or carp in the deeper water.

I was quite content to catch pike from the weir until one day something magical happened when suddenly, there on the end of my line was a silver salmon. It was quite unlike any other fish I had ever caught and right there in that moment I lost interest in casting out a spinner or a lure and repetitively winding it back in, hoping it would be grabbed by a pike. I found myself aching to cast a fly on the water, to fish more skillfully, gracefully, for the king of fish. I had effectively become a fly fisherman.

Graeme was of course experienced in fly fishing for trout and he offered to help me make a start, so over the next few years we made many trout fishing trips to local waters and became very good friends. He taught me everything he knew about this new and exciting world of fishing; the various items of tackle involved, how to present a fly on the water, timing the cast and so on. Casting a fly is like learning anything; you just have to put in enough time and energy to gain experience and allow the body to learn. Reading the water with all its different moods is also something that takes experience, and I learnt more about watercraft by simply sitting still and watching the water than actually fishing. The motto of the Fly Fishers Association is, '*There's more to fishing than catching fish*', and I have always felt this and never been disappointed by a blank (fishless) day. Something magical is always happening on the river, and over the years I came to relate strongly to the heron and the kingfisher that live there.

And so, from that day at Tewkesbury weir I began another leg of my life journey that would take me fly fishing all over the world in search of the silver salmon.

— Autumn Salmon —

My exploration into the world of fly fishing took an adventurous turn one day when I decided to try fishing for salmon on the hallowed waters of the River Tweed in Scotland. I rang up *The*

Angler's Choice, a fishing tackle shop in the small town of Melrose then run by the late Ted Hunter, and arranged for three days' fishing on a beat called Leaderfoot.

After a seven-hour drive in the pouring rain from my home up to Scotland I finally arrived in Melrose and met up with Ted who told me that I was going to be the luckiest and perhaps *only* fisherman on the river the next morning. The Tweed was rising and quite by chance I had chosen the only stretch in the area that would be fishable in such high water. Apparently the fish would gather there just above where The Leader, a small tributary, comes into the main river. Of course I knew nothing about such things since, up to that point, the only salmon I'd caught had been the one I hooked by accident at Tewkesbury weir whilst spinning for pike.

After a refreshing night's sleep in my guest house I met Ted the following morning down at the river where he was going to show me exactly where to fish. After providing me with chest waders and other waterproof gear together with some highly visible flies that he favoured for the day, Ted introduced me to the man who was going to be my fishing companion for the next three days. This was an elderly Italian fellow called Marino, a man who would become a good friend and someone with whom I would spend quite a bit of time on the river over the next few years until he passed away about ten years later.

I learned much from my dear friend Marino through countless anecdotes shared during equally countless hours spent on the river – about salmon fishing, about nature, about Italy, about food, and even about the delicious Cep mushrooms (known in Italy as Porcini) that can be found in the Scottish beech woods near the river in autumn. Fishing for salmon in those days for us was always an autumnal activity on the Tweed, a river famous for its late run of salmon or 'silver tourists'. Marino also acquainted me with an Italian restaurant in Melrose (whose name I can't recall) that he frequented where, somehow, out of the woodwork, there would suddenly appear a host of his friends who were either locals or salmon fishermen from Italy, all gathering together of an evening to swap stories about the great River Tweed. It was here that I also learned about making the simplest salad dressing with just olive oil and vinegar, and how pasta cooked al dente could be so perfect with just a little fresh tomato and parmesan cheese.

Every day we fished together Marino turned up on the river with Gorgonzola cheese he had brought from his home town of Cortina in the Italian Alps, and there was always a bottle of red wine to go with his lunch. Being in Marino's company taught me to appreciate the simple things from every aspect of life, such as taking time to appreciate one's friends and a nice conversation, never rushing, and always having time to pause for a glimpse of a kingfisher or the splash of a salmon in the tail of a river pool. Then there was the importance of freshly baked bread, something that Marino always made a priority to obtain before his fishing began. That man certainly helped me to see that life only happens now.

The first of what would be many salmon caught on the Tweed took me completely by surprise. It snatched the fly in a slow moving current away from the main flow of the river so close to the bank that I could hardly believe it was actually happening. Luckily there was a landing net close by (I later learnt how to land fish by hand) and it wasn't long before Marino helped me to net a beautiful sixteen-pounder, a fish beyond my wildest dreams at the time. I was shaking with excitement. This was fishing on a completely different level!

In those early days I would take the fish home if it was freshly run (newly arrived in fresh water from the sea), and for some years we had a chest freezer in the basement that was always full of salmon and trout that I caught. I would get one of the salmon smoked and it became a long-standing tradition to give pieces of wild-caught smoked salmon to all my friends at Christmas.

Though oblivious to the fact at the time, renewing my passion for angling had built a refuge to which I would escape and rescue my sanity in some of the turbulent times yet to come.

∞

When the renovation work was finally completed late in 1987, we all moved into *The Old Mission Hall* on the ever-increasing wave of optimism generated by my music work which was now really beginning to pay off. Matthew and Oliver were enrolled in the local primary school and Rhonda had integrated her life with the small village social scene. The only cloud hanging over us came from concern over our little toddler Allegra who had begun suffering from febrile convulsions. Apparently this is quite a common condition in infants, but it was nevertheless very frightening indeed for us, especially the time when she had her first seizure in a hotel restaurant. We were told that she'd grow out of it, but in the meantime we would have to monitor her constantly for any signs of sickness or fever that might bring on a fit.

Apart from this one issue, to any casual observer we were surely living the perfect family life. Even my brother who came to stay with us for a couple of days commented that I had such a lovely house and he wished that he could be living a 'normal' family life like me. Whether or not my life could be considered normal was perhaps open to question, but it certainly became pretty full-on after we moved into the completed house.

One of the commissions in this prolific period renewed my acquaintance with an old friend, the man who had set the wheels in motion for my brother's musical career. *Project Yankee, The Great Atlantic Balloon Challenge* documented the journey of Richard Branson and Per Lindstrand in their successful attempt to cross the Atlantic in a hot air balloon. One of the focal points of this TV documentary was Richard's sky diving training as he had to be able to bail out at high altitude if something went wrong, and there was some amazing footage of his very first jump where he went into a spin and one of the instructors had to come to his rescue. The jovial and rather shy young man whose house I had always been free to drop into for a cuppa was now a multi-millionaire entreprencur and also, it seemed, something of an adrenalin junkie! Richard had recommended me to the production company, Television South, for the job of scoring the incidental music for the documentary and later told me that he'd been following my TV work and was very impressed with it – an accolade that meant a lot to me.

Richard had had to make several more parachute jumps before he was ready to attempt the crossing, each of which presented great opportunities for me to compose some edgy music, but with his trademark tenacity he stuck with it until sufficiently prepared. Lifting off from Sugarloaf Mountain in Maine, USA, on July 2nd 1987, Richard and Per set the record at 31 hours and 41 minutes when they touched down in Co. Londonderry, Ireland, the following day. Ironically, the most dangerous part of their journey only began at that point when they had to take off again to avoid overhead power lines, eventually ditching in the freezing water of the Irish Sea where they were both rescued by the Royal Navy.

Shortly after completing Richard's documentary I was asked to write some incidental music for *Small World*, a six-part TV miniseries based on David Lodge's 1984 novel of the same name, but this must have been a pretty uninspired project as I have very little recollection of any of the music.

Soon, however, I was back to wildlife once more with *Twilight of the Dreamtime*. This was a National Geographic special about Kakadu National Park in Australia's Northern Territory that documented how the ancient aboriginal traditions were being ruined by tourism and modern ways. Having lived for a time in Australia – and of course because my wife was from this amazing country – the film was of particular interest to me. I managed to find a didgeridoo player (no mean feat when you live in Stroud!) to lay down a few atmospheric musical passages over my by-now signature moody score style with pads and flutes, then added some aboriginal style vocals that I developed through sampling some old recordings. All of this was finally blended with natural sounds from the film itself.

I received an EMMY nomination for the music on *Twilight of the Dreamtime* – which, coincidentally, was produced by Belinda Wright and Stanley Breeden, with whom I had previously worked on *Land of the Tiger* – but, based on my previous EMMY experience, this time I didn't hesitate to politely decline the invitation to attend the award ceremony.

∞

For some reason the word *resonance* had now entered my consciousness in a new and tenacious way. Specifically, the concept of one thing vibrating at a frequency that resonates with another sparked an almost obsessive new area of thinking for me. Assisted by my inventor friend, Nigel Richmond, I even made some musical models inspired by the concept, including a sort of twelve segment windmill gong based on the chromatic scale where each part, when struck, was designed to vibrate in sympathy with another. I have no idea what happened to this device/instrument but it inspired *Resonance*, my fourth album for *New World Music, and for Nigel it led to a book about the I Ching. Strange things do happen in this life...

* In response to the predominance of CD over cassette format, New World Cassettes had been renamed *New World Music*.

Digital sampling was just coming into its own at this time, and my recently-purchased Kurzveil keyboard allowed me to sample notes played on pan pipes which I could then control and apply all kinds of effects to on the keyboard in order to create interesting new timbres for the album. Nowadays I would only consider playing the actual instrument, but this was a time of innovation when lots of new musical gadgets were coming onto the market, and I have always been rather fascinated by new technology. Even today I like to have the latest versions of everything.

The solo albums were coming easily to me in what was a highly enjoyable creative process. Furthermore, they were proving popular with the global market that my record company was targeting to great effect. It seemed I had finally found my unique musical path, joining my brother and sister now in the exclusive solo recording artist club.

— Lost Worlds and New Horizons —

On top of the benefit of acquiring lots of eclectic knowledge, one of the privileges of working on a variety of film projects is that you often get to meet interesting and talented people. With the four-part BBC TV series, *Lost Worlds, Vanished Lives*, I was invited to David Attenborough's home in London where the famous broadcaster and historian discussed his passion for discovering fossils, a boyhood passion that was also the subject of the new programmes. David had travelled the world to visit fossil sites and expand upon the findings they had turned up over the years, and as he discussed this in his hypnotic, velvety voice whilst showing me an impressive private collection of fossils, rocks and amber-preserved insects, I realised the challenge ahead of me. The music I created would have to reflect the significance of the subject not only in scientific terms, but also with regard to this man's commitment and fervour. And so began another intense period of creativity and experimentation in the studio.

Such was the volume of work coming in now that commissions sometimes overlapped, meaning that I had the opportunity to work on more than one score at a time. And there was no telling what the topic of a production might be... *A Shred of Evidence*, for example, dealt with the historic introduction of DNA analysis into crime scene investigation, a procedure still relatively new at the time. (Looking back, I now see that I was involved with some productions of a rather ground-breaking nature.) Fortunately, the musical requirements weren't as challenging as the science outlined in this programme, and that freed up a bit more time for other composing work.

A Prospect of Rivers saw me indulging my two biggest passions: music and fishing. This was a one-off film for Central TV about the ways in which rivers throughout the UK provide employment for people such as engineers and distillery workers, in addition to being a source of leisure. Lawrence Moore was the producer (the man responsible for my first commission, *Mystery in the Plains*), which was a pleasant reunion experience in itself. As part of my work on this programme, Lawrence asked if I would do a piece to camera where I was interviewed about the way in which rivers have inspired some of my music – whilst standing in the river Exe in Devon with my waders on, fishing for salmon! And so it was I had my first experience of being both composer and interviewee on a project. We brought in a string quartet and oboe player for the recording sessions in the little country studio that had been rented for a couple of days, and everyone had a lot of fun doing an enjoyable job in a relaxed environment close to nature.

By the time I finished work on *Lost Worlds, Vanished Lives* I felt I had managed to capture the essence of David Attenborough's passion and vision for this series. Indeed, I had been driven as much by this man's energy as my own in the composing process which, at times, could be mentally exhausting. It was indeed an honour to be asked to contribute to this project, and to work alongside such a sincere human being who genuinely walks his talk.

— Writing Film Music to a Brief —

Working on a film always began in the cutting room with what they called a 'music spotting session'. Once contracts were signed I would be called in to the editing suite where I'd sit with all the team deciding where to put music in the film. I would then be sent the music cue sheets (indicating sections where music is required for specific parts of the production) plus a fine cut of the movie. This cut would be constantly updated and it was quite common for me to receive three or more different versions in a week, so I had to be on my toes with this – not to mention pretty flexible – otherwise a lot of time would be wasted making music cues fit the wrong bits of film. Motorbike couriers were always coming and going from *The Old Mission Hall* delivering updated U-matic video cassettes, and every week our refuse bins were full of these. There was a great deal of wastage in those days.

When working on footage I would usually start by running a click over the movie to determine how many edits or cuts/dissolves etc. the particular tempo – or BPM – of that click would randomly 'hit' in the film. By adjusting the speed of this click I could normally arrive at the most suitable tempo for each cue. This was a little trick I learnt from Hans Zimmer in the '80s (before he was famous) in his Lillie Yard studio in London while I was composing the music for *Return to Treasure Island*. Zimmer ran the studio with his then mentor, Stanley Myers, who became famous for his soundtracks on films including *The Deer Hunter* and *Wish You Were Here*. The 'click trick', a technique also used by film editors, was a piece of advice that saved me no end of time in future works. Interestingly, I have been told that 96 bpm is the most commonly used tempo in the industry!

Once I got the feel of the project and had submitted a few music cues the production team would normally leave me alone to get on with the job, but until then I was constantly talking to different members of this team to garner their opinions about the way things should be going. Some producers and editors would give me more artistic freedom than others, but generally speaking I had to take everyone's opinions on board before I could commit to any real musical direction. So, the music cues were gradually ticked off as they were accepted into the movie. I would generally aim at completing two minutes a day after which, if things went well, I'd reward myself with a nice long walk in the late afternoon. On a large series for TV there would be about twenty minutes per episode and some of these series contained over twenty programmes. It was always much more straightforward when I had the main theme sorted out because a lot of the incidental music would be based around that. Some of the producers actually insisted on this as a priority.

If I worked with a particular director or producer more than once it was so much more relaxing as they would trust my artistic integrity and let me go ahead with the actual process of composing. Most people, however, could not allow things to go ahead without actually hearing something and there was always a certain amount of re-scoring required after they would utter the phrase, '*That's not quite what I had in mind'*, so I could rarely just relax and get on with the natural creative process.

— Into the '90s —

With work once again having eaten up the largest part of another year, as we approached the 1989 winter season my thoughts turned to making a Christmas album. I decided that I didn't want to produce a typical run-of-the-mill compilation of festive songs and carols, however, and instead began to create extended original arrangements of three pieces of music: *Jesu, Joy of Man's Desiring* by J.S. Bach; *Silent Night* by Franz Gruber and my own version of *Ave Maria* (which would appear as *Star of Heaven* on the album).

I hadn't made up my mind about who I was going to approach to sing the tracks, but by very fortunate coincidence (if such things exist) my sister Sally happened to be visiting us around the time I was putting *Star of Heaven* together, and she very kindly agreed to sing all the vocal lines on the album. Although we'd previously appeared together on Mike's earlier work, this was the first time that we had actually collaborated and the recording turned out to be an absolutely seamless dream. Sally has a unique and wonderfully expressive voice that was simply perfect for the songs, and she particularly liked my version of *Ave Maria* which is the specially composed cornerstone of the album. As the last piece of music I wrote in the 1980s, *Star of Heaven* also represented a gentle and spiritual transition into the new decade, one that I hoped would last.

∞

By ever-increasing increments my attention was turning more to the production of solo albums. This was a welcome consequence of the fact that my music had a ready and apparently hungry market, combined with the well-meaning pressure imposed upon me by a record company eager to keep feeding it.

At this early stage in my career as a solo recording artist I took on board suggestions from New World Music as to what album titles might be most appropriate for their catalogue, which undoubtedly had some influence – if only at a subconscious level – on the music itself. The topic of angels and the angelic was suggested as a possible avenue to explore, but, unsure of how I even regarded these concepts, there were no initial ideas there to get me started on the music. In the end, I decided that the best way to honestly reflect this mystery was to make the music for the new album, *Angel*, really off the wall – if not pretty weird, actually – and inaccessible. My new(ish) Kurzweil keyboard was packed full of interesting developers (pads that change as you hold down the keys) and I used these to experiment with some rather obscure chords and harmonies. This was a new technology at the time which a lot of composers were exploiting to compose incidental music for films. Today I never use these keyboards as they tend to appear all over the place, making it so easy as they do to create pleasant (though entirely uninspired) sounds and effects, and fans of my music still mention *Angel* as it is so divorced from my usual style.

I had also now installed a very large Trident desk/mixer in my studio that was THE thing to have, but it would be a few years yet before I could make the big switch to a Yamaha 02R digital desk since reel-to-reel tape recorders remained in use. For all my film work I still had to stripe the tape with a 60Hz hum so that the U-matic video cassette system would start the audio machine and they would run in sync together. Oh, how easy we have things these days with our cut and paste technology!

The next album I did for New World Music that same year, *Spirit of the Rainforest*, turned out to be my bestselling album of all time, eventually peaking at over 250,000 sales. I'm not really sure why this was so; perhaps because the rainforest was becoming more topical at the time, or it could even have been due to the predominant usage of pan pipes in the music. I actually constructed my own instrument from sets of bamboo pan pipes that were all the rage at the time in New Age and tourist shops. *Spirit of the Rainforest* also featured a bullroarer, which is a Peruvian instrument consisting of an oblong piece of wood that is spun around the head on a piece of string, making a sound rather like a distant motorcycle as it turns.

I tried to imagine that I was actually in the rainforest when I was playing and listening to sections I'd recorded (through headphones), and I think the album is very atmospheric as a result of this subliminal transportation.

Sales of the album only improved the view when I looked upon the horizon of future possibilities, especially the one where I was making a living solely from my albums. At this point, however, Rhonda and the kids had stability and we were all contentedly playing our roles in the 'normal', happy family show, so for the time being I had to continue with my job as a freelance TV composer. I knew that I was in a very fortunate position now in terms of family life and work but, as with most jobs, there were times when certain aspects of the daily routine became very tedious and frustrating. Some commissions were simply an act of going through the motions in much the same way a factory worker spends the day attaching identical components onto other identical components on a moving conveyor belt. In other words, just a job. HTV's 1990 production, *Trailblazers*, was one such commission. Though quite an exciting short film about extreme outdoor physical challenges, the music – if only in my experience – was unremarkable and purely functional.

Then there was *The Second Imperative*, a follow-up to *World of the Unborn* (that lovely, successful film that had been such a joy to work on a few years previously), but in total contrast to the earlier documentary this second project was a complete ordeal. I began working with the original team from *World of the Unborn*, but unfortunately halfway through production the venture ran out of money and the backers sacked most of these people, bringing in others to take over and salvage the whole thing. It was too late to sack me as the music was mostly laid out for the series, so I was jostled about in the confusion until the production was finally dragged across the finish line and I got paid for the job after much wrangling. Unsurprisingly, the programme was not well received, but I learnt some valuable lessons from the whole experience.

Fortunately, neither financial issue nor tedium occurred while I was working on the larger BBC production, *The Birth of Europe*. This was a seven-part series covering the evolution and frequently tempestuous history of the human civilisations that had populated Europe since prehistoric times, and how these peoples thrived and conquered by utilising the natural mineral resources of the land. The opening music for this one, therefore, had to be BIG!

Somehow I managed to cram into *The Old Mission Hall* the entire choir of local singers that I'd amassed to record the epic title theme, and the whole thing went surprisingly hitch-free. Recording the impressive choir on this piece led to another serendipitous find in the form of a voice that soared above all the others. Imogen Moore has been credited with having an 'angelic voice', an oft-heard accolade which, in this girl's case, nevertheless seems entirely justified, and I would later bring her back into the studio to record vocals on my albums *Illumination* and *Celtic Blessing*.

— Time for a Little Enlightenment —

We are trying to work it all out by looking at the universe with tools that are simply not equipped for the task. Thought is basically memory recycling past experience to evaluate and reach judgements on what is happening. This whole process is essentially a survival mechanism designed to take care of the body mind in an apparent world of polarity that only makes sense when looked at through the eyes of thinking.

Working on two albums in conjunction with all the BBC projects within the space of a year had been pretty stressful, even though the flow of inspiration could at times be quite exhilarating. In order to relieve the pressures of work and family responsibilities I had taken up walking after receiving a book called *Walking in the Cotswolds* the previous Christmas, and in the proceeding months I slowly worked my way through all the featured walks, ending with a glorious twenty-five mile ramble on part of the Cotswold way. My only companion had been a walking stick I made to fend off any unfriendly dogs, and the fresh air and expansive sense of freedom – combined, no doubt, with a healthy release of endorphins from all the exercise – definitely helped to alleviate the stress of keeping up with the workload.

It was in this more relaxed state of mind that I conceived and recorded *Zen, The Search for Enlightenment*, an album loosely based on the ten Ox herding pictures that are at the foundation of Zen teaching. These pictures describe the search for the Ox (enlightenment), beginning with a deep sense of disillusionment with life, a sort of 'giving up' that happens naturally. Then there is a glimpse of the Ox that fades and reappears over time, a Will-o'-the-wisp that seems impossible to grasp. The search ends with the seeker actually riding the Ox, finally reaching the place where all is fine – the great 'Okayness' – which is basically right here on Earth but now in a relaxed state of absolute acceptance. The seeker has come to see that nothing is real and everything is perfection in a universal playground where all that is necessary is to sit back and enjoy the ride while the Ox takes care of the transportation.

When we try to look for the Ox – or something deeper – with the tools associated with thinking, or deduction, there is no hope whatsoever of achieving that goal. Thought will never stop because it is the natural ongoing process that forms the background of living in a human body. The magic begins to unfold when thought understands that its rightful place here is in the realms of knowledge and that it has no part whatsoever in the Eternal Now, the place of pure consciousness alone that is our true identity.

Thought creates an illusory self that is made of itself – thought – and only when it actually understands this can it relax its hold and let go of that frustrating and unnecessary illusion. Then it takes its proper place in the background stream of recognition, which is to use reflection or memory to guard and protect us as we go about our lives, using knowledge to drive cars and create intricate machines and walk as safely as possible upon our marvellous planet Earth.

I became so immersed in the Zen philosophy while I was composing the album that I commissioned a painting depicting images inspired by the enlightenment story from an artist friend and used it for the CD cover (the only time I have ever done this).

— Trout and Salmon Magazine and 'Wet Cel Tel' —

In the spring of 1991 Rhonda informed me that I was to become a father for the fifth time. As on all the previous occasions, the news brought a spark of joy into our hearts, somehow endorsing the notion that our lives were running just as they should, but it also increased the weight of responsibility resting on my shoulders as the family provider.

Unfortunately my brother was experiencing a crisis in his domestic situation around this time; his relationship with Anita Hegerland – with whom he'd had two children, Greta and Noah – had recently broken down, leaving Mike once again in a domestic no-man's-land. It seemed the pattern of swaying and contrasting fortunes that had existed between my brother and I since our teenage years was showing no signs of altering.

While all this was going on I had become personally involved in making a film about salmon fishing for the North Atlantic Salmon Fund (NASF) in order to help raise awareness of the plight of the 'silver tourist', as this marvellous creature is known in the angling world. The feeding grounds just off the coast of Greenland had finally been discovered by the big factory ships and they were literally hoovering the fish towards extinction. Having worked with the natural history unit at the BBC I had made many friends in the world of film making, some of whom arranged for me to get on a river beat at the exclusive Tulchan Estate in the Scottish Highlands, together with a film crew who also happened to be keen fly fishers all volunteering their services to help the salmon.

The first day of filming at the mighty River Spey took place on a warm spring afternoon. Our front person at the time was Fiona Armstrong, a keen fly fisher lady and well-known TV presenter. Also present was Sandy Leventon, the editor of *Trout and Salmon* magazine. The cameras were set up and the whole team was primed and ready, so when I began fishing there was an all-pervasive atmosphere of excited expectancy. However, it transpired that the salmon were just not taking, and after about an hour of uneventful fishing it became obvious that a change in strategy was required.

As it was sunny and the water quite low I decided to try a sinking line in an attempt to stir things up a bit, so I changed my line to a Wet Cel 2 which, at the time, happened to be a favourite of mine for such conditions. I cast out into the deeper water and within seconds had a take. At last the cameras could start rolling. Line stripped from my reel as the obviously large fish took off powerfully downstream. I handed my rod over to Fiona to allow her to play the fish, and the result was an enthralling sequence that culminated with this fine lady angler gently returning a lovely 20lb salmon to the water.

Sandy, who was delighted with this sudden turn of events, looked at me and said, 'That was a great idea to use a Wet Cel, Tel.' The English tend to abbreviate the name Terry to Tel, of course, so from then on the whole team adopted the catchy sobriquet and I was referred to as 'Wet Cel Tel'. Sandy agreed that this would probably follow me around in the fishing world, and sure enough when my article went out in *Trout and Salmon* magazine a few weeks later it was acknowledged as 'Written by Terry Oldfield (aka Wet Cel Tel).'

This was the only film for which I contributed my services as co-producer, co-presenter, financier and composer, but unfortunately the project was never completed because the only funding was coming from me and in the end I just couldn't afford to finish it. We got right up to the point of post-production, but time and resources simply became prohibitively expensive and the film had to be shelved. I did go on to write several articles about salmon fishing for *Trout and Salmon* magazine, however (under my new lyrical pseudonym), some of which documented my adventures in the more exotic places I was invited to visit solely to report the experience of fly fishing in remote areas where few anglers had ever ventured. One such place was the Kola Peninsula in Russia, a location with some wilderness rivers that I was sent to fish in and then write about at the end of the expedition. This was a once-in-a-lifetime odyssey, and one that, ironically, led to an incident that could easily have resulted in my death by drowning.

Accompanied by a huge Russian guy who would be my guide for the trip, I was dropped off by helicopter in a remote location on the peninsula destined for a river that, apparently, had never been fished before. With neither of us having much in the way of words in the other man's language, Uri and I traversed a fairly straightforward stretch of wilderness in complete silence before finally arriving at a narrow torrent that was belting past at quite a rate of knots. It looked treacherous, somehow ripe with a hidden, foreboding danger. Then I spotted the waterfall off to my right, a sheer drop of about ninety feet, and realised that this powerful stream was not, after all, keeping its threat to life a secret.

My guide casually let me know in broken English and gestures that we would have to cross the raging flow in order to reach the main river. My eyes widened at this prospect as I regarded the merciless, racing water, realising that a single stumble would result in a rapid journey to the edge of the waterfall and a drop to certain death.

There were three big stones in the stream just under the surface and Uri hopped across to the first one to test the water. His huge size meant his weight helped to keep him pretty stable on the submerged rock, so he looked back over his shoulder and nodded to tell me it was now my turn. Just before I made the leap, it flashed through my mind that I weighed around sixty-three kilos and was wearing a rather large and now suddenly destabilising back pack.

With heart in mouth and salmon rod in hand I hopped across to join my guide on the first submerged stone. The moment I flopped down onto the solid surface I instinctively grabbed hold of Uri's arm to steady my balance. So far so good! Although I did notice with some concern that my feet were having a bit of a hard time staying on the stone in the fast water. Uri turned and took another big step over to the middle stone now, leaving me on my own in the dangerous flow, so, not wanting to be swept away, I very quickly followed him. This time when I landed one of my feet was immediately swept from under me...

It's strange how in such moments of sudden, mortal danger, when life seems about to come to an abrupt end, that our lives really do seem to flash before our eyes. And so it was that a lifetime of stored memories were now unleashed in a moment's recollection in my mind – perhaps as a cerebral epitaph to what has been, or in preparation for what was yet to come.

The only thing allowing me to relay this story is what happened in the frighteningly brief amount of time it took for me to slip and fall into the watery conveyor belt to death and for my instantaneous life review to unfold. A massive hand had grabbed the hood of my wading jacket, immediately halting the momentum of my fall and thereby, in the next split-second, my being swept away for the drop into eternity. The quick reactions of my guide – and saviour – had orchestrated a move that now somehow saw me standing back on the rock, having been hauled there by a commanding, life-saving strength. We then wasted no time in leaping to the safety of the third rock which was in a much quieter part of the flow.

When we got back onto safe earth once more on the other side of the stream, Uri just carried on as though nothing out-of-the-ordinary had occurred, far less his charge's brush with death, leaving me to follow on behind, reflecting on what had just taken place and what the alternative outcome could so easily have been.

I was conducted on to the main river where, in a deep, eddying part of the flow, I managed to catch the first salmon ever taken in that remote Russian water. To this day that part of the river is apparently still known as *Terry's Pool*, but for the rest of that particular day Uri regarded all with silent interest whilst working out a much safer route for our return journey.

— The Wildman Alters my Attitude —

It was *The Wildman of China* that first signaled the change. Not an unruly individual, but a TV movie about the legend of Yeren, the Chinese version of Big Foot.

Working with most film and TV producers over the years had gone fairly smoothly, but there were times, especially with certain producers, when what seemed more like neurotic uncertainty rather than professional discernment was the root cause of what I called the '*Not quite what I had in mind*' syndrome. This of course referred to the unhelpful and uninformative response that would be uttered from some producers when they first heard the incidental music I had spent several weeks putting together. Typically, it would only be *after* I had written what I considered to be a marvellous theme for a programme or series that the fickle symptoms of this curious syndrome would present in a producer, putting me into the almost impossible situation of having to guess at what he or she might 'have in mind', followed by a great deal of time spent shooting at the musical moon in the hope of hitting it.

Had such producers been able to offer some simple clarification as to what they *did* or even *might* want then things could have run so much smoother (and quicker) for everyone, but instead there would invariably be a lot of frustrating guess work and time wasted recording themes that were also 'not quite' what the producers had in mind.

And so it came as absolutely no surprise when I asked the lady in charge of production on *The Wildman of China* what, roughly, *did* she have in mind that I received the predictable response of, '*I won't know until I hear it...*'

One of the most annoying things for any film composer has to be when a producer first needs to hear the music before they even have a clue about what they don't want. A composer must be given some degree of artistic licence in order to allow the natural creation of music, but they will of course be open to, and grateful for, some pointers in the early stage of a film scoring process. As part of this process, I personally didn't feel it was unreasonable to assume that anyone commissioning music would have the sense to listen to some of the intended composer's previous work, just to ensure they were indeed choosing the right person for the job.

In the end the *Wildman* producer got what she wanted, despite her apparent inability to offer any clues beforehand, and the project was successfully completed, much to my relief. But this one left a particularly bad taste in my mouth. Perhaps that was also partly due to where I was in my career in that, having now experienced several years as a commissioned composer, some of the quirks of the job had now been repeated enough times to become highly irritating – rather like that little affectation you hardly noticed in your spouse when you were first dating ultimately finds its way onto your *Reasons why I want a divorce* list fifteen years later!

This was something of a turning point experience for me as it triggered a loss of enthusiasm for working on commercial music scores. I was a hired tunesmith paid to come up with the goods at the whim of an employer, something which was now fulfilling little apart from financial necessity. With another child on the way, now was not the time to be considering any potentially risky changes, but I could sense nevertheless that change was on the horizon.

Constantly having to come up with the goods in a machine-like way made me feel rather numb inside and in need of some diversion, so one day I spontaneously decided that I was going to try sky diving. I went up to Hereford Aerodrome to do the basic training and soon found myself several thousand feet in the air sitting on the edge of an open-sided plane about to leap into space, suspended only by a few lengths of cord attached to a large silk canopy. I can't recall much about the first few moments of that initial solo jump (I never made a tandem jump as they do nowadays), but I do remember the relief when my parachute opened and I was floating gently downwards through the air. At last feeling alive again.

I hadn't realised just how much the pressure of composing to order had been draining the life out of me until I arranged this brief encounter with danger, and I was thankful for the reviving hit of adrenaline. I went on to make several more solo jumps from different altitudes and was going really well until the day I landed badly in high winds and injured my neck. Unfortunately that heralded the end of my sky diving career, but I've never had a problem with heights so I later took up Bungee jumping!

My other respite was fishing, and whenever possible I went on trips to Scotland with Graeme Whiting where we chased the mighty salmon together.

— My Darling Clementine —

With the exception of *Star of Heaven*, which was more of a traditional kind of CD, I had always had some resistance to using words on my music. I think that was because words have some kind of specific meaning or association, whereas instrumental music just creates a purely emotional response without awakening the machinery of association that forms the background of thought and memory.

Not until I began considering the music for the Celtic-themed album that would become *Illumination* did I decide to try using a singer for the first time in an original composition. Rather than writing songs in the traditional sense, however, I opted for a compromise that would be a sort of hybrid between instrumental music and songs and, since the album was rooted in Celtic fantasy, I didn't want the lyrics to be in English. So I began to scout around for someone to help me with Celtic words and translations.

One day I happened to mention my new album to one of the producers at HTV in Cardiff and we got talking about the connection between the Welsh and Celtic world. He was so interested in the idea that he kindly offered to do the translations for me, so I passed on some lyrics based on poems written by Carmen, co-owner of New World Music, and he translated these from English into Welsh. I wasn't particularly fussy about the meaning of the words since very few people would understand them (indeed, this enigmatic aspect was ideal for the album); the melodies and vocal timbre of my chosen phrases were far more important.

The singer on *Illumination* was Imogen Moore, the girl I discovered while recording the choir for the title music of *The Birth of Europe*. Imogen's voice would somehow embody the ancient, the mystical and the divine and, indeed, an angelic innocence on the album. Precisely the atmosphere I had hoped to conjure in an album undoubtedly inspired in no small measure by the approaching birth of my fifth child.

3: Awakening to The Dream

It was not, therefore, random selection that led to *Illumination* being played at Rhonda's bedside as she went into labour in our upstairs bedroom at *The Old Mission Hall*. It was December 18th and with Christmas rapidly approaching all the children were milling around excitedly, including Rachel, and there was a joyous, blessed feeling in every part of the house. It was a lovely, happy occasion that culminated when, as though eager to join in with the family atmosphere, my third daughter **Clementine** – aka **Clemmie** – entered the world after a brief and straightforward birth in the little room next to my studio.

In such indescribable moments of transcendent joy it seems we briefly get to look through a window that reveals all the meaning and purpose of life.

∞

Soon after *Illumination* was released on 1st January 1992 I was approached with an offer from a company called *Voiceprint Records* who wanted to release an enhanced version of the original recording of *Spiral* that I made in 1974. Taken aback but pleasantly surprised, I readily agreed to the offer and the label actually made a really nice job of cleaning up the original old quarter inch tapes that I provided. The CD was quietly released but I was very happy to see the music preserved in this way – and I still have a copy of the album, *Spiral Waves*, right here today in my Australian studio.

Around the time of *Illumination* and *Spiral Waves*, a commission arrived for a very nice little BBC film about the North American eulachon or 'candlefish' that arrive in the rivers of Alaska in huge numbers every year. Featuring David Attenborough, *When the Fish Come In* was an enjoyable interlude since not only did the subject interest me, but the music was easily put together (pretty much all flutes and keyboard pads) and no one on the production team came down with 'Producer's Syndrome'.

Unfortunately the same could not be said about the project that followed. Presented by Derek Jacobi, *The Velvet Claw* was a BBC nature series about the multifaceted behaviours of nature's predators on which I again encountered, '*It's not quite what I had in mind*'. The subject of the programme demanded a very dramatic opening theme, but I had to come up with several such themes for the producer before one was finally approved – for a reason that was never articulated any better than why he *didn't like* the others.

I had now entered a period in my life that marked the transition between making a living from composing film scores and complete independence as a solo artist. Three things were conspiring towards this specific outcome: the success of my albums for New World Music; the frustration caused by 'Producer's Syndrome'; and the fact that things were rapidly changing in the industry as a result of technological advancements in music. From now on, my commissions would dwindle and the remainder would all be for short films. My daily time in the studio, once consumed entirely by commissioned scores, was now being devoted more and more to spontaneous creation.

Meanwhile, my siblings continued on in their respective heydays. That year Sally released her tenth studio album, *The Flame*, and Mike his fifteenth, *Tubular Bells II*, which marked the twentieth anniversary of his debut album. Somehow, all three of us had become prolific composer/musicians, and whilst the sun was setting on my career as a film composer, there were already signs that this may be leading to a whole new dawn.

— School's Out —

My good friend and fishing partner, Graeme Whiting, had been talking about starting his own school. With a background of adventure and movement he was feeling a strong need to introduce his students to a more active education by taking them out into nature and presenting them with challenges beyond the academic. I was very enthusiastic about his vision for a much broader, holistic education as I too felt that my children needed more than what was being offered in the contemporary educational system. Then one day Graeme bravely decided to bite the bullet and make a start by quitting his job at the local Steiner school and begin teaching his own children at home. His hope was that other parents would eventually decide to send their kids to him, but in the meantime he and I got suited up and went to see my bank manager to ask for a loan so that Graeme could start up the school. The manager was, understandably, pretty taken aback when we told him we only had our own children as students so far – and no building! However, I was earning very well with the music at the time so, not wishing to offend, he told us that if we could provide him with some letters from prospective parents he would consider a business loan. The news generated great optimism in Graeme as he was confident that a sufficient number of parents would elect to send their kids to any school he set up.

Not long after our meeting with the bank manager I happened to find an acorn sapling whilst out walking one day in the Wye valley. It was lying at the foot of a bank that had collapsed so I picked it up and took it home with me where it grew in a pot in my studio. Some time later, on hearing that Graeme and his wife, Sarah, decided to name their new school *The Acorn School*, I gave them the sapling to plant as a symbol of their new beginnings, together with a copy of the proverb, '*From little acorns the mighty Oak doth grow*'. Like the sapling, Graeme's little home school slowly began to grow and soon he moved with his family to a larger house near Stroud where he took on more pupils. At this point my son Oliver also joined Acorn and he really loved it there.

In summer that year when he and I were fishing on the River Spey in Scotland, Graeme received a phone call from Sarah who told him that the old primary school in Nailsworth was up for sale at a very reasonable price, but a deposit would have to be forthcoming by the next day. It was too good an opportunity to miss, so I offered to put up the deposit and we cut our fishing trip short to race back down to Gloucestershire to sign the contract. Everything was carried out smoothly and the newly-purchased building went from strength to strength to become the thriving school it is today, some thirty years later. All of my children were enrolled as students at Acorn and Rhonda was taken on as an administrator in the school office, so it became quite a family affair.

∞

Following the success of *Spirit of the Rainforest*, New World Records came up with the idea of creating a '*Spirit of*' series, so I decided to make Africa the theme of the next project. Having previously visited North Africa I was inspired to do a bit of research on the music there, and it wasn't long before I had a number of musical ideas based on tribal stories about the nomadic people who reside there. On *Spirit of Africa* I made my first real foray into ethnic percussion and the music turned out to be a bit more up-tempo than my previous work.

With the creative juices in full flow, another album immediately followed *Spirit of Africa*, but this one did not bear the '*Spirit of*' prefix, nor was there any thematic resemblance to either of the other two albums in this series. *Out of the Depths* was my second album release of 1993 and would become the one that most people probably associate with my music today. It is largely based around the song of the humpback whale – which I had been captivated by after accidentally hearing it on the radio one day – and again features the vocals of Imogen Moore, whose voice curiously blended perfectly with the whale song.

The album really hit the spot at a time when the New Age movement was in full flow, and soon after its release the fan letters began to pour in. Oddly, or perhaps because I was so very busy, I took little interest in feedback from listeners in those days and am now somewhat ashamed to say that I kept a drawer full of unopened letters for some considerable time. When eventually I did start to open these (around the time that emails were taking over from standard mail) I began to realise how important and helpful my music was becoming to people, many of whom were having a hard time. I was amazed at how much the music was being used for just about every healing modality out there, as well as events such as childbirth and funerals. It seemed to have the ability to reach right through to the emotional body and actually help people relax and keep out of the restless stream of thinking. There had certainly been no intention on my part to create such an effect, but it was happening nevertheless. Looking back it was probably the perfect example of innocence in action, or what I now refer to as *being lived.*

Reading these open-hearted letters gave me a very humbling sense of purpose and a degree of satisfaction that could never be equaled by churning out incidental music. I felt I had at last found my true path in music and perhaps also in life. This mild epiphany is apparent in my creative output from then on, the majority of which consists of original albums. The following year saw another two releases in the '*Spirit of*' series which was focusing on countries of specific interest to me, this time Tibet and Australia.

Having great sympathy for the Tibetan people who were so severely displaced by China in 1959, for some time I had wanted to make a musical statement about this political travesty. So, early in 1994, I began composing an album I originally wanted to call *Tears for Tibet*, but New World Music were not so keen to depart from the 'Spirit of' prefix as the series was proving very popular, so I conceded to their preference and recorded *Spirit of Tibet*.

In 1988 when I had worked on the film, *Twilight of the Dreamtime*, a National Geographic special focusing on Australia's Aboriginal tribes and their traditions, it inspired me so much that I decided to give my new Australia-themed album more or less the same title. The ancient ways of the Aborigine were under threat by the massive influx of tourism and, rather like the Tibet album I had just finished, I wanted to make some kind of musical comment on the situation. Fortunately, this time New World Music agreed to dispense with the 'Spirit of' prefix and the CD was released as *Australia, Twilight of the Dreamtime*.

As though to commemorate both the subject and completion of that year's second album, in late 1994 I made my second visit to Australia, this time accompanied by Rhonda and the children. The trip was a welcome break for all of us, but it had a very serious and specific purpose, too, and that was to see if I could ever consider living there.

Rhonda visited her family down under fairly regularly, but in more recent times she had been talking about the possibility of us all living permanently in her native country. I was by no means closed to this possibility, so we all flew out to **Sydney and picked up a camper van** to see if I liked Australia any better than I had during my first visit in the early 1970s.

We spent Christmas in Adelaide with Rhonda's family then rented a house on the seafront there for a couple of weeks to see how we felt about the location. This wasn't a great success, so Rhonda took the girls and flew up to visit a friend in Cairns, way up in the tropics of Queensland, where she found nice rented accommodation for us at Palm Cove. We signed a lease for six months and made a go of living there as a family, sending the two boys and Allegra to the local school just to find out how well they integrated. Everything was going quite well until we hit the rainy season... Rhonda was quite happy with the heat and humidity but I found it oppressive and eventually decided to nip back to England to work on a new album. I spent seven weeks alone at *The Old Mission Hall* recording the music and only left the house for shopping and exercise, which was a bit like voluntary lockdown!

I called my latest work *Icon* and it was different from anything I had ever done before (a sort of up-tempo ambient Christian rock), probably because I was feeling quite ambiguous, or rebellious, at the time. The album went down pretty well with most of my fans, although I did get some complaints from the record company about it being a bit 'off genre', which I had expected.

When I flew back to rejoin my family we decided that the climate in Cairns was too extreme, so we rented another camper van and headed south on a big three thousand kilometre journey, calling in at various places along the Queensland coast. Eventually, we ended up at Noosa Heads and almost immediately fell in love. Stopping on Hastings Street, the main road lined with cafés and restaurants by the beach, we got out for a snack and a look around. The area was very beautiful with an air of sophistication that I liked, and it felt not too far away from the world of internet technology and online music connection that was just beginning.

It was in that moment that my relationship with Australia changed.

∞

We returned to Stroud in summer 1995 after a trip that had been quite a revelation. I had seen a different, much better – and truer – side to Australia than the first time around in my youth, and now understood just how limited that initial experience had been. Based on my second encounter, however, all the previous reticence about living there had transformed into a positive acceptance of the possibility. I found that I really liked Australia. The only issue, mainly, was my work. It was not yet possible to have conference calls or send projects such as large audio files via the internet, which would be a bit of an issue when it came to working on UK film and TV projects. However, these commissions had begun to dwindle for reasons which I knew would only continue to gather momentum, and in a process which, fortunately, seemed to be giving way to my natural transition towards a solo recording career. And that *would* bring sufficient independence to make a permanent move viable.

I had intended to start work on a new album upon my return to England but, quite out of the blue, a commission came in for a TV programme. I couldn't quite believe four years had passed already since I last worked on a film project; where had those years gone? My transition to solo album artist was perhaps more firmly established than I realized!

Wolves in White was a BBC Natural World documentary about wolves in Alaska, similar to a previous production I had worked on in 1987, *Ancient Alliance*, and indeed the title was later changed from *Wolves in White* to *Wolves and Buffalo, an Ancient Alliance*. Sufficient time had passed since my last paddle in the waters of incidental music composition to make the experience not only bearable but rather enjoyable, and there were no 'Producer's Syndrome' issues working with Jeff Turner.

As though to supplement my solo output in 1995, in addition to *Icon* New World Music released a compilation album of some of my earlier music which they titled *Earth Spirit*. I had no input whatsoever on this, but my label's decision turned out to be rather intuitive since on the heels of *Wolves in White* another commission followed, although this was for a project of an entirely different and unique kind.

— Music for the Time Machine —

Stroud artist Christopher 'Kit' Williams is well known for his bestselling 1979 picture book, *Masquerade,* which he wrote and illustrated himself. The book features concealed clues to the location of a Golden Hare encrusted with jewels that Kit had also made and hidden somewhere in the United Kingdom. As well as being an amazing painter, Kit is an inventor and skilled woodworker whose picture frames are an integral part of the artwork he creates. In 1985 he designed and helped to build *The Wishing Fish Clock* for the newly-opened Regent Shopping Arcade in Cheltenham, a creative and technical marvel which, at almost fourteen metres in height and weighing some three tons, is also likely to be the world's tallest mechanical clock. It was a major attraction for shoppers, especially those with children, as the clock had so many things going on at different times, including music that struck up on the hour accompanied by showers of bubbles that blew all over the centre. Needless to say, the kids loved it.

I met Kit in 1996 shortly after being approached by Telford Town Council to compose a theme for another clock he was designing, *The Telford Time Machine*, which was going to be a major feature in their new shopping centre. We got on famously from the start as it was an absolute pleasure to work with such a meticulous and brilliant craftsman, and soon both Kit and his wife Eleyne became good friends. Coincidentally, their home and Kit's studio were situated close to where I used to live in the Cotswolds, so we also had that in common.

The Time Machine was a massive project. Its gantry was about twenty-five metres long and chock full of happenings based around a frog and a golden ball that travelled around vanishing and reappearing in random places. The music I composed had to be an integral part of The Time Machine and it included a song based around the Latin name for the common frog, *Rana Temporaria*, for which I found a local lady singer. It all went down very well indeed and is still playing at the Telford Shopping Mall today, more than twenty-five years on.

Kit and I later worked together again on a smaller clock project, also in Cheltenham, this time aided by my four-year-old daughter, Clemmie, whose recorded laughter can still be heard on the hour.

My eldest daughter, Rachel, now twenty-two and about to begin studying for a BA degree in illustration, had set her mind on going backpacking in India that year with a friend, so I decided to join the girls for the first two weeks just to keep a watchful eye and help them settle into their unfamiliar surroundings. I had always wanted to travel in style through India ever since my first visit to the country as a penniless seeker, so here was the perfect opportunity!

We stayed at five star hotels, visited all the temples and even spent a few days on a houseboat in Kerala before parting company at Delhi railway station where the girls carried on their adventures for a further six months. When I got back to Stroud I was absolutely buzzing from the experience, full of the flavours of India, and immediately started recording some music based on Sanskrit text samples that I had found on the trip. I had no idea what the words meant, but again that suited my approach to recording at the time which was to avoid using words/lyrics that had an intelligible meaning. The end result, *Spirit of India*, perfectly suited the popular trend with New World Music at the time and provided another album for their '*Spirit of*' series.

— The Relentless March of Progress —

In the early days of my career I was given a decent budget to record my film and TV scores because I needed real musicians to play original music. Typically, that would involve small orchestras, vocalists/choirs and guitarists. Nowadays there are so many high quality samples available in digital sound libraries that it is no longer necessary to write anything new. More often than not simply pressing one key on a USB musical keyboard will access any sound from a concert timpani to a full orchestra. Originality, or the *need* for originality, has literally gone out the window, and a lot of production companies will save money by giving composing commissions to the lowest bidders. In all likelihood these will also be less experienced composers who, with all the technology at their disposal, can nevertheless produce acceptable incidental music.

With the advancements in music technology that emerged in the 1990s it was suddenly easy to compose and record music in home studios, so there was a huge increase in wannabe musicians desperate to get in on the act. The desks of all the A&R people at TV and film companies became piled high with their demos, and with the volume of submissions came an exponential drop in the quality and expertise in both compositional skill and musicianship. Suddenly anyone could start up in their bedroom with a mini recording studio comprising a computer, MIDI keyboard and software with a library of digital and sampled sounds/loops, the quality of which was sufficient for many film cues where all that was needed was an undercurrent of sound to create an atmosphere.

I experienced first-hand how the accountants at the BBC saw this as an opportunity to save money, commenting that far too much money was being spent on soundtrack commissions. The result was that all music budgets were cut drastically – right down to about ten percent of what they had been, in fact.

The Radiophonic Workshop – the BBC's in-house studio initially set up in the late 1950s to create state-of-the-art music using electronic/synthesizer sounds – was also used as a cost-cutting resource, where just a few salaried musicians/composers were employed to produce all the music for TV and films, thereby significantly reducing expenditure. Thus, financial considerations combined with rapidly-improving technology saw producers starting to favour electronic/digitally produced music over acoustic instruments – or, 'the real thing' – thereby putting a lot of people like me out of work. Why would they pay me ten times the amount when they could put maybe four people on a salary to produce all the music they needed? And so, with the exception of one or two projects whose producers loved my music, my film and TV commissions were effectively finished.

The decade between 1986 and 1996 had certainly been the heyday of my career and the most prolific period of my life in terms of musical output. It was a period of growth and development in every sense, and I consider myself fortunate indeed to have been privy to such immense creativity that also coincided with the advent of so much new musical technology. During those ten years I had honoured every commission and deadline, ever-mindful of the needs of my growing family and the many lean years spent in pursuit of what I now had. My sense of gratitude and responsibility had overshadowed almost everything else, especially personal considerations relating to workload and stress as I considered myself lucky to be 'on the spiritual path', so to speak; meditating a little and reading rather intense books about the esoteric or hidden side of things. I felt that my positive pursuits had been effectively countering the negative effects of stress and repetitious work and would continue to do so. However, shortly after the release of *Spirit of India* I was destined to discover otherwise, and hit a wall running...

— The Wall —

I walked into my studio to begin work one morning, for some reason feeling the true weight of responsibility on my shoulders. I had potential work lined up with both ITV and the BBC, and HTV were due to contact me soon about a project. I also had a new album on the go for New World Music, and of course, there was Rhonda and the children. This had been my situation for a number of years, so I had no idea why on this particular morning I should suddenly feel... different.

I went through the motions of powering up all the studio equipment and sat down to resume the music at the point I'd left it the previous day. And nothing happened. There was no inspiration, no ideas. Absolutely nothing left in me. A creative flat line. I couldn't do anything.

In the next instant all the energy seemed to drain from my body. I felt myself slumping over and –

– now lying on the floor gazing up at the ceiling.

Too weak to move. Yet my brain was somehow working in overdrive, trying to evaluate what was happening.

I had obviously collapsed.

Something terrible had either happened or was about to happen. I feared I might be having a stroke or a heart attack. Perhaps I was even about to die on my studio floor.

Panic began to set in.

I battled the ominous surge of fear, instinctively blocking out the terrifying possibilities, and discovered that if I focused only on the present moment, without allowing any other thoughts to creep in at all, then I became more capable of handling whatever was going on.

My body was numb and I still couldn't move, but luckily I was able to call out and get the attention of Rhonda who was downstairs.

∞

I sat opposite Pam in her office in the surgery, anxiously awaiting the prognosis.

In the first few weeks after my collapse I felt completely burnt out and couldn't leave the house. Unless I kept my attention on nothing but the present I would start to panic. I became convinced that there was something seriously wrong, maybe even that I had a brain tumour, so I made an appointment to see a family friend who was a doctor. I would trust her diagnosis, but I was also afraid of what that might be.

I expected pills, hospitalisation, perhaps a spell in some psychiatric unit for rehab. Maybe even all three over a period.

Having listened very patiently while I explained what had happened to me, Pam leaned forward in her black leather office chair, an action that produced a sound ominously resembling a groan of despair. Her face was now a little closer to mine. 'Terry, you've been working too hard for too long and you're suffering absolutely classic symptoms of severe stress...'

Of course. No great revelation, really. But that was just the preamble to what would be the consequences, the treatment for that stress and the breakdown that I'd obviously suffered. That news was coming next.

'...So my advice is to go home and do exactly what you want to do for two weeks and then come back and see me. And that means do *only* what you want to do, and absolutely *nothing* that you *don't* want to do.'

I'm not sure which was greater when I heard these last words; the surprise or the relief. This was not a treatment I would have ever imagined to be prescribed – probably because I'd always come to expect that doctors gave out pills and referred patients suffering with mental issues on to other specialists. This advice was so straightforward, so simple. And it also made perfect sense.

I now had sound medical advice and, perhaps more importantly, *permission* to be free of obligations. So during the next two weeks I went for long walks, watched TV, ate and slept when I wanted. I heeded the advice because deep down I knew that doing so was necessary if I were to recover. Giving myself permission to comply with such self-indulgence made me start to feel better almost immediately because obligation had been replaced with freedom of choice. Whatever I happened to be doing was now experienced freely in the moment without the 'should'. This was a revelation for me, and the beginning of healing. It would be months before I felt able to return to work, but I had already changed completely.

— Man and Soul Reunited —

If the circumstances immediately preceding my stress-related breakdown had frosted up the window between physical and spiritual reality, the situation that followed wiped it cleaner than ever before, revealing a realm of opulent colour and infinite possibilities.

I had always been interested in the spiritual aspect of life – something which started to gather momentum after reading *The Hidden Side of Things* back when I was living in West Hampstead – but during this healing period my search for meaning intensified and I experimented with yoga, postural techniques, Reiki, and so on. I found meditation particularly helpful and this soon became a daily practice that would continue for the next two or three decades of my life.

Something that pleasantly surprised me in the months of my recovery period was how everyone was so understanding and unexpectedly supportive. Even the film and TV producers with whom I had deadlines seemed to accept the sudden cessation in my output with an unexpected degree of empathy. This was the first time I ever truly felt that I was receiving support from the universe, real support, in addition to being given the opportunity to change direction.

That I had emerged from the catharsis of treadmill stress and overwork into something of a spiritual new-born was exemplified in the way I eventually approached my new album, *South East Asia*. This was a library album commissioned by Universal Music for which there was no preparation, no agenda and no deadline. For the first time in my life I just walked into the studio with only a vague idea of what I was going to do based on a loose intention (which was to compose some ethnic music), and even that tenuous plan I accepted as flexible; just a general direction that allowed for the inevitable influences of the in and outflowing tides of life. It really was the early beginnings of living, and creating music, in a totally different way.

∞

For the next two years there would be a marked drop – though certainly not a complete halt – in my output, but I wouldn't release another solo album until 1999. This was instigated by necessity as opposed to choice as I knew that any return to form would result in another breakdown. In any case, my attitude was changed irrevocably.

As this new era entered my life with the suddenness and power of a tsunami, my brother, too, had embarked on his own radical chapter. Now living in a cliffside house and studio overlooking the sea on the Balearic island of Ibiza, Mike seemed to have begun a period that might be described as a mid-life crisis where he was engaging in a carefree, party lifestyle that he'd later describe as an attempt to make up for some of the fun he'd missed out on in his youth. And so, yet another dramatic turning of the soil was occurring in the lives of the Oldfield brothers.

— Underneath the Arches with Bernard Cribbins —

Despite all the stress and challenges that came along with composing music to a brief for a film or TV production, I never lost sight of the fact that it could also be a very enjoyable job at times where I got to meet a lot of talented and engaging people, some of whom have remained friends to this day. Perhaps unsurprisingly, it was on the few occasions when my love of fishing crossed paths with commercial music-making that some of these friendships were formed. Through this amalgamation of work and passion I got to know Patrick Morris, a respected British director and producer for the BBC, the Discovery channel, National Geographic and PBS Nova, with whom I still occasionally go fishing. The late Icelandic environmentalist, Orri Vigfússon, was another; a man once described by Time Magazine as a 'European Hero' for his contributions to addressing the restoration of balance in the natural world. Orri had embarked on a specific mission to replenish the stocks of wild salmon in the North Atlantic, a quest that brought us together and one that saw me coordinating and funding a short film for the North Atlantic Salmon Fund (NASF). It was on this project that I also met legendary actor and fellow salmon angler Bernard Cribbins on the River Tweed in Scotland in 1998 when he was asked to be the front man on our film. I had enlisted the help of some BBC friends – cameramen and editors etc. – who were keen fishermen prepared to work in exchange for future fishing on the Gaula River in Norway. I, too, was working in lieu of fishing, but in my case it was alongside Bernard on the mighty Tweed, a river that had come to mean so much to me over the years.

One morning we both arrived at the river wearing all the gear we fishermen adorn for the occasion, including full-length chest waders which would allow us to walk out into the river and cast our flies more effectively. Fish were showing in the pool in front of us and the camera crew were eager to get some action, so they encouraged Bernard to get into the water quickly so they could start filming. A sullen expression had fallen upon the old actor's face, however, and he said, 'Listen guys, suddenly I really need to pee and it'll be at least half an hour before I get all these layers off...'

At first the crew thought he was just pulling their legs, until Bernard – who was in his early seventies at the time – indeed began stripping off the various 'layers'. He was amazingly enthusiastic about acting and fishing, but obviously annoyed with his body for not being able to keep up with him.

Eventually, filming got underway and we captured some nice footage on various stretches of the river. We had no fixed plan for commentary and just allowed conversation to happen as it may, influenced by whatever was happening with the river and the fishing. This resulted in a golden moment near the end of the day as we were fishing in the fading light at Bridge Pool on the Tweedswood beat, which is directly below the arches of a huge viaduct spanning across the river. Suddenly Bernard hooked a fish, a large salmon judging by the bend in his rod, but instead of whooping or calling out excitedly (the most common reaction), he calmly began singing *Underneath the Arches,* a tune he was well known for early on in his stage career. So picture the scene if you can: a calm autumn afternoon on a classic Scottish river where a classic English actor is battling a large salmon, and all the while he's sweetly singing a classic old music hall standard. Life really does deliver its own spontaneous little pearls from time to time.

I next met Bernard about three years later when he starred in *A Fisherman's Dream,* another promotional film we made (and successfully completed) in Norway for the Norwegian Fly Fishers Club (NFC). This time my duties involved presenting as well as composing and, of course, some fishing.

Through these meetings and a mutual love of salmon fishing Bernard and I became good friends and subsequently went on several fishing trips together over the years. He and his wife, Jill, live not too far from Heathrow, and I was always made to feel free to call at their home for a cuppa whenever I was passing through. On my 50th birthday Bernard even organised a surprise day's fishing for me on the hallowed waters of the River Test.

Around the time of *A Fisherman's Dream* I composed some music for *Ospreys*, a BBC Wildlife on One programme narrated by David Attenborough which was being filmed in Newfoundland. The producers on this were my fishing buddy Patrick Morris and award-winning cameraman and co-producer of *Kingdom of the Ice Bear*, Hugh Miles, so this project was more of a pleasure than a chore. The two men had also kindly offered to do some filming for the NASF film at this time, so I was invited to join them out in Eastern Canada where there would be fishing, filming and even an interview with the Canadian prime minister. Also lending his support was Orri Vigfússon whose environmental work with the NASF was so well-respected that he even managed to arrange a free helicopter for our expedition, allowing us to film in some remote and stunning locations in Labrador. Patrick ended up catching his first ever salmon on fly, whereas I nearly got eaten alive by a swarm of black flies which were absolutely terrible in the area. The things we do for love and fishing…

Actor Bernard Cribbins with a fine salmon taken 'Underneath the Arches...'

Terry warm and happy on the river in Norway

Below: Returning a double-figure fish to the river

Below: waiting for a salmon to take the fly...

Outside The Old Mission Hall in my 'Just Do It' T-shirt

The Old Mission Hall

Far left: Made the cover of 'Home Keyboard' magazine! Left: At the home studio mixing desk.

Terry, Allegra and Rachel

Oliver and Matthew

From left: Oliver, Allegra, Clemmie, Matthew and Terry

3: Awakening to The Dream

— The Bells are Ringing... Again —

On 31st August 1998 I set off to London for the concert accompanied by my firstborn child, Rachel – or Ra as she now liked to be called – after Richard Branson's PA had sent us two backstage passes for the world premiere of *Tubular Bells III* at Horse Guards Parade, my brother's first live concert in about six years.

To celebrate the 25th anniversary of the release of his first album, Mike had once again revisited the theme of his original masterpiece, this time using energetic Ibiza-influenced dance beats and sounds to weave an entirely new work that only tenuously resembled the original *Tubular Bells*.

Mike was in his caravan and pretty much unavailable to everyone before the concert, but we went backstage and got chatting to Richard who had also come along with one of his children. Despite all the intervening years since our previous meeting we picked up as though it had only been the previous day – an obviously mutual feeling since Richard suggested that, just like the old days, I should drop in for tea some time soon.

Meanwhile, as around seven thousand audience members filed into the historic grounds more accustomed to hosting royal events, the balmy early September evening was setting an auspicious scene for the open-air concert. The sense of excited expectancy among my brother's fans was palpable everywhere.

By the time Mike followed his band on stage to perform the revised modern take on the original *Tubular Bells* – now sporting a new look complete with white leather suit and short, spikey blonde hair – the heaven's had opened and rain now fell heavily on the tightly-packed audience. We weren't allowed to use umbrellas because of the filming that was taking place, but plastic macs were fortunately on sale and within minutes of the performance most people didn't seem to notice the inclement weather.

The concert went down amazingly well, receiving a couple of encores, and *Tubular Bells III* would peak at number four in the UK album charts.

At the nightclub party after the show Mike was a bit distant from me, something that was actually pretty much the norm at that time. We had lost touch and become virtual strangers, but neither of us saw this as a particular problem as we both had our busy separate lives. I do, however, remember watching Mike's daughter, Molly, crying her eyes out at one point during the concert and I had wondered whether the tears were coming from an emotional swell of pride as she watched her dad performing on stage, or whether she was just missing him.

— 1999 —

Contrary to popular belief, if the process of awakening or detachment from the illusion of a separate self happens suddenly (which was thankfully not the case with me) it can be a veritable explosion that may shatter one's hold on reality. I imagine that there could be many casualties out there who have not been able to continue to make sense of this world and have fallen by the wayside somewhere. The image of the fool in the Tarot cards and many other traditions points to this loss of identification with the rational mind. Much safer, then, if it happens gradually when the integration continues quite peacefully. Here. Now.

The final year of the twentieth century, the one in which I also happened to turn fifty, saw the beginnings of my inner desire to explore and reconnect with my Irish roots on my mother's side. The first expressions of this predictably manifested in my music, and were also perhaps some kind of consequence of my breakdown – or rather, what I now see as part of an awakening to a new way of living. By this I mean the gradual – and sometimes very awkward and painful – assimilation into everyday living of a detachment from the ever-present flow of thinking that is constantly there, like a watchful eye, in the background; a recognition factor that looks out for anything wrong or threatening to the physical body. This process still continued within me just as it is designed to, but now in a more efficient way. The big change was that it was no longer mistakenly protecting itself as a fictitious character (and inadvertently causing all the trouble) constantly on the defence against the seeming attacks on the fortress of beliefs, opinions and judgements.

Ending the two-year hiatus in solo recording, my album *All the Rivers Gold* sought to capture something of the unique atmospheres of Ireland as experienced in its landscapes, nature, and the passion and character of its people. For the first time ever I wrote my own English lyrics for the three songs featured on the seven-track album, with Imogen Moore and Katharina Heinrich on vocals, David Pash on guitar and mandolin, and another friend, Mike Smith, on uillean pipes (or Irish bagpipes). I played Irish whistles and flute, and added natural sea and wildlife sounds to conjure the rugged atmosphere of the land on the instrumental tracks, along with haunting vocals which in places are used more for their texture, like an instrument, as opposed to conveying lyrics.

This album actually instigated a musical love affair between myself and the Irish low whistle whose deep and beautifully resonant sound better facilitates the bending of notes, thereby allowing me to express some of the deeper feelings that had been coming through after the big changes in my life over the past couple of years.

All the Rivers Gold was released on 3rd August 1999, just before my 50th birthday celebrations.

The only film commission I worked on in 1999 was, ironically, a TV production with an Irish theme. I was required to write a couple of songs – including one for the opening titles – as well as the incidental music for *Celtic Fury*, a project that had initially appealed to me, but unfortunately this time I came across a producer more difficult than I could possibly tolerate.

I had enlisted a female singer for my Celtic style vocals and we booked a recording session at the studio in Cardiff where everything was going well until the producer, who was also present, started giving the singer a difficult time and generally made her feel very uncomfortable. I had a word with him about this ridiculous attitude, but he continued with his rude and shameful actions until the singer became so upset that she refused to continue. After making sure she was paid for her time, all I could do was console the poor girl and drive her back home.

When I next contacted this producer he told me that his funding had run into problems and that I would have to wait to be paid for the work. At that point all the incidental music was finished and only the titles remained to be recorded. Luckily I had a signed contract and told him that I would record the last song at home after which I would expect to be paid. He agreed to these terms, but after I delivered the final song weeks went by and no payment was forthcoming. He began avoiding my calls and ultimately refused to speak to me or answer letters. I called my music publisher's office to discuss the predicament with a contact there who had always offered me sound advice in the past, and he immediately suggested that I don't mess about but contact a debt collector he had used in similar situations. I took this advice and called the number I was given. After obtaining some information from me the debt collector said that he would get the money and take a twenty percent fee for doing so. I was pretty desperate at the time, not to mention weary of the hassle, so I agreed to these steep terms.

Within just a few days the collector called and, in a very calm, business-like tone, told me that the money had been collected and a cheque was in the post. I asked him how he managed to get the cash so promptly and he told me that it would be better if I didn't know...

It seemed then that *Celtic Fury* was responsible for what I suspect was my one and only brush with the underworld heavy mob!

— A Dawning —

As the world stood poised on the brink of a new millennium, at the end of 1999 Rhonda and I were again aware of changes on the horizon. Changes which, though insignificant when compared to contemporary global concerns relating to the environment and the validity of the threat posed by a so-called 'millennium bug', were nevertheless the biggest issues on our personal agenda.

The drifting apart had been a slow process. For some time we had both been caught up in our separate preoccupations; me with the music and my new direction in salmon fishing, and Rhonda with family and friends and, more recently, yoga classes. Another intimation of the growing distance between us was the preference I had developed for sleeping alone in my studio, a quirk that gradually became a permanent situation. It was also becoming increasingly apparent that I had inherited my father's distaste for the shallowness of certain types of social interaction such as boozy dinner parties, coffee mornings and so on, whereas Rhonda, like my mother, loved that kind of thing and was always involved in local happenings with friends. I have never liked socialising in a big way or being around anyone who is drunk, partly because more than one alcoholic drink affects me pretty badly, so I am simply not drawn to that area of life. In this respect I stood apart from Rhonda;

a reality which I now realised had been apparent even much further back in our relationship. I recalled how one New Year's Eve in Newnham I had stayed at home with little Matthew and Oliver, watching from a window while Rhonda and a group of people went cavorting down the high street at midnight, all drunk and merry. There was absolutely nothing wrong with that, of course, but it was just one of several occasions that highlighted the contrast in our personalities.

Being very different people was a chasm Rhonda and I first ignored then managed to bridge for the children's sake, but it had now reached a point where we were both feeling over-stressed mentally and physically by this elephant in the room. Rhonda was surrounding herself with people in an attempt to find levity and emotional relief, whereas I was escaping through fishing, walking, skiing or whatever would divert my mind.

A similar type of thing had happened with my own parents and it created so much angst between them that it offloaded onto Mike, Sally and myself and I was now afraid of history repeating itself in my own family. But fear has the unpleasant effect of attracting the very thing it fears, and in this respect I began to see unsettlingly familiar parallels between my dad's life and my own, specifically in how he seemed to draw into his life certain things that were completely at odds with his own nature. For instance, there was my mum's craving for alcohol and social interaction; the character of Dad's alcoholic partner in the GP practice in London, and more recently Helga, an insensitive and outspoken tyrant of a woman.

It seemed that I had definitely inherited certain subconscious patterns from my dad (the sins of the father!), but no one was at fault here. Genetics are an unavoidable physical aspect, whereas personalities evolve from a myriad influences. Rhonda could not be blamed for her nature any more than Dad and I for ours. Nevertheless, if we were to avoid creating an unpleasant domestic environment for our entirely innocent younger children, we both knew that we would have to find a way to divert – or at least delay – the pending collision from its present head-on course. Our eldest son, Matthew, had now left home and was living nearby, but Oliver, and most especially fourteen-year-old Allegra and eight-year-old Clemmie, needed the most stable home life we could provide.

Our solution, or at least the quick fix, seemed not only the wisest choice but perhaps our only option; one that, as well as being mutually appealing, also promised to resolve our steadily-growing financial concerns. It was something we had been seriously considering until my breakdown put everything on hold, but now seemed just the right time to instigate this particular life change.

With the allure of a cheaper cost of living, opportunities in greater abundance, and a chance to alleviate our relationship stresses, we were going to emigrate to Australia.

∞

Despite the resoluteness of our decision, the move to Australia would not be undertaken in a hurry; it was far too big a transition to be conducted in an impetuous manner. First, we would have to sort out the purchase of a house in an area that could serve all our needs, including the girls' education. There was lots of careful consideration and work ahead of us, but the promise of change in itself had a positive effect on Rhonda and I. **Whether** this was coming from the belief that a complete change of lifestyle would improve everything between us, or the delusion that we could simply pack up and run away from our problems, only the future would tell. In the meantime, impending change and a renewed sense of hope were enough.

The theme of new beginnings was everywhere at this time. Contemporaneous with the world entering the year 2000 and Rhonda and I planning our own radical changes, Colin and Carmen at New World Music announced their decision to pass over the label to new ownership, having received an attractive offer for the company. The news didn't bode negatively as I was confident about being signed by another label, and in fact it pleased me to hear that the couple who had led me into the world of solo album production were now embarking on a fresh new chapter in their own lives.

While all this was happening I was in the process of completing my eighteenth album for them, *Across the Universe*; a work influenced by my feelings of not knowing much at all at the time, existentially speaking, and simply coming to feel okay with the mystery of it all. For example, I had always questioned the whole idea of reincarnation and what it could be that actually reincarnates. Is it the character that I know to be an illusion? Or might it be the soul or spirit that I have no experience of whatsoever? The music of *Across the Universe* focuses around this questioning and sense of longing and the title song, recorded by a friend, Juliana, remains one of my favourite pieces to this day – such purity and clarity in the vocal! Rhonda also did some backing vocals on this album which contains two of what I consider to be my best ever recorded instrumentals.

My final album in the '*Spirit of*' series was composed more to fulfil my contractual obligations with New World Music than in response to any particular inspiration. *Spirit of the World* would therefore be my last original release with the company before it was sold, a title I chose perhaps to reflect the all-encompassing sense of completion; the end of an era. Most of the music contains examples of different cultures of the world, and although I play plenty of lyrical flutes on the album I have to say that it is not one that makes my heart sing today.

Perhaps as a sort of parting gift, New World Music released a compilation album of my music before handing over their label that year. This was *Reflections, The Best of Terry Oldfield, 1985-1995*, marking both a highly creative musical decade in my life and the close of one of its many chapters. When I regained the copyright on my back catalogue after the sale of New World Music, one of the first things I did was rename the 1994 album *Spirit of Tibet* to *Tears for Tibet*, in accordance with my original preference. Though it may sound trivial to some, I now had a sense that something important had finally been put to right.

In a very short space of time I began the next part of the story by signing up with New Earth Records who were then based in Santa Fe, New Mexico. I even flew out to meet up with company founders Bhikkhu Schober and Waduda Paradiso at their home where they greeted me with tea and homemade cake. I was immediately on board with the couple and the new label where I now felt confident my album recording career would continue to evolve.

Before I had time to contemplate the next original composition, however, I was asked to create a music library album for Warner-Chappell who offered me the commission because of my history composing for wildlife films. *Music for Wildlife* involved writing several themes for a CD that would be sent around to TV and film companies who keep such music in their editing suites for possible use on future productions. This means they only have to pay a one-off fee for music that can then be used freely, thereby eliminating the need to become involved in original commissioning or copyright issues. For this album I was given access to a recording studio with all the musicians I needed for two solid weeks. No money was paid up front but Warner-Chappell covered all expenses and the royalty split was fifty-fifty which, over the years, turned out to be well worth it.

— Goodbye —

By spring 2001 we had found and bought a nice piece of land in Queensland, Australia, with the intention of building a house and studio there. It was finally happening. We were emigrating.

The Old Mission Hall was a great house that had been perfect for bringing up a family in a friendly and beautiful Cotswold village, so, despite our firm resolve to move on, it was with some bitter-sweet sadness that we put the house up for sale. Fourteen years previously I had helped to renovate this building from its original rundown condition, and a lot of memories were now woven into its structure. Each of my five children had lived and laughed here, Rhonda had given birth to Clemmie in one of its rooms, and I had recorded some of my most memorable work in the studio at the top level overlooking the Chalford canal. In leaving this family home we would be leaving a little part of ourselves behind.

To our surprise, we very quickly got a buyer for the house – so quickly, in fact, that we had to move into rented accommodation near the children's school so that they could see out the summer term before heading out to Australia. This place was much smaller than anything we were used to and, what with all our old furniture stacked around the place, there was hardly any room to move. The sale of *The Old Mission Hall* seemed to accelerate everything, and from then on time just evaporated as we frantically made our necessary preparations.

Amidst it all I was still working on the first album for New Earth Records that I'd hoped to complete before the move, but in the end I had to stay on in England to finish recording this while my family went over to live with relatives in Australia. This arrangement suited Rhonda as she was effectively returning home at last, but there was an added keenness to introduce the kids to their new way of life as soon as possible. It also meant that someone would be on-hand to keep a watchful eye on the progress of building work on our new home since my family were living close to the site.

During this bridging period I rented a barn on a nearby farm where I could live and work – a move that happened to coincide with the mad cow disease outbreak in 2001, which meant that I had to drive or walk through disinfectant (wearing wellies!) every time I went in and out of the main gate. It was quite a strange time overall as so much was changing rapidly for me and my family, and for the next few months I lived more-or-less as a hermit while I worked on the album. It was no coincidence that I called the developing piece of music *Turning Point*, because that is exactly what this time in my life had become. I was with a new record company, about to move to the other side of the world, and at the same time continuing to integrate a new way of being into my life. The songs on the album all reflect this seeming maelstrom of change and I am still very happy with the whole thing both musically and as a true reflection of the times.

Alongside this work I put together a one-hour CD at the request of some friends in Stroud for use in their massage therapy practice. It only took me a day or two to complete the task as I used the major-minor chord progression from *Spiral Waves* to create a recurring sense of rising and falling in the music. Many years later, in 2019, this would be released as *Healing Hands, Subliminal Music for Massage*.

Feeling pretty lost and displaced during this period I began to explore the world of Reiki. *Rei* means 'soul' and *Ki* means 'energy', so I suppose I might have been trying to recharge my inner batteries. I integrated the practice into my daily life and over the next few years it became a bit of a life saver for me as I used it to realign my focus with the present. I'm sure that Reiki also helped me to overcome various physical ailments that arose through the stress I was experiencing during the transition period.

My eldest son, Matthew, had decided to remain in the UK where he was currently pursuing his own career in music, so it seemed fitting that I give him a small role in my new album, bearing in mind its significance. Matt added some great guitar work and vocals on *Turning Point*, most notably on his own song *Into the Blue*, and it was apparent from these early times that he had a promising future ahead of him.

∞

There was a certain element of relief in the fact that my film work was drying up now, but unfortunately this development coincided with another: the frighteningly rapid rise of looping and general push-button keyboard technology in mainstream music production. The march of the digital revolution had instigated huge changes in the way music could now be both produced and sourced. This was the dawning of an era when budding, would-be composers were suddenly submitting demos to film companies and offering to work for next to nothing. I remember one director bringing along his teenage son to a recording session at the BBC studios in London one afternoon, a boy who grew up to become one of today's successful TV composers originally inspired by the old ways of doing things – with real musicians – but nevertheless launched his career from the pad of new technology.

As far as the technical aspects of film scoring were concerned, everything changed so radically with the explosive advance of digital technology that it became unnecessary to have much knowledge about the way things worked since modern software took care of all that for the composer. Previously where things like tape splicing blocks and code generators were needed for syncing tape recorders to video players etc., now there was software available where music recording and film editing could be undertaken using a single computer programme. When combined with a MIDI keyboard and a library of sound samples the whole process was literally available to anyone.

The proliferation of these easy-to-use Digital Audio Workstations meant that kids could jigsaw together impressive-sounding tracks made up entirely of pre-recorded sounds, or 'loops', at their computers. As the quality and capability of the music software increased, so its cost decreased exponentially.

For the inexperienced or even non-musician this was an easy and exciting avenue of faux creation. For musicians and composers who had learned their craft after countless hours spent developing and practising their skills, however, it was something of a disaster rendered more complete by the advent of free downloading. Big music sellers were now only getting perhaps a thousand pre-orders for albums that would previously have secured sales in excess of one hundred thousand.

So now, on one hand the film and TV producers – and more commonly their accountants – saw the new potential to save money on musical score commissioning by giving the job to less experienced individuals who could produce acceptable results thanks to the new technology, and on the other, many consumers saw no reason to buy their music in either CD or cassette format when they could access free downloads.

Suddenly, the future began to look very grim indeed for recording artists – especially those with a family and other big responsibilities and financial commitments.

∞

By the time I had finished *Turning Point* and made all the necessary arrangements to move out and join my family in Australia I realised that, being a musician now almost solely dependent on CD sales for his income, my market – and therefore my livelihood – was under serious threat from free downloading and black market sales. Nevertheless, the commitment had been made. My family and I were about to begin a completely new life

3: Awakening to The Dream

on the other side of the world – whether for better or worse is something we would soon know.

One day as I was packing up my studio equipment Mike rang me up and nonchalantly said that his therapist, *Robin Skynner, had suggested that he ring and let me know how guilty he felt about being so successful. I was a little taken aback by this, but I listened in silence as my brother elaborated a bit more. Before I had a chance to say anything, Mike abruptly ended what was obviously an act of unburdening with, '…Okay, that was it', and then he was gone. Leaving me holding the phone and wondering what on Earth had just happened. He never later offered any explanation other than the brief one given that day, but the phone call had obviously been a confession, a release of a source of guilt that he'd been harbouring for some time, and in fact I have often wondered whether his song *Guilty* was an earlier expression of these repressed feelings.

— Exodus —

On the very day that I was flying out to Australia to join my family, the Disney Channel production company contacted me and asked if I would write the music for the pilot film of their new series, *Project Cobra*. I told them I was sorry but present circumstances simply didn't allow me to accept the commission. Undeterred by this, however, they offered to send someone out to meet me at Heathrow airport who would go through the details of the project, and who, with the backing of a very eager producer, could write me

---

* Robin Skynner was a prominent psychiatrist and psychotherapist who, together with actor John Cleese, co-authored the best-selling self-help book, *Families and How to Survive Them*, first published in 1983.

a cheque there and then as an advance on the contract. With some reservations I agreed, and sure enough, shortly after I arrived at Heathrow later that day two pleasant guys showed up and we found somewhere quiet to talk. I had only just come from London docks where I'd left my Range Rover chock full of favourite bits and pieces of studio gear to be freighted over to Australia, so I was feeling a little frazzled to say the least. Anyway, they made a very tempting offer and we came to an agreement that was sealed in the form of a large cheque written as an advance just one hour before I flew out to a new life down under.

∞

Compared to England where the wildlife is, by comparison, ridiculously more benign, nature in Australia is pretty full on. Spiders the size of side plates; snakes appearing overnight in the garage or curled up in a porch beam outside the house; all manner of insects requiring various levels of caution – like the mud wasps I found nesting in my bamboo flutes one day – and of course, mosquitos. Lots of mosquitos. It certainly took some time to get used to the marked change in lifestyle after England, but with the exception of the mosquitos the wildlife didn't trouble me and Rhonda so much as we had experienced such things before, and fortunately the kids weren't overly perturbed, either. And there was the other, beautiful side to Australia which, for me, found its zenith in the oddly mystical atmosphere that surrounds the land after rainfall and the rich and varied bird song that would never grow old to my ears.

What I didn't realise at the time was that things had changed so radically for me that I lost the connection between head and heart and I was still moving with the momentum of previous routines. Mind was desperately trying to find old pathways in a place where there were literally none left. I had physically made the transition to a new life but had yet to let go of all the old ways.

It would be a further six months before our new house was completed, so we moved into a rental house where I set up a temporary studio. Although I wouldn't be able to resume working as normal until I set up my full studio in the new home – for which I was also going to buy some upgraded equipment – I could still make a start on the *Project Cobra* commission and get new ideas down for my next album.

Dreamer was the very first song I wrote and recorded after moving to Australia. I played all the instrumental parts myself and managed to find a local singer called Rebecca whose voice perfectly communicated the mood I wanted to convey. This song was partly inspired by my Out-Of-Body-Experiences and lucid dreams (which hadn't ended, as I would soon discover) and what I had interpreted as a hellish experience in the cabin of the ferry during the overnight crossing to Hydra many years previously. Looking at that frightening experience from a later perspective, however, I began to regard it very differently. I believe that what actually happened was that I connected with the deepest elements of residual pain in my own mind/body mechanism, the source of rage and uncontrolled violence in us all. We resist and resist life and it all gets stored up for later, or sometimes actually causes the whole system to self-destruct because the mind cannot bear the suffering a moment longer and chooses to end the life of the body. I believe my willingness to hear and feel it all, despite the terror I was feeling at the time, had diminished the power that my deeply stored emotions held over me. Hence, the horrifying experience was never repeated despite many deliberate attempts and experiments on my part. So many insights came from that understanding.

Dreamer, often referred to later as *Shadow Dancer*, turned out to be one of my most popular songs for which countless YouTube videos have been made. Despite this seemingly auspicious start, however, the numerous personal and occupational changes that had been establishing themselves – and which I had to some extent been trying to deny – were about to instigate one of the most significant transpositions of my life.

— Turning Point —

Our new home was spacious with lots of land and we all simply loved it. Choosing to focus on the positive implications of a fresh start, Rhonda and I decided to name the house *Turning Point*, a title whose various significances extended far beyond sharing a name with my most recently released album, some of which would only become bitterly apparent with hindsight.

To the musical equipment that I shipped over in my car from the UK I had now added some more contemporary gear, but basically my new studio was fine-tuned to run on a Mac computer with two monitors. I had two sets of speakers wired in: my old JBL studio monitors and a pair of B&W DM 1200 bookshelf speakers that I had been using for many years and which I still have in my studio to this day. On the surface the new studio was perfect for purpose and as such should have sparked some motivation in me, and yet somehow it only reflected back the uncomfortable reality that circumstances within the music industry, and my life, were not going to permit business-as-usual or allow me to recreate a past that was now irretrievable.

In an attempt to counteract the growing feelings of unease from which I couldn't see a way through, I began working hard on the land surrounding our new home, planting literally hundreds of trees and countless native shrubs. Working physically like this helped to create a sense of positive achievement as well as maintain a certain balance in a life that was actually crying out for radical inner change. The music became a secondary priority through all of this and it was some time before I got around to completing *Project Cobra*, but in the end it transpired that the film studio couldn't find enough money to go forward with the full project, although I got full payment for my work and as far as I know my music was well-received. There were also contractual obligations with New Earth Records, which cajoled me into beginning work on my second album for them, *A Time for Peace*.

The multi-album deal which I had signed with New Earth Records was certainly a crucial helping hand, financially speaking, but this was still a CD-based outlet directly affected by the new ways in online music distribution, and nothing was going to hold back the global situation as it now related to music creation, distribution and sales. Music streaming was turning the tide towards virtually replacing the CD, and my income – now almost solely dependent on CD sales and royalties from past work – began to drop alarmingly.

Inevitably, the financial insecurity this caused, compounded by a sense of powerlessness to alter the situation, put a strain on my already fragile relationship with Rhonda. We both realised that things would have to change somehow in the long-term, but we also knew that the winds of change are not always pleasant and can blow away things like security and comfort. They have the power to purify and cleanse, but sometimes only if we are willing to let go of the past and surrender ourselves to them entirely.

The momentum of another ebb tide in my life was underway. This time I recognised its powerful and somehow inevitable motion for what it was and I knew that soon, together with my career and personal life, I would be carried along in its flow regardless of whether I resisted or accepted.

∞

The trend of my brother and I experiencing significant changes in our lives at roughly the same time continued to be upheld when I heard that he was soon to marry again. This time it was Fanny

Vandekerckhove, a French horse breeder twenty-four years his junior whom Mike had met in Ibiza. He had also just completed a ground-breaking musical project called *Tres Lunas*, a virtual reality game featuring a world of vistas and other-worldly landscapes that players could explore and interact with as an avatar, activating passages of original music as they went along. Mike also released a separate album of the same name, thematically linked to the game.

The outgoing tide in one part of the world always coincides with an incoming tide in another, and this news of my brother's ascending good fortune made me wonder whether the same thing was happening in the ocean of our sibling lives.

— Ebb and Flow —

Reeling from the dramatic changes, and perhaps also in a subconscious state of denial, for the next couple of years my time was shared between working in the music studio and on the acres of land that constituted most of our Australian property. This precarious and pivotal period was bolstered by one or two album reissues, including a remastered version of *Angel*, but my only original release in 2003 was *A Time for Peace*, which turned out to be a very nice melodic album with plenty of my signature flutes and some piano. Despite being quite well received, however, as with all of the more recent work the generated income was becoming pretty negligible and I was fortunate to be receiving advances on my music which just about kept things ticking over.

Inspiration for the next album, *Yoga Harmony*, came from two distinct sources. First of all, I was thinking about beginning yoga classes at a centre in our new home town of Eumundi, partly because I'd only ever practised it in self-taught isolation, but also because Rhonda was taking a class in the same yoga centre. The other influence came from a new friend I had made, Tony, who ran a local shop selling ethnic percussion. One day he agreed to bring over a van load of his instruments to my studio where I spent a few hours with him recording samples to use on the new album. There were many different sizes of gongs and bells, Tibetan bowls and all sorts of interesting things that I added to my quiver for the project. Tony also agreed to lend me a whole collection of ethnic flutes, among which was an Indian bansuri that I immediately took to and still use predominantly in my recordings today. The bansuri was a bit of a learning curve for me as the holes in these bamboo flutes are quite far apart, requiring a totally different fingering technique than I was accustomed to. To begin with I found it impossible to play the lower notes until I altered my hand positions to suit the new instrument.

Recording *Yoga Harmony* was quite a journey of discovery for me and the end result, I felt, was quite stunning. It has been a popular album since its release and one of the tracks, *Earth and Sky*, is, at the time of writing in 2020, currently leading the streaming race on Spotify.

Less of an innovative work, my second album release in 2004, *Celt*, was put together in just a few days as another venture into my Irish roots. The CD – which was released on a fellow musician's label, MG Music – comprises a medley of original and traditional Irish tunes that simply gave me a lot of satisfaction playing at the time.

Working on solo albums occupied almost all of my studio time during this period, but it was broken up by what was to be the last drop in a once flowing well of film score commissions.

The Falcon that Flew with Man was a film privately made by a group of base jumpers who were using a falcon to measure their descent speed as they launched themselves from various peaks and crags around the world. They had a falcon handler who released the bird when the jumper launched, whereupon the graceful predator would accelerate and swoop in to take a bait held in the hand of the jumper now falling at terminal velocity speed, only to fly off even faster.

The footage was exciting, but nevertheless it now felt very limiting for me to have to write this kind of music to a very specific brief. Like so many things that become clear at certain pivotal times in life, composing scores had obviously now run its course for me, and not long after completing this commission I decided to give up writing for film. I had had enough.

— Meeting with a Soulmate —

We don't always choose to do certain things or meet particular people; sometimes the universe brings everything together. I think that's the way things happen. If each of us looked back on those momentous changes in our lives, we might find they weren't the result of a conscious decision on our part. They just happened.

When we were living in Stroud, Rhonda had been going to yoga classes given by a teacher from the **Satyananda** tradition, and shortly after we moved to Australia she managed to find someone who taught in the same tradition. Her name was Soraya Saraswati, a single parent who was raising her four sons alone while running both a yoga practice and a naturopathic studio. She had taken on the Saraswati name after becoming a swami in the ashram she lived in many years previously.

Although I had practised a little yoga previously – aided by a manual when I was working on *Spiral* in the cottage in Wales – it never occurred to me to take a class until just before I began recording *Yoga Harmony* when, coincidentally, a friend suggested I join Soraya's class. Working on the album put me further in the mood for exploring the yoga world in general, so I went ahead and booked my first group session with Rhonda's teacher.

The class was totally absorbing and I felt revitalised and completely at peace when it was over – welcome feelings in my otherwise tumultuous life at this time. After the class the students were all milling about chatting when I just happened to catch Soraya's eye. There was this curious sort of lingering double take that tends to happen when you experience déjà vu; a moment's recognition of something unknown and indefinable yet somehow familiar. It was a moment we both clearly remember to this day.

The yoga classes became both a fixture and a new focus in my life, as did the philosophy explored there by Soraya, and I began to meditate **again** more regularly. This was a source of great support for me during that time, an antithesis to the downturn in other areas of my life, but it also served to fan the flames of my underlying interest in the spiritual. And so a new outlet, or portal, of spirituality opened up for me.

— Precognition —

Lucid dreaming is one step removed from lucid waking when we begin to live consciously, knowing that nothing is real but it is the only reality there is. This allows the possibility of really making the most of life and being grateful for the opportunity to explore our amazing world without the handicap of fear and insecurity. We can then enter a world without stress where we are open to everything. True freedom.

One day I would write a song about this called 'Nothing Wrong At All'.

I was walking down our driveway when I lifted my head and noticed that underneath the house, between the posts on which our Queenslander style house was built, my car had somehow, impossibly, been elongated into a shape resembling a funeral hearse. In the back a coffin was clearly visible through the miraculously over-stretched windows. Next to the car stood a man dressed in a well-tailored black suit swinging a set of car keys in his hand that I instinctively knew were mine. His smile more closely resembled a mocking sneer. 'I'm going to be needing these from now on,' he said. I responded instinctively, irrationally, with, 'Who has died?' The stranger's grimace dissolved, and the man looked more intent now as he pointed directly at me and said, 'You!'

At this point I found myself lying in bed unable to move a muscle and with a vision of sparks flying up and down my body from head to toe. I was utterly convinced that I had passed away and consciousness now remained post mortem. *This is what it's like to die*, I considered as I lay helpless. But little by little, and over an agonisingly protracted period of time, I was able to move first my fingers then gradually the rest of my body.

Now fully back in my body I opened my eyes. The ceiling of my Australian bedroom met my gaze. It had happened again.

Not long after moving to Australia another period of Out-Of-Body Experiences and lucid dreaming began for me in which this latest was the clearest and somehow most ominous thus far. Sometimes I would experience the classic scenario where I 'awoke' into the vivid or powerful dream fully aware that I was **dreaming**, whereas others were as real to me as everyday life. Frequently, too, the familiar intense vibration or buzzing sound occurred just before entering the dream or as I began to wake up.

The effect of the 'death dream' remained with me all that day, as was the case with most of my lucid dreams. It happened that that evening I was going to a kirtan or musical evening of chanting held at Soraya's house, and I went along to that in a kind of daze. When I got to the house and Soraya first set eyes on me she took a tiny step back and said, 'You look like you need a hug!'

For some reason I felt myself being moved, directed in a way that I was powerless to resist, and I burst into tears. This was the moment that marked the beginning of another new phase in my life, one that would necessarily be born from uncomfortable and painful circumstances involving the purging of deeply ingrained patterns of emotion and reactivity. Unknown to me at the time, the enigmatic dreams and OOBEs had once again been the harbingers of a big change that was about to unfold in my life.

∞

A contributing factor in my unstable emotional state were the mood swings I still experienced from time to time. I had always assumed these most probably stemmed from the effects of stress suffered in my teenage years, and yet somehow that didn't adequately account for their potency, or the accompanying bouts of depression. There seemed to be an underlying ailment more suggestive of a physical cause than one purely psychological.

My rocky state of mind naturally fanned the flames of the relationship problems between Rhonda and I, especially when combined with our equally precarious financial situation. For the sake of our growing children we had endured whatever storms had brewed over the years, somehow managing to hold things together and move along with the flow, but these storms had caused cracks that slowly widened over time, producing fissures and eventually ugly gaps between myself and my wife. The underlying differences between us, although apparent, were basically disregarded in the mélange of family life and my growing musical career. We had even successfully ignored the ominous implications behind the fact that we designed our newly-built house in Australia to accommodate a living arrangement where we each had our own bedroom and only shared a bathroom. It was obvious that we both knew the only reason we had stayed together was the children, but that situation, too, had changed. With Oliver now living on his own and Matthew in England pursuing a musical career, only our two adolescent girls remained at home, but Allegra had left school the previous year and Clemmie was already fifteen. This realisation obviously struck Rhonda at precisely the same time since she came and sat next to me on the sofa one evening and calmly said, 'I suppose you're going to leave me now?'

Although it was somehow inevitable, the question still came as a bit of a shock. Nevertheless, it opened a door for me.

'Yes', was all I said.

Above: Turning Point

Left and below: Queensland music studios

4. Awakening from The Dream

Explaining what it's like to live as awake-ness will never be possible using words in the normal or traditional way. This is because the moment so-called truth is spoken it immediately becomes untrue in the sense that it has fallen way behind the actuality of the flow of creation in the eternal Now. The moment of truth wherein the words were given voice is no longer. The real origin of truth is truth itself and there is no way it can ever be described since it can only BE, not be BEEN – see how the words become nonsensical?

This is why we have always turned to forms of expression such as poetry and music to try to convey any sense of what is true at the deepest, most fundamental level. The words in a poem, for example, are not always immediately accessible to cold reason, so an illusory distinction between art and academic study, or spirituality and reductionist science, is made by the rational mind constantly bending the truth in order to fit the realms of the explicable. This presents the illusion of a universe that is safe and ongoing, the downside of which is that what is actually manufactured is suffering, and all suffering is the result of separation from our true self or source; being A-PART from the oneness of creation.

Consciousness is not just a function that contains something separate or outside itself. Similarly, the notion of there being a world of objects inside consciousness is just another distortion of the simplicity of Being the Truth. Consciousness is also the content of itself, and herein lies the real rub of it all: there is no separation between consciousness and the objects because there has never been any inside or outside at all. Here we can refer to the ancient Chinese symbol of YIN/YANG where 'The sea is in the fish and the fish is in the sea'. *It cannot be explained any better than this in words.*

By December 2004, just over three years since Rhonda and I had made the big transition down under, all the pretence and denial had finally come to an end. I would move out of *Turning Point*, the home we had put so much into – including an unreasonable amount of faith in its ability to resolve our relationship issues – and so begin the painful process of official separation.

Luckily, Soraya was taking a group to India and she accepted my offer to house sit for her while she was away. This allowed me to transition into my new way of living in a familiar and homely environment as opposed to impersonal rented accommodation, at least for the time being.

The six weeks that followed were an intense period in which I released a tumult of suppressed feelings and went through all the insecurity of having no set direction in life any more, no shared family unit. My days were all without plan, painfully long, and I would often wake up in tears. I still remained in touch with Clemmie and Allegra, of course, trying to keep things as normal as possible for them under the circumstances.

When Soraya returned from India I had no alternative other than to rent a house nearby, but I still attended her classes as this was now the only positive thing in my life, other than my children, capable of illuminating the darkness of my situation. Furthermore, it transpired that Soraya was a musician who on occasion combined her abilities as a singer and keyboard player with yoga, so I gradually became involved with this, too, going along to her house with my flutes where we'd sing mantras or simply respond to the moment with some improvisatory creation. This added a new dimension to my life as I entered uncharted depths of expression where I felt exposed, free, and for the first time entirely supplicant to the great mystery of which Terry Oldfield the biological organism became an indistinguishable part when playing the flute; a conduit that allowed something far greater and more fundamental to incarnate through music. The respite this afforded from all the other highly unpleasant aspects of my life was immense, throwing me a life belt in an ocean I could easily have drowned in, were it not for the transcendent bliss I escaped into every time Soraya and I sat down to create music.

    I had set up a makeshift studio in the rented house I now found myself living in alone, but my life had entered a surreal limbo state in which my family life and musical career were in tatters, so this very painful time was destined to be far less productive, creatively speaking. For some reason I made a completely fresh re-recording (not a remix or a remaster) of my 1993 album *Out of the Depths* which I titled *De Profundis* (subtitled *Out of the Depths 2*). I probably decided to do this because there was absolutely no fresh inspiration available to me at the time, so putting the new digital studio technology through its paces at least allowed me to continue working. However, it also presented a wonderful opportunity to recreate the atmosphere of that album using updated musical resources – including a different singer – and thereby fully complete the experience. I feel that incomplete experience is something that somehow gets locked into the human body or mind, rather like a trapped nerve. The body-mind always seems to be working to complete our past experience; dreams are one way that it does this, and another is the constant repetition in the stream of our thinking. When we finally reach full awareness of this moment then things are completed 'as we go'. This is the natural way of things, of *being* in human form. The universe always provides us with the fastest way forward in the natural flow of change and it is our resistance to change that creates the suffering of incomplete experience. Rather than letting the current carry us, we hang onto the bank or swim around in backflow and eddies trying to control what we experience through repetition of what is pleasant and avoidance of what is not. This is the human addiction to craving and aversion, a primary cause of suffering in this world.

The album that eventually followed, *Ethereal*, was a similarly uninspired creation largely made up of various improvisations I had previously recorded on concert and alto flutes, with one or two played on Irish low whistle and pan pipes. I commonly record many improvisations whenever the mood – or the muse – takes me since these are natural expressions of how I am feeling in the moment and therefore 'real' or uncontrived music. It also means that I always have some original sections of music at my fingertips to edit into spontaneous tracks, should I choose to do so, as was the case on *Ethereal*. Throughout the years I have also gathered a vast amount of natural sounds in this way, recording bird song, rainfall, rivers, the ocean and so on – a whole library, in fact, of nature's own music.

4: Awakening from The Dream

— Sad Endings, Joyous Beginnings —

Over the months my friendship with Soraya was galvanised by the events swirling in the vortex of both our lives. We shared the common ground of being single and having several children whom we loved dearly, and of course there was the yoga and our music, but in particular there was a like-mindedness, a spiritual connection at the deepest level. Being a widow who had also lost a brother to suicide, Soraya identified with the kind of grief I was enduring and consequently could offer a unique and effective support. I soon discovered that one of her sons, Prem, was also experiencing some pretty severe emotional problems at the time, so I suppose we helped each other just by being there to lend an attentive and sympathetic ear.

By October 2005 I was in the epicentre of the tempest that occurred after the dream sequence in which I died. My marriage dissolution was about to be confirmed by divorce and *Turning Point* – our dream house – was now on the market. As though to complete a trilogy of despair, these events coincided with the zenith of the collapse of the CD market and the rise of downloads and streaming in the music industry. Consequently, my music income took a steep dive.

The universe was definitely supporting big changes in my life that were painful and yet at the same time strangely exhilarating. There was absolutely no security to be had anywhere other than within where, thankfully, there existed the beginnings of a sense of true peace at the centre of the passing storms. *This too shall pass* became my guiding mantra and helped me to stay as close as I could to the prevailing wind.

The next studio album I began working on was as much an attempt to bring a state of balance and harmony back into my life as it was a musical venture. I had been practising Reiki for about five years and I turned to this energy healing technique as the source of inspiration for what would be my only music release of 2006, *Reiki Harmony*. This is a deeply meditative work with lots of soaring, expansive melodies intended for emotional escape and the creation of a profoundly peaceful atmosphere. I invited Soraya to sing on the second track, *Om Shanti*, as I knew her vocal timbre would be ideal for its haunting lines of discarnate-sounding chant.

Since we first started playing together Soraya had been telling me that I should be sharing my music with others in a live setting, and one day she took it upon herself to organise an informal little concert at her house. Initially I was somewhat reticent about the whole idea of performing live to an audience as this was something I'd always shied away from in favour of entering my musical 'zone' in the privacy of the studio. Soraya pointed out that this wouldn't be a typical concert situation where people were only coming along to listen to music and be entertained, but rather to share in the spiritual connection we made and expressed through music. Playing in such an uncontrived way to those who themselves were open to, and actively seeking, such an experience was far more amenable to me, so I immediately felt better about the prospect of this debut event.

Apart from accompanying Julie Felix on a few songs, the last time I performed in public had been at the world premiere of *Tubular Bells* more than thirty years previously, so I was a bit scared when I walked out in front of the fifty or so people who turned up to completely fill the room we had set up for the concert. However, almost from the moment Soraya and I began playing – or perhaps *channelling* might be a more appropriate word – the audience first diminished then completely disappeared from my awareness as we entered a dimension that transcended fear, insecurity, human ego and even music.

At the end of the concert when I seemed to return from the timelessness of what had just passed, I was amazed to hear the strength of the applause, to see the joy and appreciation on absolutely every face, some of which displayed unabashed emotion through tears. I knew that something significant had just happened. Whatever it was that had to be conceived through all the recent pain and apparent misfortune in my life had now just experienced a glorious birth.

It finally seemed that the universe, having first inflicted a very painful – albeit necessary – wound upon me, had now begun a healing process that was destined to bring about positive changes.

The highly successful concert gave me the confidence I needed to begin travelling along a new pathway of exploration into the amazing world of playing to a live audience, something that would become an enormous part of my life and relationship with Soraya. From then on we played together in group and informal concert settings as a natural accompaniment to the existing work

Soraya had been doing with people, and our union felt so 'right' that it was impossible not to regard it as something preordained rather than the result of a mere lucky coincidence. The compatibility and ease with each other that had quickly formed a close friendship was slowly, inevitably, developing into something far more intense.

Three momentous things then happened in close succession. Firstly, I moved from my rented accommodation into Soraya's house where, secondly, she and I decided to take our music to a much wider audience in the form of a European concert tour in 2006. The third event resolved a puzzle that had troubled and confounded me for almost thirty years.

— The Celtic Curse —

In the mid 1990s a genetic abnormality was discovered among those of mainly Celtic origin. Now more commonly known as 'The Celtic Curse', hemochromatosis is a disorder which causes excessive amounts of iron to be stored in the organs of those affected. The condition is especially prevalent on the west coast of Ireland where one in about eighty people have been found to suffer from it. One theory why this particular genetic change happened is that it evolved during the Viking era to help sailors survive long sea voyages when lack of iron in the diet would cause serious problems. Another theory is that loss of blood in battle would deplete iron levels. Ironically, donating blood regularly is now the main treatment for the condition.

4: Awakening from The Dream

After going for a routine medical check in my fifties the blood test revealed that my iron levels were very high (a symptom of hemochromatosis), so my doctor arranged for me to be checked for this condition that I had never even heard of at the time. Thanks to my good diet, regular walks and active youth I have always been very fit, so initially I dismissed the possibility that I could have been harbouring such an ailment for more than fifty years. I learnt, however, that the symptoms don't usually manifest until middle age, and this gave me pause to recall how my stamina was never great whenever I pushed myself to any extreme, as doing so often resulted in exhaustion and a headache. Also, I have generally suffered from mild depression and mood swings all my life, and my body energy levels have never really been constant and balanced. So, what with my Celtic genes, I began to think that, perhaps...

The test indeed turned out to be positive. I had been host to hemochromatosis since the day of my birth.

The news came as a bit of a body blow, of course, but there was satisfaction – relief, even – in learning that an underlying physical imbalance had been contributing to the erratic mood swings and stress that had plagued me on-and-off for many years. Another thing that struck me more powerfully than the diagnosis itself was the sudden realisation that my poor mother had experienced the symptoms of this condition long before it came to the attention of the medical fraternity. Naturally outgoing and vibrant in her earlier years, Mum, too, began to suffer from lethargy, depression and mood swings as she entered middle age (classic indications of the iron overload associated with hemochromatosis), and almost certainly had the condition as it can only be passed through genetic inheritance. And whilst my mum's problems undoubtedly began after she gave birth to her fourth child, the proven emotional disturbances linked to hemochromatosis could also have been a contributing factor in some of the terrible difficulties she experienced. How sad it is that we commonly assume such symptoms are always the result of a psychological disorder or a disturbed personality, perhaps without ever considering the possibility that the person may be at the mercy of a purely physical condition that is erratic in nature and beyond their control.

Fortunately I was diagnosed well before there was any lasting organ damage (which can happen if the condition goes untreated), and followed the advice of my doctor as well as doing some research of my own. The main treatment lies in regular phlebotomy – having blood taken to reduce the iron levels in the system – so I became a blood donor at the Red Cross and kept a close eye on my iron levels from then on. In the long term it was quite miraculous how my overall mood improved and I began to feel better and happier than ever.

— A New Dawn and a Tin Shed —

As Soraya and I fell more deeply in love, one of the outward manifestations of our relationship was playing music together. Our mutual beliefs, philosophy, love and, indeed, the personal journeys that had taken us to this point found expression in every note we played. The decision to start recording our developing repertoire was a natural development from this, added to which we began the first forays into composing together. The first song we co-wrote in Soraya's yoga studio was *Make Me an Instrument*, inspired by the prayer of Saint Francis of Assisi, '*Make Me an Instrument of Your Peace*'. This song set the foundation for our work and future travels together, and has been a sort of mantric motto ever since. In our own way we both wanted to be an instrument in whatever direction the universe decided for us, and it was with this song that we took our first baby steps towards being lived, responding to whatever was happening. This feeling of surrender would be the inspiration for another song we later wrote together, *Thy Will be Done*, from our 2016 album release, *Namaste*.

    The new possibilities presented in our lives now led Soraya and I to purchase a very basic house in Eudlo, a small town in Queensland, situated on thirty-two acres of land. The biggest attraction for us was the enormous tin shed – which was more like a huge barn, really – that came with the property, as it offered a lot of potential for running events there. The whole place had an oddly disquieting atmosphere about it after we moved in, but we did what we could to transform the house and land into home and called it *Mandala*. Despite our positive outlook, this was nevertheless a difficult time of transition for both of us in which we had to negotiate a lot of emotional and familial baggage along with the new directions in our work, literally transforming ourselves as we learnt to melt into the ongoing flow of things. Personal growth is seldom ever comfortable as it necessarily involves letting go of old ways of seeing and doing, surrendering more to the Tao, the natural flow of creation and destruction.

As soon as Soraya and I moved into our new place with the four boys I set up what was probably my worst ever recording studio in the big tin shed that we also used for yoga and accommodation. It was in this metal cabin that I rather hurriedly cobbled together my next solo album, *Labyrinth*, probably driven more by habit or the mistaken belief that I had to keep putting music out there than a genuine desire to create. I don't think it had fully sunk in with me that the music scene had changed beyond all recognition either, and that I was going to have to fall into line with the new ways of using music platforms to promote my catalogue. I was also in the process of shaking off some of the drainage from illegal sites that had been hanging on to my work for so long, and this, combined with repercussions from my divorce with Rhonda and other stuff that was going on with Soraya's children, caused distractions that are reflected in the lack of a clear musical direction on *Labyrinth*.

Containing five meditative instrumental pieces, this album was one of two I worked on that year for Gemini Sun Records, the second being a collaborative work with Medywn Goodall called *Om*. There were no issues with the production of this second album, and it was received well enough, however on a personal level it highlighted how my mind set at the time had moved towards a preference for working independently as a solo artist, rowing the boat myself with two oars, so to speak. Undoubtedly my more unsavoury experiences with some TV producers over the years had contributed to this feeling and so, with the exception of working with Soraya, *Om* would be my last fully collaborative work for many years until my approach became one where I responded according to the whim of the day and the project.

∞

Our first European concert tour in September 2006 was a huge learning curve in several ways. To begin with, we carried far too much gear with us and consequently struggled with the enormous weight of stuff. Luckily, the stringent airline baggage regulations of the present day had not yet been introduced and we got away with a lot that either wouldn't be possible now or would cost a fortune in excess baggage fees.

Our first port of call was Brussels where we were met by Patrick Niels, a man who was to become a close friend over the years and who, on that very first occasion, fortunately arrived to pick us up in a large van which easily accommodated all our equipment!

The inaugural concert of the tour was attended by nearly two hundred people, and we also ran some yoga and mindfulness workshops that were filled to capacity. When the events all sold out we decided to put on extra days to accommodate the demand, and that was a very pleasant surprise for myself and Soraya, not to mention a strong affirmation for what we were doing. It also demonstrated how public appearances could inevitably be a useful platform for boosting CD sales as a result of people wanting to take something away from, or extend, their concert experience.

Most of the music we performed had been gathered over quite a long period of time amidst difficult issues in both our families, and included a collection of mostly Sanskrit mantras with lots of bansuri improvisation and, of course, *Make Me an Instrument*, the first song we wrote together. Much of this material was soon to be brought together on our debut album in 2007, *Forever One*.

That first European tour was a wonderfully exhilarating adventure and a very encouraging start to what would become an annual event for us until 2020 when the global Covid 19 pandemic suspended all travel and public events.

— A Different Life Begins —

Our wedding took place on October 2nd 2007 on a beautiful afternoon in our garden at *Mandala*. We had built a stone circle and thatched Bali hut especially for the occasion which was shared with about fifty of our friends and relatives (including Allegra and Clemmie), and a magical day full of joy and blessings unfolded perfectly. For our honeymoon we went to a local resort for two nights, leaving the four boys in the good care of their grandparents.

Soraya, my best friend and soul mate, was now my wife.

We set out on our new life together as husband and wife in a rapture of musical creation and, in addition to our debut album, *Forever One*, that year Soraya and I released *Dancing Through the*

Chakras. This is a single track CD that takes the listener on a sort of guided journey through the seven bodily chakras, each of which are expressed in music and the character of individual instruments. The two albums in their own unique ways also announced to the world a personal and professional union that was set to endure.

∞

After completing our second successful European tour in 2007, to further showcase the music we were playing live on stage Soraya and I recorded *Mandala, Circle of Chant*, which was released on New Earth Records in 2008. Featuring the music which now formed the backbone of our live repertoire, the eight mantras on this album – predominantly with Sanskrit wording – are an expression of our growing love for playing in front of a live audience. We made the recording at *Mandala* in the 'tin shed' where I was still not happy with my studio location or the operation of my equipment, since the internet was a constant problem and updating software a complete nightmare. However, through all of this, not to mention a house full of teenagers and the echoing waves of divorce and displacement, somehow we **managed** to come up with a very nice recording from the chaotic dance that was our life at the time. Out of that maelstrom came the beginnings of the true peace that we now live with together through thick and thin; a time when we learned the true meaning of acceptance through a willingness to go through the actual experiencing of present reality as reflected in circumstances that were simply the appearance of incompletion in the past, or the natural repercussions of resistance to what is. From there we attained a state of being that we have lived ever since, where there is only full participation in the human race.

∞

The next album we did was based upon an ancient yogic practice that Soraya had been teaching for years known as yoga nidra, or psychic sleep, where the body goes to sleep but the mind remains awake in a state of emptiness or no thought. This was a meditation CD, guided by the dulcet timbre of Soraya's Aussie voice, on which I added background music that we both felt would work well to create just the right peaceful atmosphere. Using a similar format we also recorded *Chakra Clearing and Healing Sounds* around the same time, another meditative album that focuses on the listener's well-being.

Despite Soraya's significant contribution on these projects, they were both released on New Earth Records with my name up front for commercial reasons, since they probably wouldn't have put them out without the Oldfield name in prominence to help them along. A sad fact of life.

Regardless of musical politics, Soraya and I had begun to soar in our collaborative musical activity and ease into a smooth flow of daily life. The nature of life, however, is to present us with contrasting and vacillating scenarios which delight, challenge, enlighten, push, torment and sometimes even bring us to the brink of despair.

— The Ultimate Tragedy —

I was driving back home from Brisbane one afternoon in September 2009 when my phone rang. Soraya had been dealing with yet another difficult situation with Prem and was calling to tell me that she had decided to take him away to stay with her family over a thousand kilometres away. I suppose I was getting rather tired of the endless drama surrounding my stepson and remember saying to her in the heat of the moment, 'The more you try to help him the worse it gets.' These turned out to be unfortunately prophetic words since only a few days later Soraya called me at three a.m. with the devastating news that Prem had tried to take his own life and was in the ICU on life support. I quickly made arrangements to fly down with two of my other stepsons, Kumar and Aruna, to join my wife at the hospital later that morning. Soraya's family also began to arrive later that day and there began a painful process of realising that Prem was not going to recover and would therefore be taken off life support. Each family member and friend took turns to spend a little time with him and eventually only Soraya and I were left there with Kumar while the doctor prepared to remove the breathing tube. This turned out to be too much for poor Kumar who hurried out of the room to join the rest of the family, leaving his mum and I alone with his dying brother. It was terrible to watch as Prem's breathing began to struggle. We had been told it would not be long until he passed, but eleven hours of painful waiting unfolded before he finally took his last breath. During those seemingly endless hours I mostly just sat quietly in the room, trying to be something of an anchor on which Soraya could ride the waves of grief. At one stage I briefly left the room only to return and find that Prem had gone. There was a feeling of quiet relief for the poor boy, but Soraya was of course devastated and reality suddenly began to play out like a vague dream for both of us.

In the weeks that followed we stayed quietly at home until the initial force of the terrible shock gradually abated and we were able to arrange a celebration of Prem's life with all his friends and siblings present. This was a way of bringing the whole thing together, of laying a lot of incomplete things to rest, and from there we slowly, very slowly, began to move on with our lives. A key part of this process for Soraya was to eventually start writing a book in memory of the son she had lost. This memoir would be an integral part of her healing, but also perhaps the finest tribute she could ever give Prem.

— Mangalam —

We moved out of *Mandala* in December 2010 at the height of the Australian summer when it rained continuously for three weeks over the Christmas period, creating huge floods in Brisbane. This was a very fortunate time for us to relocate since *Mandala* was in a flat area where the flooding was quite bad, whereas the new place was situated at the top of a hill. The house itself, which we called

Mangalam, was too small to accommodate a recording studio, so we built one just a short way from the main house; quite a simple construction with some basic soundproofing, but it had a nice feeling to it and a great view. From then on my working days would often begin in here with a warm north westerly breeze, carried from thousands of miles of outback desert, wafting in through the open studio window and portending a hot day ahead. Australia is indeed an exciting place to live, a landscape of extremes and wondrous flowing change.

My only commercial release in 2010 was the Christmas album, *Silent Night, Peaceful Night*, which I put together at the request of New Earth Records who thought it would be a good idea to have a seasonal recording. In order to get the album out quickly, I used two singers: my sister, Sally, who recorded *Silent Night* and my own version of *Ave Maria*, and another professional singer, Ashleigh Muekenberger, for the eight traditional carols featured.

Despite the fact that this album had been recorded in the *Mandala* (tin shed) studio with all its attendant difficulties, putting it together was actually quite an enjoyable experience as I didn't have to compose much original material and could simply work in my own way as tunesmith and engineer/producer.

Also recorded in the *Mandala* studio prior to our departure was *Healing Sound Journey*, another collaboration album with Soraya whose title perhaps says something about where we both were at that stage in our lives. This was a pretty spontaneous work with lots of improvisation and forays into wilder singing which, combined with some unusual harmonies, demand more of the listener, but I think it turned out to be a nice diversion from our previous musical directions. Two of the tracks, *A Walk in the Forest* and *Butterfly*, became live concert favourites of ours as they offered a versatile platform for exploration onstage and consequently were always a bit different with each new performance. They were very popular with our audiences, too.

From now until 2017 I would release no more than one album a year. This was a consequence of several factors, the most significant of which was undoubtedly the absolute acceptance of living in the moment, free from illusory attitudes towards things such as commercialism, which Soraya and I shared on an even deeper level now since Prem's passing. I believe, however, that every album from that time until now has unsurpassed original character and depth, in which case this is maybe an instance where *quality over quantity* really does apply.

— He Ain't Heavy —

My brother Mike had invited me to play on his first four albums between 1973 and 1978 (*Tubular Bells*, *Hergest Ridge*, *Ommadawn* and *Incantations*) and I was delighted when he reciprocated by agreeing to play guitar on some of the tracks for my 2012 album, *Journey into Space*.

With me in Australia and Mike now living in the Bahamas, however, the recording had to be done online – quite a common and highly convenient thing to do these days. My brother told me that his current way of improvising a guitar solo was to take two passes at the song then choose the best bits from each and edit them together, which is exactly what I did with Mike's contributions. It was a pretty seamless process, really, but at the same time quite impersonal as there wasn't the usual interaction between musicians that can happen face to face. The end result was great, of course, and Mike was happy with my editing of his performances. I think working online like this definitely gets the job done, but the divide created by such physical distances caused me to recall one magical evening way back in 1975 when I visited Mike at *The Beacon* where he was living at the time. The house was in complete darkness apart from the basement studio where my brother was busy working alone at his massive mixing console. He had just recorded the African drums for *Ommadawn* with the group *Jabula* and was keen for me to have a listen. Excitedly, he pressed play and the tape reel began to turn... I was about to be one of the first people ever to hear the drum ensemble track in the closing section of part one of what would become one of **his** best-loved and most iconic albums. The raw energy of the drums sounded fantastic and Mike was over the moon with the way the album was going. He had asked me to bring along my pan pipes to do some overdubs, and I remember the delight he took in listening to the way this new sound contributed to the overall mood and how everything was generally coming together. That we were making a little bit of musical history was something to which we were of course completely oblivious at the time. That night in the basement studio we were just two musicians who happened to be brothers having a bit of spontaneous fun, and for me that was probably the highlight of all the musical moments that Mike and I shared together.

— Inspirations and Challenges —

The first album Soraya and I recorded in the new studio at *Mangalam* also launched our own label, Global Spirit Records. A reflection of our developing skills and the inspiration derived from working together, *Peaceful Hearts* speaks of our personal transformation mirrored in the new house and the land we call home, as well as the interactions we were having with people and our travels around the world that were slowly increasing as our musical sharing and confidence grew. On this album we sing mostly in English as that was the new direction our live concert work had begun to take.

I was also to be steered in another, less likely, direction around this time by my sons Matthew and Oliver, who suggested that I compose something a bit more up tempo and accessible to youthful tastes. Always open to new ideas, I decided to take up their challenge and put together nine tracks in a racier, modern style for an album I eventually released myself called *Making Tracks*, a title which seemed perfect for this 'family' project. It all turned out a lot better than I expected and the boys and their friends seemed to like it, so that was a case of *job done!*

A few of the European concert dates that year were in Germany, so **Soraya and I** took the opportunity to go and visit my dad in Stuttgart. When we arrived there I was shocked to find him in a rather poor condition; he was now ninety years old and hadn't been in the best of health for some time, added to which Helga was not the most empathic carer. So, we called Sally and Mike in Nassau and after a quick discussion arranged to put Dad in a care home.

It was a very powerful and sad lesson for me to watch someone as polite and gentle as my father – so unconscious of the powerful patterns that were running in his life, particularly around his relationships – digging himself deeper and deeper into suffering to a place where nobody could reach or help him. I tried many times to rescue him as I had with my mother, but sometimes the patterns are just playing out too strongly and the suffering will have its wicked way no matter what.

That turned out to be the first of several emotional challenges to descend upon us in the following couple of years, the next occurring on May 17th 2015 with the sudden death of Mike's son, Dougal, aged just thirty-three. My nephew had died of natural causes completely out of the blue and our entire family were very deeply shocked. Combined with the terrible sorrow, his death was yet another reminder of the fragility of life here on Earth and how quickly and suddenly it can be taken away.

∞

By the end of 2015 Soraya and I had now completed several European concert and workshop tours and run a couple of retreats in India, a land with which we shared a certain affinity. Our family-related problems were gradually fading and we began to live peacefully at *Mangalam*, content with the way things were coasting along smoother than ever for both of us. Soraya was also approaching the final stages of the writing process in her memoir dedicated to Prem. The completed book, *Shining Through: From Grief to Gratitude*, would be published the following year, thereby ending part of a long grieving process and fulfilling a promise made by a mother to her son.

From this position of peace and gratitude came our album *Namaste*, a collection of songs whose title track became quite popular and for which Soraya made a lovely video. It is a very optimistic collaborative work and the music, whilst still containing that element of searching that would soon vanish entirely from our lives, fills the listener with hope and radiates a feeling of happiness.

This was to be the second release on our own label and by now we had done a lot of work to clear the air between the catalogue and the internet. Although CD sales had more or less vanished apart from at concerts where we still had a good turnover, the streaming stations were starting to come into their own and these were doing better all the time.

∞

One day early in 2016 Soraya and I received an unexpected email from the agent of a Spanish musician named Carlos Garo inviting us to join him on tour that year. We had never heard of Carlos, but soon became aware that he had quite a prestigious reputation in Spain where he is highly respected as an artist and composer, so we were delighted that he had expressed such an interest in our music.

Although it was all a bit of a mystery to us we were nevertheless open to new things now, so that year Spain became a date on our European tour in May. The concert collaboration was a great success in every way since we got on extremely well with Carlos, so much so, in fact, that I ended up working with him on some tracks that later became the album, *Sky Dancer*. This collaborative work embraced the changing face of music production technology in that it was put together over the internet between our studios in Spain and Australia in about three months. I found this way of working quite effective because both of us had artistic control over our own mixes and sounds and generally our tastes blended very well. The composing and playing work was divided equally between us and our skills in the studio were also well matched, so everything went very smoothly indeed.

Sky Dancer turned out to be a very nice chill out album that hit the spot for both of us and went down very well with our own fans. I think if we had released it twenty years earlier it would have been a much bigger success, but the global musical trends at the time caused it to be swallowed up in the massive pile of new releases from so many budding musicians in a world where new internet platforms were arising almost daily. Consequently, our album went the way of so much modern music and barely paid for itself in the end.

The world had never seen such a glut of new music, much of which, regrettably, seemed rather shoddy and quite forgettable; an unfortunate development that prompted me to look back on the heydays and thank my lucky stars that I was around for the very best of it. Nothing lasts forever, of course, and soon I came to adopt the old adage, *'This too shall pass'* as an inner mantra that applies equally well to both good and bad experiences. As I would soon be reminded.

— Another Farewell —

A tribute of thanks to my dad who just passed away this morning. At the time I am born in he is leaving. Much peace to you my wonderful father. Thank you so much.

With these simple words I said goodbye.

Having journeyed here for ninety-three years my dad, Raymond, left this world at around one a.m. Australian time on the morning of my 67th birthday. Soraya and I had just returned from our European tour and recently visited him in his care home in Stuttgart. He was not in a good physical condition at all and, looking back, it was apparent that he'd definitely had enough of life. He had been refusing to eat and was mainly receiving liquids which, as a doctor, he'd know would of course hurry things along.

When he first saw me as he awoke from a nap, obviously a bit confused, he said, *'How did you find me..?'*

Heartbreaking.

It was clear that this would be our last encounter and Dad made a big effort to come out into nature in his wheelchair and have a cup of tea and some biscuits with us. One of the nurses later told us that this was the first time he had eaten anything solid in a week. Soraya massaged his feet as we sat in the garden, quietly chatting. A sullen sadness hung in the air and I wished that I could help him in some way to go peacefully from a world that clearly held no attraction for him now.

At the end of our visit I gave him a final hug and said goodbye, holding back the tears as I left, knowing that I would not see him again. Just a couple of weeks later he passed away. I was alone at home when I received the news as Soraya was on a trip to **Uluru in the Red Centre of Australia.** Later that day I lit a bonfire in the garden and sat in solitude toasting my dad's passing with a beer.

— A Hole in the Sky —

Soraya and I love to walk at night under the stars here at *Mangalam* where the sky is particularly clear and beautiful. The lack of light pollution serves to reveal the complete majesty of the cosmos where the more familiar constellations are almost obscured by the billions of other stars and galaxies that spray the dark canvas with tiny points of light. The wondrous show is rendered all the more awe-inspiring on moonless nights where the spiral arm of the Milky Way in which our solar system was formed is visible as a nebulous line of wispy gas cloud directly above.

For some reason I have always been particularly aware of the constellation Pleiades in the night sky. Also known as *The Seven Sisters*, this cluster of stars would draw my gaze whenever I was travelling and I now refer to them as *my travelling stars*. After moving over to Australia I even bought a Subaru because that is the Japanese name for the Pleiades constellation and the symbol they use for that car (昴, スバル, すばる).

It was while star gazing that I started to notice what I lightheartedly referred to as a hole in the sky; a blind spot that seemed to be getting bigger. I was also beginning to see random flashing lights when I closed my eyes, especially lying in bed at night. I had known for several years that there was a Nevus or freckle on the inside of my right eye, an apparently common thing that had originally shown up in a routine eye test a couple of years previously when I was told it was nothing to worry about. 'Just keep an eye on it', the optician had said jokingly. Prompted by the new symptoms, however, and Soraya's insistence, in October 2016 I went for another eye test.

The Nevus had doubled in size and this time the optician told me that such a change was very serious and immediately arranged an appointment for me to see a specialist that same afternoon. Suddenly there was a foreboding sense of urgency in the air and things began to move at a dizzying pace.

Soraya accompanied me to the appointment and we sat in the waiting room feeling dazed by the surrealness of it all. A day that had started off with what I thought would have been just another routine eye test was transforming, alarmingly quickly, into something quite sinister.

'I'm certain that this is a choroidal melanoma,' the consultant announced dispassionately. 'There's a likelihood that it may already have spread throughout the body and the next six months are going to be pretty intense for you.'

At that point I remember looking at Soraya in a state of shock and utter disbelief. Did he really just say those words? Did they apply to me in the here and now or to some other patient in a hypothetical scenario? Where had all this come from, this sudden state of emergency, on what is surely just another day?

Much of the remainder of the conversation with the consultant passed as a sort of aside to reality, after which Soraya and I wandered off together in a kind of numb daze to digest what we had just been told. We were set to leave for India two weeks hence to run our annual retreat in Kerala, and after talking things over together we decided that nothing really needed to happen in a hurry and we should put off any decisions about my eye for the time being and go to India as planned. The following day I made an appointment with an eye specialist in Brisbane for when we got back and, after also talking to my doctor, I agreed to go for a PET scan in the meantime to check whether there was any metastatic spread.

On the morning of the scan I awoke early for my usual tea meditation in the garden and was acutely aware of a feeling that, yes, I really could be facing the abyss. My thoughts turned to my five children who were spread all over the world and I decided to let them know the situation as soon as I had had the PET scan results. The melanoma in my eye was bad enough but if the cancer had spread then that would be another matter entirely.

Later on that morning as I was driving to the hospital for the scan, a feeling of acceptance came in like a wave; a sensation of peace and quiet indifference to what was happening. The feeling seemed to come quite unbidden, not through any philosophical rationalising on my part but from something outside of me. It was in this state that I arrived at the hospital perfectly prepared to go with the flow.

Part of the scan procedure involves being injected with radioactive glucose that attracts any cancer cells and shows their presence in the body. I was told that I would be receiving the equivalent of about seven years of background radiation in one hit! There was no turning back now. All I could do was undergo the test and wait in a state of emotional limbo for the result which, having already made an appointment to see my doctor later that same day, I would receive in just a few hours.

That afternoon the sun blazed into our car, coolly unaffected by the world's cares, as Soraya and I made our way to the clinic. The chit-chat of feigned levity had given way to silence as the hypnotic conveyor belt of pale greens, fiery browns and ochres of the landscape cascaded steadily past. Abruptly, our wandering thoughts were broken by a rude mechanical tune announcing the arrival of a text message on my phone. It was from the doctor I was on my way to visit.

Good news. No metastatic spread!

4: Awakening from The Dream

My initial reaction was strange in that I took the good news with the same calm acceptance that pervaded during the scan that morning. I did feel a sense of relief, naturally, but there was no explosive surge of it as one would expect, or any sense of euphoria. I now see that this was the beginning of something that remains with me to this day. I was coming to trust in the rightness of whatever is happening, that all is indeed well and whatever may turn up in life is supposed to be there. An amazing intelligence is running the show and that is the only thing that really knows what it is doing. So, a couple of weeks later off we went to India as planned.

Our retreat there was based in an Ayurvedic (traditional Hindu medicine) Centre, and this presented me with the perfect opportunity to prepare for whatever might lie in store upon my return home. The doctors at the retreat were very supportive and put me on a course of treatment for the eye. My blood tests also came back with very positive results and I was assured that I had nothing to worry about as far as the rest of my body was concerned. This news fortified my overall sense of acceptance and trust in the unknowable plan, and I used the time at the retreat with Soraya to relax and grow accustomed to the possibility that my right eye might have to be removed.

The retreat was wonderful as usual, and we both returned home in a nice relaxed frame of mind. I was open to whatever was to come in my immediate future, and so when we went to see the surgeon in Brisbane and he suggested an urgent enucleation, or eye removal, the news came neither as a shock nor a surprise. I was given the option to be placed on the surgeon's private operation list for the following Tuesday, five days hence, to which, after a brief consultation with Soraya, I agreed.

We spent the weekend absorbed in some of the things we love to do together, like walking in the forest and pottering about in our garden. Our conversations were neither especially intense nor imbued with the kind of pretend frivolity that goes hand-in-hand with the avoidance of a weighty subject. There was no sense of a heavy storm cloud moving ominously into our lives as Soraya seemed to share my acceptance that everything was playing out exactly as it should.

On the day before my operation we visited a favourite part of the nearby rainforest where I made a little video in which I talked about my last day of normal vision. Looking back on this I seem to come across as quite resigned and relaxed about the whole thing, which on one level I was, but there was a definite tinge of sadness creeping in at that stage, too.

∞

I had expressed some concern about the possibility of the wrong eye being removed, leaving me blind, but apparently this is a common fear with enucleation so, after I had been wheeled into the theatre on the morning of the operation, my surgeon – who happened to be from India – appeared in his scrubs and special headgear with a marker pen and mirror in his hands. Though wearing a mask that covered the lower part of his face I could tell from his eyes that he was smiling. He positioned the mirror so that I could see my own reflected face and asked me to point to the eye with the melanoma. This was of course just for the sake of my own peace of mind, and when I pointed to the right eye he used the marker pen to make a little cross just below the lower lid. As he bent over to conduct a careful close-up examination of the eye, a golden Om suddenly appeared in front of me from the end of a chain worn around the surgeon's neck. It remained there, gently swaying to and fro, for the duration of the examination. Somehow I knew then, even when the anaesthetist stepped up to administer the drug that would close my eyes and my final moments of normal vision, that I was in the right hands.

∞

From the moment I awoke in the recovery room it was obvious that life as I'd always experienced it was gone forever, and I had now entered what was going to be a very difficult time.

My vision had changed so dramatically that I could hardly imagine ever getting used to seeing the world in this new way. It didn't feel like reality, somehow, and my mind seemed to be sending signals for the right eye to open in order to escape this 'not right' situation and restore normal vision. Although at a deeper level I had already accepted that everything was just as it should be within the great and mysterious journey of life, I knew there would be lots of frustration and sadness, perhaps even moments of despair ahead of me, because part of that journey often involves painful pathways where suffering must be experienced in order to be confronted and overcome.

And so began the long days of healing.

There was of course the physical healing process, the natural way in which the body deals with change, but the greatest challenges I encountered were emotional; letting go of all the old ways of seeing and doing as the brain got used to the missing right hand field of vision. My right eye, coincidentally, had been the dominant of the two, meaning that the left now had to work overtime to adapt to its new burden of processing everything. Consequently, I would have to wear glasses most of the time, which was a bit of a daunting prospect in itself since, before the operation, I was fortunate to have enjoyed extremely good sight. I was also taught how to use the prosthetic eye that had been specially made for me. This artificial creation, whose detail and stunning life-like qualities though undoubtedly capable of inspiring aesthetic admiration if regarded with the separation of an art lover studying a portrait in a gallery, to me represented little more than a vulgar cosmetic mockery of what once was. Unlike a prosthetic limb that has the potential of restoring a high percentage of function after months of physiotherapy, my artificial eye would only ever be capable of stagnant, one-way reflection. There could be no rehabilitation, only acceptance and adaptation.

There was one particular morning when I woke up and burst into uncontrollable sobbing, suddenly hit by the enormity of what I felt I had actually lost. Before the operation my surgeon had told me that losing an eye is akin to losing a close family member and suggested that I may need some counselling afterwards. It was obvious that I had indeed now entered a grieving process that would require time to run its course, but once again a belief in the old saying, '*This too shall pass*', was absolutely crucial in helping me to move through and accept the maelstrom of feelings that were coming up at this time.

The long days evolved into weeks and eventually months in which my body slowly, gradually, often distressingly, reset to the new parameters and I began to experiment with things I used to do before the operation, like gardening and making music. I even joined a Facebook group called *Lost Eye* from which I derived a lot of comfort. There were many people going through the same thing I was, and that is always reassuring as there is something intrinsically human about finding comfort and security from being part of a tribe. I also came across an audible version of the biography of Sammy Davis Jr., the one-time member of the famous 'Rat Pack' who, at the age of twenty-nine, lost an eye in a car crash. I found this especially helpful and inspiring since, after a long period of adjustment, this man went on to become one of the world's most accomplished entertainers, and was once considered the greatest entertainer ever to grace an American stage.

One of the things I have come to regard as positive about the whole experience of losing an eye is that there has been a noticeable calming, or slowing down, in many areas of my life, including my stream of thought. I have learnt to move more slowly, always aware of the blind side, and consequently now take a bit more time for patient consideration in all things. Life since the operation has given me many lessons in this, but one that particularly stands out is the time I was in a crowded restaurant one afternoon with Soraya and, preparing to leave, I stood up from my chair not having seen the waitress passing my table with a very large tray full of food. Inevitably, everything on the tray got knocked up in the air, only to land in the lap of a fellow diner. From that experience I learned that in such situations it doesn't really help to say, 'Sorry, I only have one eye', because the responsibility to adapt, to take the necessary care, is mine, especially since my highly realistic-looking prosthetic eye means that most people can't tell that I have impaired vision.

There is one very interesting thing that happens, though: whenever there is an unexpected or unusual sound close by I *see* that sound in my right field as a reddish flash of light. I think this is the optic nerve – which is still alive – trying to pass information back to the brain without the camera of the eye.

This is indeed a holographic universe which, without the conversion and interpretation of the brain, would be just a vast ocean of swirling energy.

As I began to adapt, there came an unexpected and powerful inner transformation that was to find expression in a surge of musical creativity. Though initially throwing me into a state approaching despair, the experience of losing an eye ultimately guided me onto a path of deeper awareness and

4: Awakening from The Dream

increased creative flow, so much so that I came to recognise it as a blessing in disguise.

As well as the album *Sky Dancer* which had been put together with Carlos Garo the previous year, I released two further albums in 2017. *Pure Flute* was my first solo album for some time, one in which, as the title suggests, there is only a simple and pure exploration of the inner self expressed in music.

The other album, *Temple Moon*, continued in a similar vein as *Namaste* in that it comprises more of the music and mantras that Soraya and I had now added to our live concert repertoire. Amidst our daily life at *Mangalam* we spent several months pouring our hearts into recording this music which flowed as a natural expression of our current direction in the world. Later that year while we were on tour some filmmakers put together a nice video of one of the tracks, *So Ham Shivoham*, at the Suryalila Retreat Centre near Seville where we gave a workshop and concert. This event came at the end of an annual European tour that marked a ten year collaboration anniversary for me and Soraya, after which I also went on to do a few concerts with Carlos Garo in Valladolid and Madrid to promote *Sky Dancer* before finally flying home to rejoin Soraya in Australia.

∞

My spate of unrestrained creativity continued on into 2018 with the rapid production of an album that came along as a big surprise to me. I genuinely have no idea where the songs came from; they simply flowed through like melting butter on hot toast. The first was *Reach Out*, which began on our wooden deck at *Mangalam* one morning as I watched my stepson Jaya texting away on his mobile phone at lightning speed. I happened to be playing my guitar at the time and the words '*Is there anybody out there?*' came out as a lyrical line that developed into '*Is there anybody home? Is there anyone not online? Is there anyone not on the phone?*' I sang this as a kind of joke to Jaya, but it quickly formed into a song for which Carlos Garo put together a video with the aid of a professional film crew in Spain. The other songs that eventually formed the album came through over the next couple of months and they *really* surprised me in that they wanted to be put out in a much more up tempo and racy style than is usual for me.

On Fire is a song that seems to mirror what I was going through at the time when I felt like I was moving through the fires of creation and destruction, leading more and more to the present moment where this is a constant: birth and death, living and dying, all at once in the eternal now. It was the first time that I used a kind of rapping style to convey the lyrics, which seemed to work better than melody in some places. I also used the rap style in one of the other songs on the album, *Moving On*.

All six songs on the album speak of a major transition from a habitual life based upon planning, will and direction to one of no plans, no will and no direction. In other words, leaving everything to run all by itself. Nature does this all the time. It is in perfect harmony with itself as it unfolds effortlessly as a unified and universally complete whole. The song, *No Resistance*, tells of the need to surrender to this natural flow and take all our personal irons out of the fire. No resistance is the key to peace and happiness. To the ego personality this is death because there is no room for separation in oneness.

Carlos and I performed some of these songs live at a few concerts in Spain, which was a very interesting experience as we played in venues and clubs that were 'high use', with dressing rooms full of graffiti made by years of bands and musicians passing through. It brought back to mind my roadie days in the 1960s and also something that my brother Mike told me when he'd announced his retirement from touring after travelling for twenty years throughout the 1980s and '90s... '*The atmosphere in those backstage dressing rooms is always depressing and cold. They're not the sort of places you want to be.*'

Mike has passed on to me some little gems of clear insight over the years and a couple more spring to mind here that I often remember and apply to my life now: 1. '*It is wonderful to walk barefoot in the snow and enjoy the warmth and comfort of a roaring log fire afterwards.*' 2. '*I love to take a siesta in the early afternoon because I get to begin my day again afterwards.*' Thanks Mike!

My audiences and fans seemed to enjoy the new direction I'd taken with the *On Fire* album, and Tom Newman who was a co-producer on *Tubular Bells* was so impressed when he heard the songs that he very kindly offered to remix and produce the title song for me. A particularly nice comment he made afterwards was,

'Terry, this music has the potential to take you onto the world stage.'

Immediately following on from this I recorded an album that was something of a showpiece for the bansuri flute. Each of the ten tracks on *Rhapsody* are flute improvisations with an Indian atmosphere created with the assistance of studio samples and keyboards plus an app called *Itabla* that I downloaded to my iPhone. With this kind of spontaneous yet profound music creation I am totally in my element and most in flow, and the whole album was done and dusted within about a month. It really can be quite incredible when we take the easiest pathway, the one where all our musical skills are well-honed and we are completely present – with the thinking mind out of the way – to allow the muse to come out and play through this mind body that is an image in the mind of God.

Next came *Soundscapes for Awakening*, an album similar to *Rhapsody* in approach, but always with unique expressions, rather like same-species trees that assume different shapes according to the lean of the slope they grow on or the predominating wind direction. Their individuality is not born of a thinking and calculating mind that uses the past to project onto the future, but evolves in a natural and uncontrived way.

During this period I also made quite a few videos for these improvised and studio-polished flute tracks, all based around nature with some quirky slow-motion shots taken on my iphone and edited in Final Cut Pro on my studio Mac. I love adding visuals to my music – especially in these days of easy sharing – using the sort of condensed filming technology and equipment that at one time required a backpack and muscles of steel just to carry around! Many wildlife cameramen and women have entered later life with back problems resulting from carrying their gear in wild places all over the world, and we certainly owe them a large debt of gratitude.

— Return to Celtic Roots —

Over the years when I was growing up I had come to know a little about my mother's culture through her stories and long Celtic poems – even her cooking! She didn't speak so much about her family, though – with the exception of her father who was a gamekeeper and had been a soldier in the First World War – or of the place where she grew up. She only told us that her hometown was Charleville in Cork, right down in southern Ireland, a place she left when she was about nineteen to work as a nurse in Essex, England. It was while working at the Royal Surrey County Hospital in Guildford that she met a young intern who was destined to become both a GP and her husband. My dad had been raised in the Protestant faith so, unfortunately, when the young couple decided to marry it created a rift between Mum and her staunch Catholic family who strongly disapproved of betrothal to a non-Catholic. Mum was virtually cut off from her relatives from then on, and consequently the Oldfield's had no contact with that side of our family.

I had long been curious about our Celtic roots, however, and over the years had often toyed with the idea of visiting Mum's home town of Charleville in County Cork. I had visited Ireland three times before, once with my brother, but had not then felt inclined to go to Charleville. I think there is a right time for everything and unless we are clearly moved to do something at a particular time then it isn't going to happen just yet.

When he was preparing his biography Mike carried out an investigation into our mother's history by hiring a private detective in 2005 and I had seen the resulting family tree, but that wasn't enough for me. I wanted to actually go there and visit the very streets where Mum had walked and played as a young girl known as Maisie.

Through all the confusion and uncertainty that sprang up around the UK Brexit issue in 2017 it suddenly dawned on me that, having had an Irish mother, I could apply for Irish citizenship which would then allow Soraya and I to continue our music tours in Europe without first having to apply for visas from Australia. So, in 2018 when I set the wheels in motion for obtaining an Irish passport, other cogs immediately began to turn towards the idea of visiting Mum's home town. This time the idea, the timing, felt right, and when my passport application went through without a single hitch, it appeared that everything was conspiring to facilitate the process.

In my experience it always seems to be the case that when a 'right' idea arrives at an appropriate time in a person's life the universe will collude to remove any obstacles that may hinder the wave of progress, nudging that person in a particular direction. And it was perhaps for the same reason that, while riding this inspired Celtic wave, I also got to thinking about including a concert in Cork as part of a future tour. **Soraya** and I had already arranged our 2018 European tour at this point, so the earliest that an Irish visit could happen was 2019. The fact that 2019 would coincidentally be the year in which both the 100th anniversary of my mum's birth and my 70th birthday occurred made me feel that I really was being guided to make the trip the following year. Everything was falling into place – so far, at least.

∞

One of our tour destinations in 2018 was southern Spain, where we would give two concerts and a *Sounds of Inner Stillness* workshop. The first concert took place in Gibraltar and the second, a much larger event in aid of World Peace Day, was held at a venue in Marbella.

By a rather fortunate coincidence, our Scottish friend Joe McGowan was at the time living close to where we were based in Sotogrande for the week, and he became part of the team who organised the events. A musician himself, Joe assisted with the sound system for the concerts and premiered a new peace song he had written, and at one point towards the end of the week I happened to mention my idea about including Cork in the following year's tour. Joe's eyes widened in astonishment before he told me that he and his partner, Sharon (originally from Cork), were preparing to move there in just a few months' time! When he immediately offered to help set up something for Soraya and I as part of our tour the following year, it seemed that yet another piece of the puzzle had been comfortably guided into place.

I was now becoming very excited about the Cork visit (which, apart from everything else, would give me the chance to use my new Irish passport for the first time; a prospect I found oddly thrilling), and kept in touch with Joe over the following months as he explored various options for a concert over there. I was soon amazed to receive an email from him with some attached photos of The School Yard Theatre in Charleville, a possible venue which just happened to have been converted from the old building where my mother went to school. This sounded perfect, not least of all because it offered the opportunity to actually play in the building where Mum had spent so much time as a schoolgirl, and again there was the sensing that somehow all of this was meant to be. The suggestion of predestination was only enforced when Joe visited the venue for the first time and the theatre manager agreed, without hesitation, to host the concert at a time that fitted perfectly with our 2019 tour schedule in Europe.

Apart from any nostalgic compulsions related to my age, I also had a very specific personal intention behind my visit to Ireland, and that was to lay to rest some old ghosts that had haunted me for most of my life. Mum had been deeply troubled for a fourteen-year period beginning in 1961 with the birth of her Downs Syndrome baby, my brother David, and ending with her untimely death in 1974 when I was twenty-six. Prior to that she had been an energetic and bubbly presence in my life, a light I clearly remember shining brightly in my childhood. But the light abruptly became dim and unstable, began to flicker out of control. Occasionally its once benevolent glow would be rekindled, but seldom for long. The instability always returned until, one day, the light just went out.

Her suffering, to which I had been a childhood witness, was only part of her troubled story, though. There was also the more ambiguous aspect surrounding the estrangement from her family in Ireland. Being suddenly cut off from her parents, her brothers and sisters, apparently for no reason other than the fact that she had married a Protestant, seems an unreasonably extreme reaction in our more tolerant times, but within the highly oppressive religious climate of Ireland in the 1940s, Maisie would have been seen to have committed a pretty grievous sin. What had she endured as a result of this? There had been rumours, whispered comments here and there when I'd been growing up, but children are unable to comprehend the weight or significance of such adult issues, since these are things that can only come with age and life experience.

Consequently my sympathy for – and the number of unanswered questions about – Mum had increased exponentially with my emotional maturity. Major life events such as emergent and broken relationships, domestic troubles and the birth of my own children had all served to increase the sense of empathy for her – and indeed for both my parents, as is so often the case in our lives.

At the start of 2019 when plans were finalised for an October concert in Charleville as part of the Irish leg of our European tour that year, some old ghosts began to make their presence felt again, reminding me that whilst they may have been silent, dormant, all this time, they had by no means disappeared completely. All my life I had been carrying around these nameless entities in a secreted little bundle; subliminal imposters spawned by events that occurred years before my birth. These callous spectres had suckled on personal misery and emotional family ties and continued to feed and grow on sadness, suffering, pity, guilt and the impotent disquiet of unanswered questions. But now a date had been set for me to face all of those ghosts.

The mysterious inspiration that had guided my feverish creativity throughout the previous two years began to regulate, as though finally satiated, in 2019. Though there would be three album releases I only worked on one since the other two – *Forever One* and *Healing Hands, Subliminal Music for Massage* – had been recorded several years previously. The former was a straightforward re-release and the latter an album compiled from music I had put together in 2001 for the massage therapy practice of some friends in Stroud. The new composition, *Music for Relaxation*, was a continuous one hour piece of music based around flute and bansuri improvisations that I had originally conceived to be played via my YouTube channel as an aid to relaxation and meditation. The music was woven from many improvisations edited together to make a nice flowing track that could easily be looped up for use in spas and therapy centres.

4: Awakening from The Dream

— A Long-Awaited Confrontation —

By the time Soraya and I arrived at Cork airport in late September we had been travelling around Europe for several weeks and our annual tour was drawing towards its conclusion. Beginning in Greece and set to conclude in the UK and Sweden, our tour, titled *Terry Oldfield and Soraya, Return to Celtic Roots, 2019,* had comprised Norway, Spain, Belgium, The Netherlands, Slovenia and now, of course, Ireland.

Having celebrated my 70th birthday the previous month I suppose I should have been rather proud of my ability to tour like this but, although **Soraya** and I enjoy good health, air travel and living out of a suitcase for an extended period does become tiring, and we both seemed to have registered that perhaps the time had come to think about giving ourselves a less punishing schedule in the future.

Nevertheless, I was enlivened by the significance of this leg of the tour which, for me, would be so much more than playing a concert and meeting friends. There was also the small fact that on October 2nd, the day before the concert at The Schoolyard Theatre, Soraya and I would celebrate both her birthday and our wedding anniversary.

In order to allow some time for exploring my mum's old home town, we had arranged to spend a couple of days in Charleville at the end of the visit, but for the first part of our week-long stay in Ireland we were based in the lovely coastal town of Kinsale.

The first thing that struck me upon stepping out of the car when we reached our hotel was the quality of the cool, early evening air, the freshness of which was rendered even sweeter by the fact that we'd just spent the previous hours in the cabin of a plane. The crisp, coastal ozone was suffused with the characteristic smell of the sea and its weed exposed by low tide, whilst hints of wood smoke from a nearby chimney concocted an infusion that hinted at times past. For several moments I imbibed on that evocative air as though it were a potion thoughtfully prepared for my senses alone, an essential part of my Irish odyssey, every breath of which seemed capable of conjuring the very history of Ireland. And my roots. There was a sense of connection. Faint, distant, yet distinct.

Our first days were largely spent exploring Kinsale and some of the more local areas including Cork City and Bantry, before we moved on to Charleville in preparation for the concert on October 3rd. Charleville is a small, historic town whose streets are shared between some very old, traditional buildings and those with more modern aspirations. The kind of place, not unique in southern Ireland, where a run-down looking pub with a faded Gaelic name above its door will stare defiantly at the small yoga centre across the road, or a second-hand shop whose window wouldn't look out of place in a photo from the 1970s sits parallel with the vibrant edifice of an organic café and take away. Curious juxtapositions that hint at towns defiantly clinging onto their past, or communities with an aversion to change – or who, perhaps, simply take an uncommon pride in their history. Whatever the reason, or reasons, it is something charming rather than banal or pitiful.

Wandering through the town of Charleville, absorbing its motley past-present atmosphere, it wasn't difficult for me to pick up impressions of the past, or to sense the presence of Maisie walking these same streets and pathways as a young girl almost a hundred years previously. I envisaged what it might have been like back then when the sounds of horse's hooves and wooden cart wheels trundling over cobblestones would substitute the modern cacophony of internal combustion engines intruding upon the present scene; synthetic vehicles passing by like a perpetual mechanical conveyor belt.

Occasionally I would stop outside a shop front whose appearance suggested that it might not have changed much in the years since little Maisie had gazed in through the same window at all the toys and games, or the now old-fashioned jars of sweets, and wondered how she had felt living there at the time.

At the far end of the town, sitting in a position of slightly higher elevation with its majestic spire reaching skyward, is the Holy Cross Catholic Church. Built in the late nineteenth century in the gothic revival style, this building would have had special significance for my mum and her family, and therefore it was the place we visited first.

Most churches have a serene, spiritual presence, but for me of course there was the added emotional poignancy of family history. Here I touched the font where my mother was baptised as a baby, faced the altar at which she would have received the other catholic sacraments of communion and confirmation, stood in the imposing religious surroundings where she would have attended Mass every Sunday. Her parents were married here, too; a young Irish couple with a large family who, at the beginning of the 20th century, lived a hard life together just outside the main town here in one of the many small houses that had been relegated to ex-servicemen and their families after the First World War.

Outside again in the cool afternoon air within the grounds of the cemetery, while gazing upon the grave that was the final resting place of my grandparents, Michael and Mary, I contemplated how circumstances wouldn't have been easy for them or their many children. Cramped living conditions, near-poverty and the lingering after-effects of the First World War had seen to that.

Our friend Joe had arranged for us to visit the house where my mum grew up (a surprise he disclosed when he'd picked up Soraya and I at the airport a few days previously), and I was now eagerly anticipating this highlight of the trip. But that was two days hence. First we had the momentous concert the following evening.

∞

On the morning of October 3rd we awoke to media warnings of an imminent storm set to hit the Cork area later that evening. There had been talk of *Storm Lorenzo* – originally a category five Atlantic hurricane – the previous day when local news channels had debated the level of threat posed by the diminishing strength of the approaching winds, but that morning there was less ambiguity. The official met office declaration now was that south west Ireland would be affected by potentially dangerous high winds and rain peaking between the hours of 9 pm that evening and 6 am the following morning, and that during this time people should stay at home if possible and certainly avoid making any journeys that weren't absolutely necessary.

After everything having apparently conspired, successfully, to get me to this point, it seemed strange now that the peak force of what was being referred to as one of the worst storms to hit the area in recent times was going to coincide with the time Soraya and I were on stage that evening. There was no doubt that the storm would have an adverse effect on audience numbers, a deflating realisation that became worse when we arrived at The Schoolyard Theatre that afternoon to do our sound check and a solemn-faced theatre manager told us that the concert may even have to be cancelled. How on Earth could this be happening?

We continued to set up our equipment on stage with a *What will be will be* attitude, and after a straightforward sound check I took the opportunity to have a look around inside this old building where my mum had attended school. From the size of the place I estimated that no more than about a hundred children would have attended, and the minimum amount of renovation undertaken meant that much of the interior remained as it was a century ago, making it easy to become immersed in the atmosphere, the stories, exuding from the exposed original stonework. If one remained still enough. And so I sat alone in different spots, feeling the presence of Maisie and her schoolmates walking around and laughing, learning, dreaming…

∞

Looking out at the small audience sitting in the first few rows of the theatre I picked up my guitar in preparation for the opening song, *All the Rivers Gold*. The storm warning had prevented most people from venturing out, but in this moment I realised that that was quite perfect. We certainly weren't here for profit, so there was no disappointment from a commercial viewpoint, and having a smaller audience actually removed all the pressure from me and Soraya as performers and created an environment where we could simply relax with friends and immerse ourselves in the atmosphere of The School Yard Theatre.

Among the intimate audience was a young couple with a child who had come all the way from Sweden, and a long-lost Irish friend, Colette, who was there with her husband Sebastian. The last time I had met this lady was around the time of my daughter Rachel's birth in London in 1974!

It seemed, then, that right up to the last important detail of the freak weather conditions the universe had orchestrated the perfect scenario for me to fully engage with and exorcise the ghosts of the past. Even as we played the opening notes of that first song I sensed their crooked, wispy forms slowly beginning to fade, and all the troublesome patterns of the past somehow just falling away and disintegrating.

In the end the forecast storm never amounted to much more than a light gale on an evening that Soraya and I played our hearts out. Between pieces I talked about my mother and how it felt to be there, having traversed seventy years and seventeen thousand kilometres to arrive at that place in that moment in time. Because, of course, it wasn't just about playing a concert or knowing all the relevant history; it was about being there with an open heart, fully absorbing the feelings that had seemed to detach themselves from the walls, and the act of cleansing the very essence of the place, exorcising the ghosts, with the love in each note of the performance. As we reached the end of the final song, *Into Your Hands*, I experienced a deep sense of completion. All the questions and angst had dissolved into the peace of the moment, and if there had been any remaining ties there in that building for my mum, or me, they too simply vanished. The music and the love that Soraya and I had cultivated over many years had finally laid the ghosts to rest.

∞

Next morning as we awaited the arrival of the local historian who would drive us to my mum's childhood home, the gentle winds mocked the previous day's storm threat drama as little more than an over-reaction. Had it all been real? Did such an anticlimactic event really transpire, and with such ironic timing, within the brief period of last night's concert? It was another lesson in letting go, a case for simply living in the moment.

After a short car journey we arrived at the far end of Harrison's Place, a horseshoe-shaped estate about half a mile from Charleville town centre. Almost as soon as we stepped out of the car, the front door of a nearby house opened and an elderly man appeared, raising his hand in salute. This was the house.

As I began walking up the pathway to the house, the emotional significance of the occasion rapidly began to magnify in my mind. I was, after all, now truly walking in my mum's footsteps.

After some brief introductions were made by our driver/reporter/historian, I crossed the threshold into the narrow hallway, just as Maisie would have so many, many times before me, and immediately felt overwhelmed by the sensation that I was stepping straight into my family's past.

Waiting to greet me inside were the owner's wife – a very jolly little Irish lady – and her friend, and then, with perfect politician's timing, the local counsellor suddenly appeared, all smiles and handshakes. By the time we had all gathered in the little sitting room it was standing room only, so after a brief but fascinating little chat about my mum and grandparents and their lives in this very house, only Soraya and I were shown upstairs.

Looking in at the tiny bedrooms where Maisie and her siblings would have slept, perhaps dreaming of bright and exciting futures, I had a much clearer understanding of my mum's situation back then. With two small single beds and a wardrobe each room was just about filled to capacity, and I struggled to imagine how a family of ten had possibly coped in such cramped conditions. Little wonder my mum had wanted to escape this situation and find more space in the outside world as soon as she was old enough.

Next, we went outside to see the garden shed which, I was told, had remained unaltered since the time of my grandparents. It was in here that I really felt a connection with my grandfather the gamekeeper and fisherman who would have used this shed to store his equipment, prepare game for the table, or maybe just take some brief respite from the relentless tribulations of life. I happened to look up and there, immediately above my head, a large old rusty nail jutted out, still solidly, from the wooden support beam into which it had been hammered by hands long deceased. Hands with which I shared a blood tie, a unique DNA sequence that forged an unbreakable bond between us down through the years and the passing generations. Fleetingly, I felt Michael's presence in there with me, watching with my mind's eye as on that very nail he hung up a pheasant, or one of the plump silver salmon my mum had enjoyed at many a family meal.

That poignant experience concluded my visit to the past, and so much more. Soon afterwards we left Mum's old house and hometown, stopping off at Blarney castle – where Soraya and I both kissed the legendary Blarney **Stone for a bit of fun** – before heading back to Cork in preparation for the next day's early morning flight to England and the penultimate leg of our tour.

I now truly felt that all the old hungry ghosts were finally at rest and that this visit to Ireland had given me an amazing insight into how everything is, really, always perfect. Absolutely okay. Soon I would write a song called *Nothing Wrong at All* inspired by everything that came from my return to Celtic roots.

∞

When our three month music and workshop tour of Europe came to an end early in December 2019, Soraya and I were both pretty tired when we boarded the flight to Singapore. We had booked a two-week holiday in Thailand leading up to Christmas and were happy to be heading there for some rest and recuperation before returning home to Australia.

At this point there had been no talk of the new panic about a virus that would shortly become a global pandemic, so when we arrived in Thailand and Soraya began to display flu-like symptoms we weren't overly concerned, assuming that this was simply a consequence of our nomadic lifestyle over the past few months. Unperturbed, we therefore openly mingled with tourists from all over the world on the busy streets of Phuket. Before long, however, poor Soraya became quite ill with what we would later associate with Covid 19 symptoms: cough, fever, respiratory problems and loss of taste and smell. What was supposed to have been our holiday was severely curtailed as a result, and even a couple of weeks later when we arrived home on Christmas day Soraya still had a serious cough. By this time I too had developed similar symptoms which ran their stubborn course, so either I had picked up Soraya's flu or we'd both been infected with the emerging virus. There was indeed speculation months later that the virus may have been around in certain parts of the world much earlier than initially presumed, and certainly well before it came to general public attention, but in any event Soraya and I never took on any of the fear that was about to be unleashed upon the world.

— 2020. Challenges and Opportunities —

After recovering from whatever ailment we'd both come down with, **Soraya** and I settled back into our quiet life at *Mangalam* and soon began making plans for our 2020 European tour, which included booking June flights to England. We were now starting to hear about something called Coronavirus, or Covid 19, but didn't really know quite what to make of the situation until things suddenly took a very serious turn in March when the world entered a pandemic situation. Not long afterwards, social distancing was introduced and we were **very soon** cancelling all tour dates and applying for refunds on those June flights. I was particularly disappointed to have to cancel an event at a summer music camp in the Czech Republic as I regarded the prospect of giving a master class to seasoned professional musicians both challenging and exciting. Plans had also been made for a concert in a **state-of-the-art** contemporary theatre with a great sound system but, sadly, it was just not meant to be.

Around this time the media seemed to be busy generating fear twenty-four hours a day, conspiracy theories developed to massive proportions, and Australia became famous for running out of toilet paper! A lot of musicians were now turning their attention to playing online, so Soraya and I decided to make our daily practice a live concert over the internet just to offer a little respite to those who were confined to their homes, some of whom would be feeling lonely and afraid. It wasn't too big a step to incorporate our practice into the live social media scene since we always have our instruments conveniently on hand in the lounge in case we feel like playing a few songs, so for the next fifty-five days in a row we performed a half-hour song set to an online audience from all over the world. It was very moving to see all the emoji hearts flying in on-screen as we played, and to know that we could reach out in this way and share our feelings - quite magical, actually.

When the initial period of lockdown was relaxed in Australia and people began to venture out of their homes, we reduced our online sessions to just one a week before finally stopping when things appeared to be slowly returning to normal. This of course turned out to be a prematurely optimistic notion, as later developments concerning the virus would prove.

With our European tour cancelled and social interaction heavily curtailed, Soraya and I, in pleasant isolation at *Mangalam*, turned to other creative projects that otherwise would have been put on the back burner. There was a lot more gardening, some small renovation projects and, inevitably, much musical creativity, including a number of new songs for which I put together videos that I uploaded online. To begin with, I wrote *A Sense of Wonder*, a soaring piece that has the sort of yearning and spiritual quality that can only be expressed when it is genuinely and deeply felt – I really must have been in the zone at the time. Next came a song originally released as *Only Love Remains*, whose title I later changed to *A Perfect Song* as it is about the perfection that THIS is, and how we are witnessing the perfect song in the everyday flow of things. For the final mix I hired a cello player from an online source to perform some of the melodic lines, which is something I had never done before but it worked out very well and was quite affordable. I have since heard that many musicians and composers are using this kind of online platform now, and it seems a great, mutually beneficial way to sustain music with live musicians as opposed to using sampled sounds.

Somewhere in between these songs came a re-release of *Spiral* and two instrumental pieces, the longest of which, *River of Gold*, was an expression of my gratitude and love for the Gaula River in Norway, a place that had been my saving grace and refuge from overwork and family responsibilities for a number of years. A composition perhaps also partly influenced by the conditions of global isolation and the theme of sanctuary in which it was written, each of the twenty-three tracks – or movements – comprising *River of Gold* represent a personal memory of different pools on the wondrous river. Every year when I returned, usually in early June, the river would have changed its mood and course and I had many favourite perches where I loved to sit and be inspired.

Still loosely connected to the theme of angling, the second instrumental piece that just 'popped in' one day was *Fishing for Stars*. This is a tranquil work featuring pan pipes with alto flute, piano and guitar that I simply couldn't help recording. It only took me a day to set down the music, after which I made a nice little accompanying video – with lots of water in it, of course. This is the kind of music that literally flows easiest for – or rather *through* – me. No pun intended!

'*There is nothing either good or bad but thinking makes it so.*' These wise words from Shakespeare's *Hamlet* perhaps best summarise the meaning of the next song that came along, *Nothing Wrong at All*, which tells of the way I see things now. My life philosophy condensed and expressed in a single song.

For the final sound mix again I hired the cello player previously used on *A Perfect Song* and also a pianist from the same online source, so here I had certainly found an invaluable resource that was beneficial to composer, working musician and, ultimately, listener. Judging by the amount of positive feedback and comments I received for this song (and indeed for *A Perfect Song*), it appeared that many people really got the message behind it, suggesting that we are all beginning to see things differently now. And maybe just in time.

— Isolation and the 'Doing' Energy —

The restrictions imposed on daily activities by the Covid 19 pandemic, where everyone was asked to stay at home as much as possible, presented a certain opportunity for us to look inwardly in a way we usually don't have time for because what I call the 'Doing' energy is exercising powerful control over us. This is something we all have to come to terms with eventually, where the constant movement of thought is towards recreating the past and casting those memories ahead onto an apparent future. This future is only apparent because it is a reflection of the past and therefore has no reality other than as an idea. It is a difficult thing to notice because it's something that is learned over a lifetime and has an unconscious presence. From early childhood we are given a description of the world around us and soon we have a name for every object until everything becomes so familiar that we no longer see the beauty and freshness of things. We lose that sense of wonder experienced through the eyes of a baby who knows nothing about the world. Everything is experienced as a mystery until we begin to name it all, thereby gradually integrating ourselves as individuals into a description of the world that turns most things into a mundane experience based upon repetition. This leads to a false sense of security in what the greater part of humanity calls consciousness. It is nothing short of automation. All our planning for work, family, travel, recreation and the like is such an addiction and an identity we are so deeply immersed in that we become mesmerised and unable to see out. The whole plethora of things we do and make arrangements for has become a preparation for something we call 'life' in which the Doing energy effectively steals us away from the present moment where every true experience takes place. This so-called life then becomes a phantom-like idea that has no actual substance, one that seems akin to something like Christmas dinner where all the elements we hold so dear actually come together, such as family, friends, food, love and ultimately, dare I say it, happiness. It is this last thing called happiness that we are always heading for; everything we think we need in order to get to happiness is the craving that the Buddha referred to, and everything that gets in the way of that apparent movement towards happiness is the aversion. Craving and aversion are the bottom line, the foundation stones of suffering. Happiness is an idea until we discover that it is actually who we really are. Happiness is our true identity and is the only thing that remains after all the dross of the Doing energy has been stripped away.

With the chance to spend a lot more time at home I often sat and watched the movement of the Doing energy, noticing the way it is constantly trying to take over the muscles, the nervous system and the mind by projecting images onto an idea of the future; endlessly dredging the past for new ways to influence the road ahead. The way it works is now so clear to me that I have found myself bursting into laughter whilst sitting on my sofa, or just noticing a smile form on my face as I gaze through the foliage in the garden. The background of thought continues 'in the background' but is no longer taking me over. I am free now in the very place where happiness has been hiding all along. This present moment.

We can all go back to that place of not knowing if we learn how to 'stop the world' and enter into the mystery once again. The secret is to just notice **the thoughts** without getting **drawn in**.

For many of us 2020 was a wakeup call, a time of many changes and much speculation, but above all it was a continual unfolding of something that will always remain a mystery to us.

That is, until we give up trying to find a solution to something that always resolves itself in the end anyway. 'Panta rei' (*Everything flows*, Heraclitus).

The last song I completed in this strange year of global lockdown, *Running on Empty*, was an attempt to bring a bit of humour and light into the anguished situation, but it also has a deeper meaning which I always like to have in a song. I wanted to extend to everyone a message that we are all part of nature and therefore truly united. No separation. Human conflict always arises over beliefs and opinions because our entire illusory substance as separate personalities – or his/her stories – constantly needs to be defended or added to. And these perceived entities will never be satiated because they literally do not exist. They have no substance. When we disappear as an object facing other objects we reappear as the solitary subject that contains everything. And everything means the entire universe! Humankind is the universe gazing at itself in wonder.

With such a realisation comes empathy, peace, healing and mutual respect; a way out of the dark.

∞

The extra hours that became available for contemplation in 2020 turned out to be a very positive thing for me both inwardly and creatively. I began to look back on the years of drama that had thus far constituted this life of mine and, alongside my musical compositions, I started making notes of another kind. Memories. Musings. Snapshots of youth and lessons learned in adulthood. The joy of new life and the sadness when it has to leave. A spiritual journey with many treacherous pathways. A life shared in memoirs. And reflections.

On the road touring the globe with Soraya

Soraya and I on our wedding day

Mixed family blessings

Left: Brothers in arms. Outside in Mike's garden in Nassau. Below: With my sister. Bottom: A trip on Mike's boat in the Bahamas.

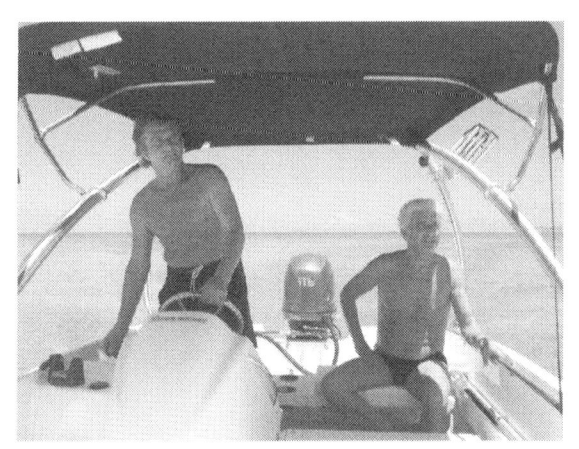

Me and Dad

Right: On the spot where mum and dad were married

Left: Outside my grandparents' (Bertie and Mabel) old house in Margate

A long road ahead after the enucleation.
But it will all happen now.

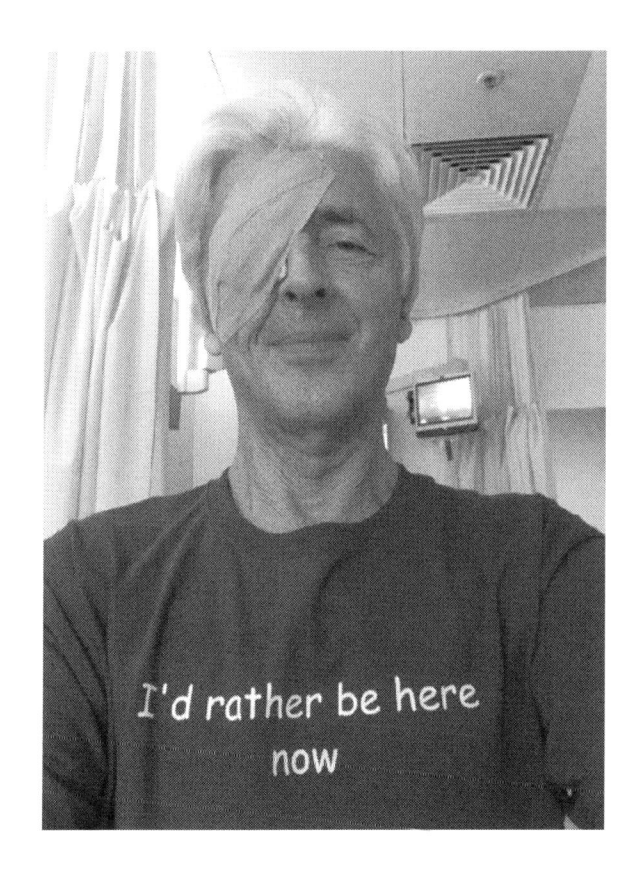

Return to Celtic Roots, Charleville, Cork 2019

The Schoolyard Theatre in Charleville; concert venue for Terry in 2019 and school for Maisie in the 1920s

Outside Maisie's old house. From left: Joe McGowan, Jerry O'Brien, Soraya Saraswati, Terry, Bridie O'Brien, Councillor Ian Doyle

Pictured with Terry and Soraya, a young Swedish family who made the trip for the concert on October 3rd, 2019.

Reflections

Reflections

— Glimpses of Truth —

Looking back there have been some pivotal moments in my transpersonal awakening process; poignant events often referred to as *epiphanies* in our apparent lives that I would call glimpses of the obvious.

Glimpse 1. This came from reading *The Hidden Side of Things* by Bishop Leadbeater when I was living in the shared house in Pandora Road in London. It began a process of looking deeper, accompanied by a growing sense of dissatisfaction with the norm, and from this came the desire, the need, to keep looking. I now see this as the raison d'etre for travelling and seeking in general. The first footstep on the path.

Glimpse 2. The second glimpse came from another book, *Freedom from the Known* by Jiddu Krishnamurti, which I read early one morning whilst lying in a hammock in Bombay. I have no idea which particular words triggered the shift, but I suddenly found myself unable to formulate a thought and spent the rest of the day wandering around the city in a state of peaceful reverie, sitting and watching the amazing world drift around me without the usual internal commentary going on. This is the different way of living that can be so hard to get used to and is in fact impossible to communicate to another person because language itself is caught up in the very substance, the actual working mechanics, of the illusion. The feeling didn't last as I simply wasn't ready for the big change required, and I needed several more years to infuse the experience of this incredible, enlightening day into my being.

Glimpse 3. The next occurred at the weekend Exegesis seminar that I was introduced to by my brother, Mike, where I was brought to the realisation that I was repetitively indulging in reactive or instinctive behaviour 'loops' that were draining my energy through causing me to live as a separate character. Following the revelation there came a sudden, explosive release – or redirection – of this energy, making it available to me now in a way that was both exhilarating and disturbing at the same time.

The Exegesis experience brought about a far stronger integration of the different or new way of Being into my life, and this time the true sense of living differently continued for several months.

Glimpse 4. The day I suffered a breakdown in my studio in 1996 was probably another glimpse, even though that happened as a result of over-work and stress rather than a conscious act of seeking. However, the effect of this seemingly catastrophic event – which was both mental and physical as well as much deeper and longer lasting – literally stopped me dead in my tracks from continuing to go off at a tangent from the mainstream flow of creation. The doctor's advice to give myself permission to do anything that made me feel right for at least two weeks (basically advising me to follow my heart rather than my head) on that occasion was what got me back into the flow more resolutely than ever. The advice turned out to be the best ever and I'll always be grateful for it.

Glimpse 5. This happened after the vivid 'death dream' I experienced in 2004, one of many such lucid dreams I experienced over a five-year period after moving to Australia in 2001. Following that particularly poignant dream there began a series of major changes in my life, circumstances that I could never have brought about from my previous state of consciousness or reality.

— Awakening, Life, Death and Meditation —

One of the things which has profoundly affected my life is the development of an ability to move on, or not to become attached to any specific thing in the flow of creation. That's because if I'm not moving with it then I'm trying to swim against the current, and that realisation has given me much more happiness and flexibility with less reactivity. It has actually allowed the completion of a lot of **suppressed** emotion, giving me permission to be who I am now as opposed to an idea of what I think I **am or should be**. This permits access into a world of not knowing, and not knowing isn't such a negative thing because it is wilfully entering into the mystery of life. If you haven't got a fixed or preconceived notion of knowing then anything is possible. Knowing blocks off certain paths, whereas not knowing allows for infinite potential.

Consciousness, the authentic 'I Am' presence, the sense of being, is not just the emptiness that contains everything, it is also the everything that it contains. In the same way that the reality of a dream is real to us at the time, so the universe is real to consciousness in the 'dream time'.

The sage sees the unreality of the real and the realness of unreality, living fully and consciously in a world where nothing especially matters whilst acting – or playing along – as though everything is important. One so wakened doesn't mind what, in particular, actually happens because everything is seen and known to be essentially equal. This is the world of the spiritual warrior who moves through life in a state of conscious waking, knowing that all of this is a dream and every actor or persona in the dream is an avatar of consciousness.

Whilst knowledge is essentially the product of thought and memory (and in that respect alone it is necessary in practical terms), wisdom on the other hand is closer to *being*; the representation of the present moment which is timeless and therefore has no place for time-based thought. Being in The Now requires a letting go of any idea of what *should be* happening and moving with the flow of what actually *is* taking place.

The separate thought-made self looks upon the present moment as emptiness because without itself as the centre of everything there is literally nothing. This is not an empty nothing, but rather a nothing that contains everything.

I find it helpful to remember that there is essentially nothing wrong with any level of experience. This game of life is a holographic journey that has been programmed with many levels to satisfy all players. Nothing in it really matters but there is nothing else that matters more than this. Hence the mystery, the paradox, of living.

There is only one question I regularly ask myself these days: *Is this – what is happening right now around me – enough?* In other words, am I moving towards something in the future or am I simply being here with whatever is happening right now in this moment? This is not some sublime or grandiose state of consciousness that has been attained or reached, but rather our natural state of innocent watching; the condition of being present in the background of what is happening all by itself. This is the place that children look from, only with the added dimension of certainty that all is indeed well and that no matter what may or may not arise here it doesn't assume the status of *problem*.

I am moved to act or not act according to the will of an intelligence that is the untouched pristine awareness which contemplates the world without interference. The action is indeed afoot but the movie is already 'in the can'.

Death

The basic fear of dying is the foundation for all our resistance to the flow of life, and in my earlier life there was never an exception to this norm. Any change of perspective or point of view that has occurred within me seems to have been quite erratic in terms of why I became dissatisfied enough with the normal or accepted view of reality to begin to look into things more deeply. As a new-born I was merely an expression of pure awareness with no idea about what the world is or even who or what I was. Then I gradually entered into an agreement with my parents and society to think that I am just this body and began to live under the shadow of the huge inevitability of death. I observed that everything and everyone arises and passes away, a process which, some day, would include this body and this personality called 'Terry' that I identified with so dramatically. And so began the search for something more than *just this*.

It all started with the fear of death and, I suppose to some extent, the search for a way out of that fear. This naturally involved religion and the afterlife, but also making myself so busy that I didn't have time to think about it. If we are open enough and given a little grace to help us along, we can begin to see through all of this quite easily and come to realise that any obvious question like *What is it that survives death?* will only open up a Pandora's box of mysteries that cannot be answered. The most important thing I have ever discovered is that there is no answer, and any attempt to find one is looking for a way out of an impossible conundrum. Eventually the mind boggles and just abandons all hope and gives up. This is the moment that we enter the real death, the ending of resistance to what is. The surrender that all the sages refer to where *I don't know* is actually a perfect answer. It is the ultimate act of humility from a personality that is made up of memory and stories.

I feel it is really important to keep 'Joe Black' close to us in life; to live knowing that there is a real possibility that death may come on this very day, to understand that waking in the morning is both a bonus and a blessing, and that with each sunrise we have the chance of a new beginning. I believe that going to sleep is a kind of rehearsal for dying and the only thing that makes it feel okay is our intrinsic belief that we will wake up in the morning. But what if we went to sleep each night without such assuredness that our eyes would be open again? I think we would live more fully, no longer taking things for granted or worrying over ultimately trivial matters and effectively dreaming our lives away. Not just awake but completely conscious of – and in – each moment with the absolute knowledge that the Grim Reaper is our constant companion. Ironically, we live in fear of the yawning emptiness of death without realising that death is perhaps our truest friend because it is the one thing that we know for sure; the reality that all things, including ourselves, must pass.

Meditation

My very first encounter with meditation was in the 1960s after I read a book on the subject in Romford Technical College library that outlined a method focusing on relaxing with each outbreath. The first time I tried it I found myself entering a deep state of relaxation that culminated in a dreadful sense of falling and losing touch with my bodily sensations. This in turn triggered a panic attack as I struggled desperately to regain contact with my body, an experience that scared me badly. I persevered with meditation from time to time, though, but nearly always came close to the deep sense of falling into nothingness and that dreadful panicky sensation of having nothing to grasp, nothing to hold onto as I began to fall.

Years later on Hydra when I was talking to my wise friend Roger about this he told me that he'd experienced the very same thing until one day he just let go and allowed himself to fall. He explained that it was basically the fear we all come across when asked to confront the abyss that lies at the entrance to awakening to who or what we truly are. Because our essential nature is consciousness, the mind interprets this 'gateway' as a void and therefore seeks naturally to turn away from what it sees as emptiness. It is a confrontation with the bare truth of what we really are, and in that sense it is the only real death.

And so I continued to gaze over the edge of the chasm inside, each time taking a little step further, further, until one day I literally just let go and leapt into the deep unknown. And the amazing thing was, nothing happened. No panic. No drama. No horror. Simply and uneventfully nothing. In letting go, the fear just fell away as the experience of emptiness or consciousness without an object was embraced as part of life. Living and dying happening together as we move from a world of time and measure to the only place where everything really happens. The present moment.

For more than twenty-five years I meditated every morning with the view that there was something to be gained from leaving the physical and entering into some kind of extrasensory realm where lay all that could be deemed spiritual. It was something akin to an addiction, actually. Now, however, I feel the spirit so deep within my bones that it enables a physical connection with our marvellous Earth that is so very nourishing, bringing me the inspiration to play music from the heart that communicates with others. When this occurs and 'I' disappear, becoming like the open tube of the flute through which the wind blows, that's when the magic happens. The less I Am the more powerful is the sharing with those who recognise themselves in the magical vibration of music.

People tend to use my music for healing, relaxation, inspiration, creative endeavours and yoga (it has also been dubbed 'Inspirational background music'), and I think, even if sometimes only subconsciously, they recognise that they are listening to something that has been channelled from a different place; familiar and yet perpetually mysterious. With this comes the desire to make a connection with it, to immerse themselves more deeply, however fleeting or tenuous the experience may be.

I have always used listening as a precursor to the meditative state, but for me it doesn't really matter what sounds are happening; they all simply arise from nothing and go back to nothing. The secret is to allow them to rise and fall naturally in consciousness, and this is what leads into the meditative state. Consciousness without an object.

Nowadays I don't practice any formal meditation as such, but having been 'on the cushion' for more than twenty-five years in the past, I've reached a stage where the cushion is the world and meditation has become integrated into life in both action and rest.

— Addictions —

Like most people I've had mild addictions along the way through my life, none of which have caused me a major problem. Events could easily have turned out very differently, however, were it not for some innate bodily aversions and, in some cases, a fair helping of luck.

Drugs

Having a Dad who was a GP meant that in my youth I had some access to prescription drugs that were newly on the market, and I remember the 'circulars' from drug companies that used to come through the letterbox with a couple of sample pills taped to the top corner of the glossy ads. I clearly recall the heading on one of these: *'There is nothing so conducive to sleep as a good book, except perhaps Nodulen 25'.*

It was literally a time of open experimentation on whatever guinea pigs would peel back the tape and take the medication. I was given pills for just about every kind of symptom – pain, anxiety, depression, insomnia – more or less at the drop of a hat.

In his mind, and of course due to the ignorance of the times, Dad was just being a doctor and helping me as best he could, but at the age of thirteen I couldn't go to sleep most nights without first taking my tranquilisers. I now know that I had become addicted to them, but for some reason the seriousness of such side effects was either unknown or largely disregarded back then. I have no recollection of how it happened, but over the next couple of years I managed to stop taking them altogether. It could have been that my dad realised the danger just in time for me, but unfortunately this wasn't the case with my poor old mum who spiralled downward through prescription drug dependency into terrible anxiety and depression which eventually resulted in her tragic early death.

Cigarettes

I remember my first cigarette at the age of thirteen. I had been attracted to the smell of tobacco for some time, so when a friend opened a new silver case full of Gold Leaf ciggies one afternoon and offered me one I fully expected a pleasant experience. I certainly wasn't prepared for the lung-wrenching coughing fit that came from that very first inhalation of tobacco smoke. There are some things that stick in the memory and that was one for sure. The problem was that being thirteen years old I didn't want to lose face with my friends so I had to persevere until the poor old lungs gave in and accepted the situation. I think peer pressure is how most of these bad habits begin; through wanting to be part of the gang or avoiding the possibility of becoming an outcast. I'm sure this goes back to ancient times when exclusion from the tribe meant certain death. So I trained myself into casual smoking in my early teens then later, when I could afford it, I became a real smoker, a true nicotine addict. I smoked No.6 and Old Holborn roll ups for a few years, but fortunately managed to wean myself off them again over a period of time. I was never tempted to resume at any point, although I did smoke a few rolled up leaves called *Beedies* during my time in India.

Cannabis

I also clearly remember my first experience of cannabis, that first drag on a joint, and how my body immediately seemed to reject the substance. Within seconds I felt faint and weak and had to lie down. Not long afterwards I was violently sick. When I looked in the mirror a pallid and ghostly caricature of Terry Oldfield was reflected. After that initial experience I was naturally terrified to try it again, but as with smoking cigarettes in my teens the fear of alienation from the group was too strong, so I had to endure several more nightmare sessions before my body eventually surrendered to the drug. By the age of sixteen I was a regular dope smoker, and when I later became a roadie for *Formerly Fat Harry* I had the additional responsibility of keeping the band, and myself, well supplied with the drug. Lord knows how we survived all those road trips over Europe with me driving around half-stoned most of the time.

Alcohol

With alcohol I was more fortunate because although the pressure was there to join in with the sessions of drinking endless pints in the pub, my body literally put its foot down and refused to give in to the situation. Every time I tried to get drunk I vomited and was incapable of doing anything at all apart from lying flat and feeling dizzy. To this day I can't have more than one drink without experiencing these severe effects, and I thank the universe for protecting me in this way. I do love the taste of peaty single malt whisky, but thankfully I'll never be able to drink more than one measure at a time.

LSD

Hallucinogenic drugs were a different story again. In my late teens and early twenties I experimented considerably with these, including things like mescaline and magic mushrooms, and I can even remember once driving through London whilst 'on a trip'. It felt as though the van was actually bending around the corners, and I was extremely lucky that this did not end in disaster. Thankfully, I was never tempted to try any of the harder stuff such as speed, cocaine or heroin, and I stopped taking drugs altogether around the time I began travelling.

— Creating Music —

There are nearly eight billion of us here on planet Earth, all with different viewpoints of the same mental landscape. We each look out upon the world from a unique vantage point and therefore see things differently. When Terry plays his flute he is sharing a personal and authentic view of things as we all do in our own myriad ways. As I sit in my garden in the early morning listening to the sounds of nature, every bird I hear singing is doing that very same thing; all one consciousness playing through the apparent separateness of itself.

This explains the wonderful diversity of taste and expression in music, why we are all the same and yet very different. Consciousness *is* everything so it can express itself *as* anything. The way I play the flute is different to how others play, yet ultimately it is the same flute player. As the Hindu myth reflects, *With his flute Krishna creates the universe.*

The thinking mind with its abundant potential for acquired knowledge is both wonderful and, of course, absolutely necessary, and we learn to play a musical instrument in much the same way that we learn to ride a bicycle or drive a car. The technical or physical side of things crucially must be addressed. When I began to learn the flute my fingers needed many hours of intense practice to reach a place of ease in finding their way about the strange key work. Producing enough pressure in the breath to create a nice tone was hard work, and learning how to breathe properly was not easy either. It all needed determination and effort over a period of time because it is absolutely essential that the body is attuned to the instrument in a way that allows the mind to take over the practical running of things, just as the heart beats and the breath happens by itself. This skillful blending of practised technique and 'not knowing' or emptiness allows a freedom of expression to come through that is unique to the instrument but at the same time not special, because it is always the same thing, the same player. No separation. No single act of expression is more important than another. It is all the same and all things are equal.

Really profound expression comes through wherever there is a genuine lack of self-importance. Authenticity is key here. A musician is only a musician when playing music; everything else is merely an idea. When I say, *I am a flute player*, that is only an idea or a concept, whereas true musical expression comes from a place of uniqueness and authenticity that is not merely reflecting past experience or telling a story; it is when thought drops away and the musician becomes the instrument for divine expression. This authenticity shines through so clearly in the natural world and that is why I find just being in nature so restorative and inspiring. There I know I will always find my own true nature and if there is authenticity here it will be naturally reflected back in an ongoing process of self-revelation.

It is very easy to get stuck or to dry up whilst dealing with the so-called 'Muse' because she never gives away any of her secrets outside of the present moment. The false Muse, or Maya as we sometimes call her, is always impersonating the real thing by pretending that what she has to offer is fresh and new, whereas all she can ever dip into is the past which is then flung out upon the future. This is actually exemplified in the world of music sampling and looping; the practice of copying and pasting sound fragments or bits of half-forgotten inspirations that were true in their time, but now exist as part of a huge pile of patterns that many modern day musicians assemble like musical jigsaw puzzles and then put their names to these. I may sound rather haughty in saying this, but in the world of truth there is nothing but truth. And real truth is an ongoing thing that has no opposite.

Quite often when working with live musicians – particularly those who are used to playing in an orchestra – I have noticed that between their performance parts they will pass the brief periods of inactivity by flicking through a newspaper or magazine which they then deftly put down just before playing again. They are very skillful players, yet these are often the ones who ask me how I learned to play and improvise so freely. I point out that I have had no formal training and that mine is not a learned skill but actually something quite the opposite; an 'unlearning' that needs the emptiness of a beginner's mind. To start with, the fingers and the breath need much physical practice in order to develop technique, but there comes a time when focusing on all of that needs to fall away and the body itself become part of the instrument, leaving the heart open to the ebb and flow of the divine melodies of creation.

These days when I finish a song or a piece of music I have the privilege of being able to say that I really like it, or not, because I have no feeling of ownership in the sense that it is not *really* my piece; it happened just as the heart beats or the garden spade moves through the earth with a crunch, or the kookaburra titters in the tree above. An artist is only an artist when in the act of creation. If I say I am a musician that would be true only when I am playing. In other words, I am all that stands between 'the singer and the song'.

There is often, of course, a mundane and practical side, too. After all, most artistic creation is, usually through necessity, a product the artist hopes will be popular and sell, and I am certainly no different in that respect. An audience is therefore essential, but thoughts of the recipient never enter my own creative process – the only exception to this over the years has been when I have made a few remixes purely as a commercial venture. I do love engaging people with my music, whether it's used for healing purposes, meditation, relaxation or a brief respite from the chaotic outer world, but it's not a purely altruistic thing because I only really think about the listener when the work is finished and out there. It's more a matter of having to do it, mostly because of the focus, the edge to life that it gives. That feeling is addictive and I find life rather difficult and less meaningful if I can't work, but other artists, not only musicians, say the same. It's not merely an urge but, I feel, an energy flow thing that manifests as a compulsion which, if not indulged, makes the artist restless, irritable and feeling unfulfilled.

Creating music is a wonderful tool for bringing the whole maelstrom of thinking to a halt (and I often wonder whether I would still compose if nobody ever listened), but I'm sure that any naturally expressive person would consider all creative processes rewarding in how they put the creator in touch with him/herself and the inexhaustible flow of energy and power that is always there, but only in this present moment which is eternity unfolding.

— Why the Flute? —

When we speak, we can only speak from what we know. Otherwise, it's called channelling, which is what happens when I make myself available while improvising with the flute.

In my youth I listened to a great deal of music – often while stoned of an evening at the shared house in Pandora Road, and also when working in Virgin's shop in Notting Hill Gate – but I can't say that any musician has ever strongly influenced me or my playing, which I think was a good thing because it allowed me to find what I believe was my true and authentic path in music. A possible exception might be Leonard Cohen, whose expressions of life and philosophy in music certainly did resonate with me. Leonard even offered to record a track with me one time, but other plans got in the way and I had to decline. I since regret turning down that wonderful opportunity to record a song with him as it would probably have been my greatest hit!

Apart from that, the only musician I have ever perhaps come closest to emulating is American composer and flautist Paul Horn, particularly on his live album, *Inside*, which was recorded in the Taj Mahal.

There was a bit of a confused time when I tried to learn to play the saxophone and the oboe, but I gave up both when I read somewhere that they would be bad for my embouchure with the flute. I know that a lot of saxophonists also play the flute but I have noticed that most of them have a rather breathy sound when playing the latter instrument, so in the end I gravitated back to flute and pan pipes. Nevertheless, I have played a number of instruments on my various recordings, including keyboards, guitar, ocarina, Indian tabla, Irish whistle, Irish low whistle, piccolo and pan pipes, in addition to various types of flute such as the alto, bass, concert, bansuri and shakuhachi. And, of course, vocals!

Reflections

When Mike and I formed our band *Barefoot* in 1968 I had no real musical talent and just strummed away on the three guitar chords I had learnt or played a little bit of bass, somehow managing to get away with it up to a point. I was literally busking it, trying to pass for something that I really didn't believe I could be at the time.

Similarly, when I discovered the flute I had no idea at all what was going to happen. By that time I knew that I wanted to be a musician but still could not bring myself to believe it was possible. I practised and experimented with the instrument, harbouring no real hope of success but doing it anyway, taken over by an energy and aspiration that seemed totally beyond any meagre efforts of mine to play music. This is the conundrum that we all have to face; taking the great leap of faith into the void, going beyond a self that is made up of all our limiting beliefs and patterns. The feeling is like being possessed by something that knows its way clearly beyond anything that the personal self could ever attain. This is the awakening of intuition where a deeper connection with the inner sense of 'just knowing' is made, where true knowledge is allowed to be expressed in the freshness of creation, and without which there is little chance of stepping into freedom from the known. I think that is why I love to improvise so much when I play; not improvising in the commonly accepted rock or jazz sense, where certain specific and somewhat constraining rules have to be observed, but in the sense of complete freedom of expression, following only the natural physics of harmony rather in the way nature herself adheres only to the rules of the harmonic web of creation.

Perhaps the Covid 19 pandemic, which at the time of writing seems to be instigating a reprogramming of humanity, is one of those rare exceptions when nature breaks the rules. Throughout the world there currently exists the same resistance and pain that I experienced in those early days whilst making the transition towards becoming a real musician, and there is also the impression that, despite our best efforts to explain and control the natural and inevitable changes that are happening, we are being taken over and carried along by a force majeure. After all, we are just one of the myriad species on this planet and nature will most likely deal with us as she deals with everything else.

— My Way of Composing Music —

I have often been asked how I compose new music. Is it all recorded or feverishly written down as the muse wanders by? Do I sit down at the computer with a particular idea in mind, tap *Record*, and improvise for a period of time, inspiring myself with the unfolding music and perhaps saving the best bits?

There is an underlying tendency for we humans to think far too much about most things (certainly more than is actually necessary), the result being that we create enormously complex explanations in a futile effort to understand something that cannot be understood in that way. This is when the *need* to understand overrides true understanding. We are encouraged to do this from early childhood and so in that respect become disadvantaged from the start. This is all part of the game of life where we get caught up in the illusion of our own importance.

The truth is, with nearly all of my albums – and certainly those since about 2015 – the entire process is spontaneous, including when I enter the studio and pick up the flute. For me, that's the way it *has* to be if the music is to be real. A lot of people who enjoy my music say how my playing touches their heart, seems to somehow, enigmatically, communicate with their souls. Blogs and reviews comment that I have a special talent or 'gift' which allows me to play in a way that resonates deeply with the listener, which is very humbling and satisfying in the sense that it gives me joy to know that people can be moved, soothed or healed just by listening to the music that comes from **this apparent** me.

When I comment that I'm just the vehicle, or conduit, through which creation expresses itself, many naturally assume that I am being modest, or perhaps deflecting the embarrassment of such a hefty compliment, but I am simply stating a fact that I have long since come to recognise. I can only play in this honest and powerful way if I make myself open and available to something immeasurably greater than myself. It's understandable that people want to examine, pin down, or quantify the specific 'secret' elements responsible for the creation of such music in order to completely understand them and, in the case of other musicians, perhaps also replicate. But instrumental technique, breathing and the person of Terry Oldfield are just the essential physical aspects – the automation – required for the music to happen (just as the flute itself without a player is little more than a silent lump of polished metal with holes in it), whereas the music itself is a non-physical thing wherein lies the power, the very essence of The Great Mystery. That's why I mostly have no idea what each successive note is going to be when I play; it really does unfold in the moment, and it's a 'process' that is every bit as moving, exhilarating and, frequently, puzzling to me.

The 'enigmatic connection to something profound yet familiar' that my listeners often claim to feel is in fact this recognition of oneness, or creation itself, that flows through here. In this sense they are quite correct to use words such as 'recognition', 'familiarity', 'connection' and so on to articulate their experience, but less accurate in crediting Terry Oldfield as the only source from which the music originates. I am at best an essential link in a communication chain through which the universe can speak to all of us. Think about it: after a fulfilling, pleasant or emotional conversation with a loved one, how many of us will give exclusive credit to the telephone?

It is wonderfully enlivening to play a musical instrument without knowing in advance what note you're going to play next, and that is perhaps the best way I can describe it in terms of musical performance. It's rather like what might happen if you ask someone to spontaneously sing or hum a passage of notes which expresses how they're feeling in that moment. If the person is stressed or angry, the notes that emerge are likely to be short, erratic or loud, whereas a more serene mood will result in soft, sustained and pleasant tones. I do pretty much the same except my voice is the flute or panpipes, but of course, playing these wind instruments is quite close to using the human voice in that I also use my breath, tongue and lips to produce each note.

Some musicians find this idea of simply allowing the music to unfold with each moment in time a very scary notion indeed. Classically trained performers would probably regard it as the polar opposite to their desired scenario, which is to clearly know every passage of notes in every piece of music to be performed. If something is written down and practised for performance there is of course some scope for interpretation, but pure, fresh inspiration comes through being available to be 'played'.

Nowadays I never know when I'm going to start composing a new piece. I could just amble into my studio and several hours later something has been born. I couldn't walk in and think, *Right, I'm going to compose some music now*. I really have no idea what's going to happen.

That certainly was not, *could* not be, the case when I was writing film music, which has to be composed to particular specifications involving set visuals, pace, mood and strict timing – not to mention a deadline. That in itself wasn't especially restrictive as there was still plenty of opportunity for personal creativity within those parameters; rather, it was the attitudes of some of the producers that could be inhibiting. Having to please such individuals – which often equated to pandering to their fickle personalities – was an aspect of the business that I had particular trouble with, and the main reason why I never really loved composing for film and TV. I have always preferred to work alone, so I'm very grateful for the complete musical freedom I now enjoy where I hardly ever plan a project; it just falls into place as part of the natural flow of things.

For me, being creative and composing music is therefore simply about making myself available to that which is, and then it all happens by itself or through me. That's why the question, *'How do you write music?* is impossible for me to answer because I honestly don't know. It can only happen when I (thought) am no longer there to get in the way.

— My Peaceful Passion —

I have always preferred to spend time with people on a one-to-one basis and never liked, in the words of D.H Lawrence, 'trooping off in a crowd'. I like it when two individuals can just relax and connect on a deeper level. Group situations often activate the ego in a way that sees people just voicing every thought that wanders through with an over-inflated sense of importance, or rehearsing their next line in the conversation, waiting to be the one to speak, the knowledgeable one, rather than listening. There is no opening up or sharing, only an eagerness to score points or earn approval, which only enforces the sense of separateness that is actually the root cause of all suffering.

Fishing has taken me to some of the most sublime places on this Earth, moving me to stand in great rivers, sometimes under the midnight sun. I have made countless trips to the River Tweed over the years – which almost became a home away from home for me – where my biggest fish has been a thirty-five pounder, taken from Norham on the lower river. A photo of me with that salmon made the centrefold of *Trout and Salmon* magazine, for which I have written several articles on salmon fishing.

On another river I saw a moose swim across the flow through a morning mist that blended with his breath as a heron glided past, and there have been times when I've laughed out loud and jumped for joy with only the kingfisher as silent witness. I have also wept bitterly upon the river bank. Nature tends to bring our feelings to bear upon her with such innocent compassion and a recognition that is more akin to being. The answer to any question is right there in the flowing waters, and as I would raise up my eyes from river to forest the flow continued in the greenery; the trees alive with a movement that overflowed into everything, and what would be looking was stillness itself. The very thing perceived.

As a boy growing up in the 1950s I was accustomed to meals of meat and two veg, and as a young angler I was also inured to killing and eating some of the fish I caught. Being part of a Catholic family meant that I always ate fish on Fridays anyway, so back then I thought nothing about these habitual and ritualistic eating habits.

I now believe that if I am going to eat something I have to be capable of harvesting or killing the food myself. When I first reached this moral conclusion and realised that, for me, this would exclude certain animals, I simply gave up eating them. These days I very rarely eat a fish or a bird either, but I rest in the certainty that I am actually capable of killing one if I need to. We tend to leave all of that messy business – the part we'd rather not contemplate – to abattoir workers, commercial fishermen, butchers and the like, adopting attitudes similar to those surrounding death in Western society; sweeping it under the carpet and, like the rabbits of *Watership Down*, living in a world of convenient denial.

When we were living at 21 Monks Way in Reading I used to cycle down the lanes to a small bridge over a stream called *The Holy Brook*, a small tributary of the River Kennet. I remember the feelings that ran through me as a seven-year-old boy gazing down at those magical waters. I learnt to long-trot a worm (allow it to float naturally downstream) on a float from that bridge, and caught many of the chub and fiery perch that were lying in wait there, facing upstream in the current among the waving weeds, poised to snatch a morsel of food or ambush an unsuspecting aquatic creature. I got to know about these fish through reading a book called *Mister Crabtree Goes Fishing*, in which father and son explore the vast world of angling together. I also used to get *The Angling Times* delivered along with my Beano comic... how spoilt was I?

In 2019 I had the opportunity to take a trip down memory lane and visit the old house in Monks Way. Strangely, I felt very little connection there – that is, until I began to wander down the lane towards *The Holy Brook* where all those childhood feelings began to be triggered by recollections of fishing trips with my bike. Unfortunately the landscape has changed so much that I couldn't find the bridge where I used to fish, but I made a promise to myself that I would return one day.

Months later I had a dream in which I was walking with my backpack and carrying a fishing rod along Monks Way in search of

The Holy Brook bridge. I awoke with a deep sense of lingering peace, soon followed by an idea that flashed into my head. I grabbed my phone from the bedside cabinet and, taking advantage of modern technology, zoomed into the Reading area and Monks Way using *Google Earth*. With the speed at which a friend's face is recognised in a crowd, all-of-a-sudden I saw *Holy Bridge* and realised where I had gone wrong searching for it the previous year. I now have a definite plan to go back and stand on that bridge when travel opens up again after the current pandemic situation.

Another spot on the River Kennet I frequented in those early days of angling was the bridge at Burghfield, next to the gravel pits, where large pike were reputed to dwell alongside the legendary tench and carp. I remember arriving there one day in the dead of winter when most of the water was frozen over apart from just a few parts where the river flow was faster. I was so keen at that time that I endured the pain of cold hands and feet as I fished in those little bits between the ice, hardly looking up from the water, happily catching perch and chub even if the pike were proving to be elusive.

One late afternoon I lost track of time and my dad came looking for me when it had become too dark for me to cycle home safely. There he found me, standing on the frozen surface of the water, lost to everything but the magic of the river, nature and fishing. This was another spot that I failed to locate in 2019 but, again thanks to *Google Earth*, it has been added to the itinerary of my next 'memory lane' trip.

Some of these more special or poignant angling memories, like old, dead friends, occasionally come to visit in dreams or spontaneous recollection...

Happy Birthday

On my eighth birthday Dad gave me a pike rod and I was absolutely delighted. Not long after (it might even have been that very day) I was speeding off down Cow Lane on my bike with the sole purpose of catching my very first pike. To me this was something of a mythical beast full of lurking, predatory guile and, frankly, from the pictures I had seen of the species, I was a little afraid of the prospect of landing a creature with such deadly-looking sharp teeth.

I didn't stop at *The Holy Brook* on that particular occasion as I had spotted an old man fishing for pike further on across the fields on the River Kennet. He looked like he knew exactly what he was doing so I positioned myself at a respectable distance from him, but close enough to be within the 'hotspot' if indeed that was what this area was. Almost trembling with anticipation I made my first cast into the depths and slowly began retrieving my big spinner in a focused attempt to imitate a small, vulnerable fish heading towards the river bank. With every cast I imagined those large and cunning eyes catching sight of my lure, triggering the pike's predatory instincts... a swish of its big forked tail raising it from the river bed... now giving chase to my artificial meal, moving stealthily behind it, preparing to strike... I tensed up in readiness for the scenario that played out over and over in my head, willing it to become reality, fingers tightening their grip on my new fishing rod in preparation for that moment.

When it came, I was ready. The strike was sudden. Sharp. Deadly. Had my lure been a live fish rather than a metallic imitation of one, it would have entered oblivion in the blink of a human eye. The fight was lively but surprisingly short since the pike that had taken my lure that morning was no more than a foot long. But I was over the moon with happiness. It was both my first pike and the biggest fish I had ever caught, and that was all that mattered to me. My cat Ming was pleased, too; I gave it to her for supper!

Thames Trout

Thames trout are very rare indeed. Thanks to the merciless activities of the industrial age, pollution of the mighty Thames and its tributaries at one stage almost saw the river being declared 'dead'. Happily, things have steadily improved in more recent times, but even now it is still something of an event when a brown trout or a sea trout turns up in an angler's landing net.

With many thousands of hours spent on this marvellous river between the ages of six and sixteen, over the course of ten years I was fortunate enough to catch just two of these elusive fish.

Each one has its own story...

The Island at 'The Springs'

My friend Paul and his family lived on a property called *The Springs* on the middle reaches of the River Thames. It was a beguiling place that had a small island opposite a stream originating from the spring after which the property was named. I was lucky enough to be granted permission to fish there whenever I wanted, and this island became my favourite place for a number of years until my focus turned outward from fishing towards the world at large. I very rarely saw another soul when I visited 'my island', and this was the place where I fell deeply in love with solitude.

The little stream flowed into the main river at the end of the island, and it was there that I would stalk the giant chub lurking just under the bank using a so-called free lining technique where no floats or weights are added to the line. I would simply tear off a chunk of bread from one of the loaves of fresh white bread I took with me and squeeze this into a paste on the hook. My preferred method then involved throwing a few loose bread pieces into the stream just above the island end where the two currents met. The bread would sink gently towards the tangle of roots that made a hollow under the bank, the place where the big chub lay watching for any morsels that might pass by. I would then wait until a fish emerged to take the bread, giving it time to develop confidence in the menu and a taste for the next piece that would follow; the one disguising my hook. With my heart galloping I would then cast out, every nerve on edge as I watched the bread slowly sinking on its course downstream towards those roots. Suddenly, a big chub would take my bread and the battle would begin.

I lost many of these fish in the tangle of roots, but some of them stayed on long enough to be landed, whereupon they would spend the next few hours in my submerged keep net until I released them at the end of the session after one last admiring look.

One day the chub seemed to be absent for some reason, so I changed tactics a little and rather nonchalantly cast the bread out into the centre of the stream, watching it disappear into the depths as it was carried along in the current. To my great surprise the line suddenly went tight on this first new cast as a large fish took the bait. I assumed it was a chub that had moved out into the stream, but when the golden flank of the fish came into sight just below the surface I was dumbstruck. I had absolutely no idea what it could be until, as I guided the thrashing, writhing thing into my landing net, I saw the spots and realised that I had caught something amazing. A Thames trout. One of the rarest of fish.

After weighing and admiring my wonderfully coloured prize – five pounds of pure magic to a ten-year-old boy – I returned the beautiful creature to the river and watched, entranced, as it swam away. I remember sitting down on the bank for quite some time before I had any urge to cast again, knowing that what I had just experienced was so special that it could never be repeated.

Reading Weir

One winter morning I asked my dad to drop me off a few miles upriver from Reading weir on the River Thames, with the understanding that he would then pick me up at the weir later that day. Carrying only a small backpack along with my rod, landing net and a selection of lures, travelling so light would enable me to cast and walk comfortably as I steadily made my way back downstream towards the prearranged rendezvous with my dad in a few hours' time.

Since I would be spinning for pike and perch, both of which were plentiful in the river at the time, this plan also meant that I'd be covering a lot of ground, giving myself a better chance of hooking more fish. And so I began to spend what would be several hours in a world of my own creation, lost in the effects created by current and light upon the water, happily casting and walking whilst carefully avoiding the many waterfowl that abounded along the banks of the Thames.

By the time I arrived down at the weir I hadn't caught a thing, but I was in a tranquil mood as I looked over the parapet at the fast and bubbling water below. Here again there was an island separated by a small stream, and as I crossed over the bridge I saw a big splash in a swirling pool close to the bank. Assuming this was a foraging pike my disposition immediately changed to one of avid concentration as I carefully approached the water. The first cast led to nothing, but seconds after the spinner hit the water second time round there was another splash and the rod bent over as a fish dived back down into the furious flow.

This must be a big pike... The pleasing thought entered my mind without realizing at the time just how instrumental the powerful whirlpool was in helping the fish to go down into the murky depths. I struggled to regain the line that had stripped from my reel until suddenly the fish came up and jumped clean out of the water! Never before had I played a jumping fish and I very nearly dropped my rod in surprise. After a lengthy, hefty tussle the fish finally came to the net and for the second time in my young life I saw the golden flank and tell-tale spots of a Thames trout. Hours of fishing had passed that day without so much as a bite, dissolving my hopes of success, but I had been grateful for the time on the river spent in magical tranquility. Then completely out of nowhere, as though rewarding me for my gracious resignation, it felt like Mother Nature herself had just gifted me something really special; a second jewel from the crown of Old Father Thames.

Connecting with the Prince

An enduring memory was forged through my friendship with the late environmentalist and entrepreneur, Orri Vigfússon, whom I met while working on a film for the North Atlantic Salmon Fund (NASF) which he founded. Orri and I once travelled together to Asturias in northern Spain – and the most southern rivers of the salmon migration – to spread the word about the plight of the Atlantic salmon, and I had even visited his Icelandic home where he was kind enough to take me to his private club to fish on the big Laxa River.

Through our association with the NASF, Orri invited me to a fundraising dinner in Aberdeen in the 1990s where Prince Charles, a patron of the fund, was guest speaker. After checking into the host hotel amid an assault course of security, that evening I adorned my formal gear and went down to the dining hall where a group of NASF members were all lined up to greet the prince –

who eventually arrived, to the tune of bagpipes, wearing a blue tartan kilt! As the heir to the British throne steadily made his way along the assembled line shaking hands and making light conversation with certain individuals, I tried to imagine what, if anything, he might say to me in order that I might prepare a response. When the prince eventually arrived in front of me he seemed to hesitate for a second and then, to my astonishment, closed his eyes and raised his joined hands in the traditional gesture of *Namaste*, before bowing gently and continuing down the line. To this day I have no idea why he did that. I was the only one of at least twenty people whose hand he didn't shake. Perhaps he thought I was Indian, or maybe there was some kind of spiritual recognition. I just don't know. But it was quite a mysterious happening, to say the least.

Dancing with Death

Statistically, fishing has a surprisingly high accident rate, ranging from painful falls on rocks or river embankments to barbed hooks becoming embedded in fingers (an injury that invariably requires the intervention of a medical professional), all the way up to drownings and other fatalities. It's not something we tend to consider much as we prepare for our relaxing day on the river when thoughts are more likely to be dominated by images of specimen salmon, sea trout or whatever the quarry may be, but the potential danger is always there nonetheless.

In the early spring of 1991 I was standing on the banks of the river Wye watching the swollen river with rod in hand, wondering how to approach the fishing. I remember the year because I had just bought a new CSK special edition Range Rover and it was sitting proudly behind me a few hundred yards back from the river.

As I was contemplating the water, a huge section of the ground beneath my feet suddenly gave way. Somehow I managed to turn and sink my hands into what was left of the muddy bank, which prevented me from falling into the water but left me hanging on for dear life with the lower half of my body immersed in the powerful river current. Bizarrely, I remember being concerned that I had dropped my fishing rod in the fall – which says something about we fishermen – but after about a minute I realised that it wouldn't be possible to climb back up the slippery sheer wall of the river edge, and there was no one nearby to help me out of the predicament. So I only had one option. I just let go and allowed the current to carry me to my fate.

I had watched a film made by Hugh Falkus on how to survive after falling into a fast current wearing waders and that probably saved my life because I didn't panic and literally just went with the flow, carried along the river on my back, gazing up at overhanging trees that allowed occasional glimpses of a powder blue sky. Luckily there were no rapids ahead, so I began to steer myself gradually towards a shingle bank where I found my feet and was able to stand up. I was freezing cold and shaking like a leaf, but my car wasn't too far away and thankfully I always packed a spare set of emergency clothes in the back for just such an occasion. I quickly dried off and changed clothes in the spacious Range Rover, and with the engine and heater running I began to warm up again.

It wasn't long before I felt completely normal once more, almost as though nothing had happened, so I went back to the river to see if by some great fortune I could find my fishing rod and was delighted to discover that it got snagged up in a branch not very far from where I fell in. Once again I had experienced that little touch of the green, the luck of the Irish (thanks Mum!).

Another time I experienced such uncanny good fortune was while fishing on the Bridge Pool on the River Gaula in Norway when I dropped my favourite fly box into the water while wading deep. It contained my own wonderful collection of flies that I had spent many happy hours tying in the music studio in between recording. There was a gut-wrenching feeling of sadness – and probably a couple of loud heartfelt expletives – as I watched the box floating off downriver. I even remember thinking at the time how much better it would have been if instead I'd dropped my wallet into the bubbling flow of the river.

Later on that afternoon when I had just about recovered from the initial disappointment of losing all my precious hand-tied flies I moved five miles further downriver to a pool we called Langoy. Now standing on the river bank rather than mid-stream, I was intensely focused on the line being slowly retrieved by my left hand, expecting a fish to take at any moment, when to my absolute bewilderment the lost fly box floated in gently at my feet. At my FEET! I looked down at the box in profound disbelief for a few moments before it occurred to me to pick it up, and for a while afterwards I just sat on the bank with the open box, staring at the jewels inside. Miracles, sometimes, do indeed happen.

Places of Power

One of the things I enjoy most in life is revisiting spots where I have sometimes paused from fishing or walking just to sit quietly and ponder for a while. This is particularly true of rocky perches on river banks and old logs or benches somewhere out in nature where I might have rested – perhaps many times – over the years. For me there is an ambience still there, an echo of those moments that compels me to sit once again and bask in the feeling. Sometimes I will go out of my way to do this and I've often wondered what it is, exactly, that draws me back to these places. Like a turn in a spiral, each new pondering seems to vibrate on the same note but at a different octave. The simplicity of presence is noticeably pronounced, more focused, and time seems to vanish in the haze of almost remembering as I sit quietly listening and watching the ever-changing patterns of nature. Somehow the magic of past moments is instilled in the enormous presence of just being there, being here, where I always am, morphing into nothingness.

— Family —

In over seven decades of living in this dream of life I have met many wonderful – and some not-so-wonderful – souls who have brought joy and challenge in various degrees, but I think each encounter has probably taught me something. Throughout my journey I have gained knowledge, some wisdom (I hope), five wonderful children, four stepsons, several nieces and nephews and, between Soraya and I, thirteen grandchildren – so far! Along with all the things that can be considered achievements, I made decisions or behaved in ways that I now consider inappropriate or insensitive, but that is all part of the learning process we all have to go through.

Unfortunately the way I suddenly left Lynne in 1974 has left a deep rift between us, but my relationship with our daughter, my firstborn child, Rachel, has deepened over the years. She was very hurt by the separation of her parents, of course, and I will never forget one heart-rending occasion in her childhood when we were all seated at a table with some friends and she suddenly burst into tears and screamed out, 'I just want you both to be together!'

It is the birthright of all children to have a secure and happy home with two parents who love and support them through thick and thin, and it makes me so sad that I could not provide that for Rachel – Ra as she is known today. But that little girl, now all grown up, has turned the tables on me and has a beautiful family home in Stroud with her husband Darius and three happy, thriving boys. I am so very happy for her, and so proud, as is the case with all my children.

My marriage to Lynne was, sadly, a result of the fact that I could not countenance the idea of being alone back then and, much sadder, I cannot honestly say that I was ever in love with her in the accepted sense. Unfortunately for her our relationship was born out of my own lack of self-caring and love. I was terrified of the yawning chasm of *not having*, whether it be a relationship, money, home, love... whatever label I might apply to it, and there was certainly a great deal of dishonesty on my part. I only came to see this clearly much later on in life when I was able to recognise and accept full responsibility for the suffering that spun out from all these unfolding patterns of irresponsible behaviour.

It was the same situation with Rhonda, actually; we, too, were very different people brought together by an initial physical attraction and held together, for a time, by children. I suspect this is an even more common scenario in our modern world of fast turnover marriage and divorce.

Looking back, I believe it was the same with my parents. They had a bit of a fling together and found themselves with child, then the inevitable social ties of their time bound them into something that they perhaps would never have wanted. Maybe this is a natural consequence of the capricious and impulsive side of human nature – or perhaps consciousness itself, which is everything, really – that just wants to explore every possible angle on its every reflection. The more intense and complex the scenario, the more interesting it becomes. The sponge will often be wrung out no matter what the cost in terms of human suffering.

Without wishing to mitigate any of the responsibility for the suffering that my own insecure behaviours have inadvertently caused in the past, only now from my place of security and complete trust in the unfolding of a divine will – a place so totally beyond any delusions of control that I had at the time – can I see that the relationships with my now ex-wives were born from the folds of negative patterns. These patterns originated from my own insecure tenure on life between the age of twelve (when I was sent away to boarding school) and nineteen when I began my journey into freedom by leaving England to travel the world in search of my true self.

My son Matthew who now works in the area of mental health and sees a great deal of family disharmony recently raised a question about a period in the past when I was in my late forties. Remembering how I expressed quite a bit of anger in the family around the time that I had my meltdown in 1997, he felt that this was completely inappropriate behaviour and decided to bring up the matter with me in order to help clear the air and 'complete things', as he told me. In my mind Matt and I have always been close so I was quite taken aback by his comments which I felt in turn contained some resentment and anger towards me. I have reached a point in my life where the ability to move on may seem unfeeling to others, but to my mind this moving on contains the all-important and elusive nature of forgiveness that allows others to move on also, removing things like guilt and regret, blame and resentment. It provides self and other with a freedom to flow onward with the moving finger of creation and destruction.

My son and I had a good long discussion and managed to work things out between us enough to move on in an atmosphere of acceptance and love. The importance of fully experiencing life 'as we go' and not creating the residue of incompletion has never been as important as it is now in this intense time of global **fear and suffering around the Covid 19** pandemic. The emotional triggers that are present for us all are so powerful that we have no choice but to face up to life as a spiritual warrior, willing to face the music as it really plays and sounds.

I don't think it is necessary to trawl around in the past looking for reasons for what we are feeling now. I believe that patterns are always repeating until they are played out in the **wheel of Karma** which endlessly provides a new version of past events arising naturally in the present for us to re-experience and complete. These patterns or waves will then all melt back into the ocean – which reminds me of the time when Leonard Cohen arrived back on Hydra after spending ten years in the monastery at Mount Baldy in California. Having just disembarked the ferry from Athens he was sitting alone on a wall in the port, bags by his side, and I asked him how he was. He simply smiled at me and said, 'I'm **just happy for no reason.**'

Sally and Mike

I find it startling that between us my siblings and I have so far released close to one hundred albums; startling because I have no idea how we each ended up becoming musicians let alone artists of note. I think people often assume, understandably, that some musical influence was passed on to us from our parents but, speaking for myself, it came from a need to find a mode of self-expression after the nightmare of school in my early teens; an outlet for all the suppressed emotion that had atrophied into depression and anxiety. It was much the same for Mike, too, except his trigger was the situation that existed at home between our parents, and more specifically with Mum.

Generally speaking, during the main period of our musical careers we siblings were far too focused on our individual paths to take a particular interest in each other's activities, and consequently we didn't have much contact. There were occasions that brought us together, of course, but we weren't especially close in the accepted sense. Sally had a whole period of living and performing in Germany when she was working on a career that I knew very little about, and I hardly ever saw Mike when he was on the road touring in the 1980s and '90s. Of the scores of concerts he did in that period I think I only went to about two. I undoubtedly responded to invitations to these, but I was so busy with my own family and music that I probably wouldn't have been able to make any commitment to attend. I'm pretty sure that Mike and Sally felt the same about me, with no animosity felt on anyone's part. I remember once in the late nineties in Stroud when I was in the process of buying a motor bike for my son Oliver's sixteenth birthday the salesman telling me that there had been another person named Oldfield in the shop recently looking at bikes. Shortly afterwards I discovered that Mike had been living within twenty minutes' drive of Chalford for quite some time!

I did, however, retain a certain degree of closeness to my sister that Mike and I never **really** had together, which I'm sure stemmed at least in part from early childhood when Sally and I were playmates before our new baby **brother** arrived on the scene. Looking back, to be quite honest I think I always just saw Mike as the little brother who was there but held little interest for me – an attitude many big brothers find themselves adopting. I think Mike may well have resented the closeness between myself and Sally a little in those early years, however, and later on when he became so successful I felt he had a tendency to hold it over me a bit. I remember him being a bit **bemused** one time when he asked me what I wanted for Christmas and I told him there was a particular flute, a Couesnon, that I had my eye on, but at £700 it was (back then) very expensive. His answer was, 'Terry, honestly, what would *you* want with a £700 flute?' Little did he know that my entire future career would centre on that silver tube! In the end my mum bought the flute for me but, years later, I was devastated when it was stolen from my car while I was on holiday in Wales. Perhaps I just wasn't meant to have that particular instrument.

My siblings and I are pretty distant in both senses of the word these days and I know very little of their lives and loves. Communication is infrequent with Mike over in the Bahamas but a little better with Sally who stays in touch online. I think the closest we all came to talking on deeper levels was during the Exegesis period in the late 1970s, but that was quite a raw awakening for us that had more to do with surface tensions being released. It was an important development but only a first step in the greater scheme of things.

— Now —

Through a deeper understanding it is quite possible for our true nature, pure consciousness, to detach from the stream of inner dialogue; that seemingly endless succession of thoughts that has captured us in the web of Maya, the veil of illusion. Then, the inner dialogue with its naming of objects will continue to run in the background whilst allowing us, as consciousness, to experience the world as it appears in this present moment. This is what is commonly known as enlightenment. Living in the world fully awake to what is really going on.

As this book of memories draws to a close I find myself gazing transfixed at the phantasmagoria of complexity that is literally going viral around the world in the current situation of pandemic. There are so many avenues being explored, so many opinions and judgements that the mind boggles in the maelstrom of desperate solutions that are arising on a daily basis. Humankind is doing its utmost to solve the seemingly very real problem of a new coronavirus that is entering a virome already comprising billions of viruses in which we already live and breathe. Surely this innate multi-million-year-old immune system is capable of welcoming just one more into the fold?

But hidden in the midst of all this apparent chaos are two words that echo through the elusive canyons of now from the ancient sages of India: *Leela*, which means 'play', and *Maya*, 'illusion'. These two words speak of the ultimate viewpoint from the lofty pinnacle of humankind's evolution upon planet Earth. Life is a play or *Leela* in which consciousness plays every part, a world where *Maya* casts her veil before our eyes and makes all the complexity seem so real. The truth? *My* truth now is that life is absolutely *meant* to be experienced as real. We willingly drink from the waters of the River Lethe, the ancient Greek river of forgetfulness, to forget who we really are; intentionally becoming lost in order to play the game of not knowing and walking the pathways of remembering. What a fantastic creation!

Like so many people during this strange time of enforced separation Soraya and I have turned our attention more to the garden and nature, but we are very fortunate to live here at *Mangalam* in what is such a beautiful, natural place. Leaving home was always a fairly infrequent occurrence for us anyway, unless it was to go for shopping or a walk on the beach or in the rainforest, so our lifestyle hasn't really changed much at all. The greatest inconvenience has been the inability to travel and share our music, and that situation which has affected a lot of musicians may yet continue for some time, but we are optimistic that 2022 will be different. However, having now travelled to over forty countries together and seen so much of our beautiful world, travelling with Soraya and playing music together has been one of the most fulfilling aspects of my life, and that is more than sufficient compensation.

∞

Bernard Cribbins once passed on a little pearl of life wisdom to me: *'Terry, if you have any ambitions remaining in your life get them achieved before you turn sixty, because after that you'll have more of a preference to sit down quietly with a nice cup of tea.'*

Actually, it's only now that I'm closer to the age Bernard was at the time that my energy has begun to wane, just a little bit, but I still plan to go fishing in Norway again whenever the opportunity presents itself and sit, quietly pondering, in some of my favourite spots on the river - perhaps under the midnight sun?

Now I find myself in a space that is sufficient unto itself where every day provides its own entertainment in the waving of branches in the wind, or the way the clouds bring sunlight and shade; a space where a new song will manifest here from time to time.

Now is a life without any particular direction, of simply moving in the gentle, guiding flow of what is happening; not an easy thing to describe and impossible to understand. What I've discovered and what has helped me **most** is seeing that essentially at the core of who I am is something quite mysterious, not something that's fixed or easily pinned down or explained. If you can discover this within yourself you'll be a happier person, more inspired, and far more able to deal with life's issues because you know that there is only this present moment. There is only The Now. And that's where we all are anyway, *always*, whether we experience it or not. Only right here. Only in this moment.

Only Now.

Me and Sally on either side of our mum, Maisie, with Mike on her lap

The next generation! My youngest daughter Clemmie with her own baby, my grandson Dominic.

Suggested Further Reading

The Hidden Side of Things by C.W. Leadbeater. Book Jungle, Mar. 13, 2008

Freedom from the Known by J Krishnamurti. Rider, Jul. 2010

The Power of Now: A Guide to Spiritual Enlightenment (20th anniversary edition) by Eckhart Tolle. Yellow Kite, Feb. 2001.

Shining Through: From Grief to Gratitude by Soraya Saraswati. Amazon KDP, Aug. 2016.

The Wisdom of Insecurity: A Message for an Age of Anxiety by Alan Watts. Vintage Books; 2nd edition, Feb. 2011

Cutting Through Spiritual Materialism by Chögyam Trungpa, Shambhala; revised edition, August 2002

Journeys Out of the Body by Robert Munroe. Doubleday, Jan. 1971

Pathways Through to Space by Frank Merrell-Wolff. Harmony; second edition, May 1983

Printed in Great Britain
by Amazon